PSYCHOLOGICAL ASPECTS OF POLARISATION PHENOMENON

Psychological Aspects of Polarisation Phenomenon

DAMODAR SUAR
Research and Planning Department
Xavier Institute of Social Service
Ranchi (Bihar)

Foreword by

M.B. SHARAN
Department of Humanities and Social Sciences
I.I.T., Kharagpur

CONCEPT PUBLISHING COMPANY, NEW DELHI 110059

The Indian Council of Social Science Research gave the financial support towards the publication of this work. However, the responsibility for the contents of the book — facts, opinions, conclusions, etc. is entirely that of the author and not the ICSSR.

ICSSR Consultant : Prof. Jai B.P. Sinha

ISBN 81-7022-413-6

First Published 1992

Published and Printed by
Ashok Kumar Mittal
Concept Publishing Company
A/15-16, Commercial Block, Mohan Garden
NEW DELHI 110059 (India)

Lasertypeset by
Microtech Advance Printing Systems (Pvt.) Ltd.
H-13, Bali Nagar
NEW DELHI 110015

Dedicated
to
my mother and brother
whose efforts have made me what I am today.

FOREWORD

Common sense suggests that the decisions reached by groups are generally more conservative than those recommended by individuals. Initial experimental findings, however, seemed to suggest that group discussion may often lead to a risky shift – movement by the group toward more daring or risky decisions. Further research has now revealed that the effects of group discussion are actually somewhat more general in nature, involving a movement toward polarisation. This polarisation phenomenon, which has more important implications than the existence of a shift toward risk, has become today the focus of a great deal of interest and attention in Social Psychology. Dr. Damodar Suar has to be congratulated for having dealt with this kind of complex phenomenon in his book and making a significant contribution to our knowledge.

There are five chapters in all in this book. The first chapter traces the historical development of this phenomenon and reviews the literature critically. The second chapter deals with two major questions: whether the shifts on dilemma items are dependent upon risk-oriented instructions; and whether the dilemma items measure the attitudinal judgement. Chapters 3 and 4 are concerned with theories of polarisation – persuasive argument theory and social comparison theory. The fifth chapter summarises the main findings of all the three studies and suggests avenues for further research.

The book is, thus, of great value from the point of view of research in the area of Experimental Social Psychology. It also provides a wealth of data in Indian setting which is so far regrettably lacking for teachers and students of Social Psychology in this country.

Professor of Psychology
Department of Humanities & Social Sciences
Indian Institute of Technology, Kharagpur

M.B. SHARAN, Ph.D.

PREFACE

Psychology has moved from arm chair theorisation to experimentation in field and laboratory to understand, control and predict human behaviour. Employing this method, this work is an attempt to understand some psychological aspects of attitudinal judgement polarisation.

Polarisation phenomenon refers to the strengthening of posterior response in the direction of prior response following an intervening variable. For example, if individuals are mildly in favour of a particular view or course of action, they favour it strongly following group discussion or comparison with others in group. It occurs over a wide range of tasks and stimuli ranging from opinions, attitudes, person-perceptions, gamblings, risk-taking to group counsellings. Being partly methodological, this research makes an attempt to understand how human minds and hearts can be changed.

Of central concern to this work is the two basic questions : first one dealing with the methodological and the second one with the theoretical aspects. Their logistics are discussed in the first introductory chapter. Chapter 2 deals with the methodological aspects. Despite the frequent use of choice dilemma items in polarisation (or shift) literature, it is not clear whether the observed polarisation is contaminated by the risk-oriented instructions in the items; and whether the dilemma items measure attitudinal judgement. The dilemma items yield significant choice shift and polarisation irrespective of risk-oriented and neutral instructions. The dilemma items measure the attitudinal judgement. This study clarifies the shaky difference between choice shift and polarisation. It suggests the use of choice dilemma items in attitudinal judgement form and a concentration on polarisation phenomenon for further research.

Using the choice dilemma items in attitudinal judgement form, Chapter 3 deals with the theoretical aspects. Another experiment tests the concepts of two theories over which controversies continue. They are persuasive argument theory (PAT) and social comparison theory (SCT). PAT is concerned with informational influence and SCT with normative influence. Does informational influence induce normative influence or vice versa? The magnitude of polarisation on dilemma items, evaluation of conceptual parameters of the theories along with the other findings support the persuasive argument explanations. The subjects' additional access to verbal, non-verbal and self-generated information yields larger polarisation and larger shifts in conceptual parameters of the theories following group discussion. Only the subjects' additional access to self-generated information yields smaller polarisation and smaller shifts in conceptual parameters of the theories following social comparison in group context. Thus, informational influence proves to be the basis of polarisation in both the theories.

In Chapter 4, still another experiment tests the theories by relating the situational, message-level and interpersonal variables along with the personality traits to the magnitude of polarisation. The situational and the message-level variables operate in a manner explicable in terms of PAT. The personality traits reflecting a concern for others' opinions and a tendency to be aware of differences between one's own opinion and that of others – traits that should augment the impact of social comparison – do not relate to polarisation. These findings strengthen the earlier results supporting PAT. The final chapter summarises the findings, describes a broad framework and states the implications. It also suggests problems for further study.

This book not only provides a review and synthesis of past and present findings but also incorporates methodological and theoretical contributions. This would, therefore, be of interest to methodologists and theorists in psychology, sociology and management science.

I take this opportunity to express my indebtedness to my affectionate teacher and supervisor Professor Mithila B. Sharan (IIT, Kharagpur) for his suggestions and inspiration during the course of the present research undertaking. This work is highly influenced by the writings of professors, Amiram Vinokur (ISR, Michigan), David G. Myers (Hope College, Michigan), Eugene Burnstein (ISR, Michigan) and Robert S. Baron (University of Iowa). I, therefore, express my gratitude to each one of them.

I am also thankful to the teaching faculty of Sambalpur University, Jyoti Vihar, Orissa for encouraging their students to participate in the experiments embodied here. It could have given me pleasure, if I could have mentioned the names of all the participants and thanked them individually. But for reasons, they must go unnamed. I am grateful to the authorities of IIT, Kharagpur for providing research facilities and scholarship, and to Father Louis Francken (Director, XISS, Ranchi) for granting me leave to complete this work.

I am grateful to Professor Jai B.P. Sinha (National Fellow), consultant of Indian Council of Social Science Research (ICSSR), New Delhi, for evaluating this research and offering editorial advices. I offer my thanks to ICSSR for supporting this publication financially.

Research and Planning Department
Xavier Institute of Social Service
Ranchi 834 001

DAMODAR SUAR

CONTENTS

LIST OF TABLES

LIST OF FIGURES

1

INTRODUCTION

The study of polarisation has moved through a series of transitions from risky shift to generalised shift, group dynamics to individual dynamics and theories of attitude change to theories of thinking and memory. A huge array of empirical facts has been collected. Psychologists, sociologists, educationists and management scientists have tried to understand the mystery of individual's behaviour in small groups and their effects on change in his opinion, attitude and value. The knowledge gained so far in this field claims wider scope, generality and applicability. It has made a substantial contribution to theorisation and understanding of individual change in social situations. In spite of this, the authenticity of the popular research protocol used in polarisation is doubted; theoretical controversies are still unsettled; and their practical implications are not fully realised. If at all an appropriate theoretical formulation for polarisation phenomenon can be justified, it will help in guiding research and understanding polarisation in social situations. It will define the conditions for the occurrence and non-occurrence of polarisation and predict the effects on other situations not yet studied. Definitely, it is a challenging intellectual puzzle.

With this back-drop, the research on polarisation demands a methodological and theoretical approach to understand and bring about change in individuals' opinions, attitudes, values and judgements. In our two primary sectors of economy – agricultural and industrial – we frequently face the problem of changing attitudes, values and decisions of people from an undesirable state of affairs to a desirable one. If the applicability can be extended to this extent, all facets of polarisation including its history, conceptual maturation, generality and theoretical controversies, deserve thorough specification and scrutiny.

From Risky Shift to Polarisation: Historical Development

Long back, both social psychologists and laymen believed that people were more conservative and less daring in groups than alone. In order to test this old popular belief, Stoner (1961) started his research at M.I.T. His procedure, worth describing here, was followed by a series of experiments. He had given to M.I.T. subjects a series of hypothetical story problems called choice dilemma questionnaire (CDQ), developed and used by Wallach and Kogan (1959, 1961). The stories covered a wide range of themes: controversies about career choice, heart operation, monetary investment, playing strategy, university enrolment, war-camp escape, political office acquisition, research problem selection and marriage decision. Each story portrayed a situation in which the central person confronted a choice between a certain and an uncertain course of action. The subject was instructed to assume the role of an adviser in each story and indicate the lowest probability of success he would demand before recommending the uncertain alternative or would recommend the certain alternative. The following example illustrates a similar sample item.

Mr. L, a married 30-year old research physicist, has been given a five-year appointment by a major university laboratory. As he contemplates the next five years, he realises that he might work on a difficult, long-term problem which, if a solution could be found, would resolve basic scientific issues in the field and bring high scientific honours. If no solutions were found, Mr. L would have little to show for his five years in the laboratory, and this would make it hard for him to get a good job afterwards. On the other hand, he could, as most of his professional associates are doing, work on a series of short-term problems where solutions would be easier to find, but where the problems are of lesser scientific importance.

Imagine that you are advising Mr. L. *Please check the lowest probability that you would consider acceptable to make it worthwhile for Mr. L to work on more difficult, long-term problem.*

Mr. L should choose the difficult, long-term problem if the chances are at least:

– 1 in 10 that Mr. L would solve the long-term problem.
– 2 in 10 that Mr. L would solve the long-term problem.
– 3 in 10 that Mr. L would solve the long-term problem.
– 4 in 10 that Mr. L would solve the long-term problem.
– 5 in 10 that Mr. L would solve the long-term problem.
– 6 in 10 that Mr. L would solve the long-term problem.
– 7 in 10 that Mr. L would solve the long-term problem.

- 8 in 10 that Mr. L would solve the long-term problem.
- 9 in 10 that Mr. L would solve the long-term problem.
- Place a check here if you think Mr. L should *not* choose the long-term, difficult problem, no matter what the probabilities.

Initially subjects reported their decisions individually on such items. Then they assembled in six-member groups and discussed each item until they arrived at a common decision. Surprisingly, on all the items, group decisions were significantly more risky than individual prior decisions. In group decisions the probability to choose the uncertain alternative became still lower. It dubbed the phenomenon of 'risky shift'. Situations depicted in dilemma items possessed attractive features of social realism and the findings were replicable using a wide variety of subjects in different nations. Subsequently, the choice dilemma paradigm continued to dominate researches in this field.

In CDQ, the average shift per item was roughly one scale unit (Belovicz & Finch, 1971; Burns, 1967). In spite of this, it attracted an ever-increasing number of researchers to this field. Common sense prevailed that individuals in group would avoid expression of extreme opinions. By that time, psychologists (e.g., Allport, 1962) had already discovered that the group decision represented a compromise among individuals' prior decisions. The shift towards increased risk-taking in group challenged the conventional wisdom and the compromising tendency. Second, the cause of shift was not obvious. It stimulated much theoretical controversies. Third, if groups adopted extreme risk, it would help understanding the decision-making activities of juries, military councils and religious groups. It was anticipated that solutions would yield some new ideas about human behaviour which would be a real accomplishment of social psychology.

Gradually an important fact began to emerge. Researchers developed dilemma items that demonstrated shift towards greater caution or higher probability in the same paradigm (Nordhoy, 1962; Myers, 1967; Rabow, Fowler, Bradford, Hofeller, & Shibuya, 1966; Stoner, 1968). Even item 5 dealing with the building of a plant and item 12 dealing with the marriage decision in standard CDQ showed robust cautious shifts. But item 2 in CDQ dealing with a delicate heart operation elicited neither any predominant initial inclination nor any significant shift (Burnstein, Miller, Vinokur, Katz, & Crowley, 1971; Myers & Arenson, 1972; Vinokur, 1971; Wallach, Kogan, & Bem, 1962). These observations cast strong doubts on several hypotheses advanced earlier to explain risky shift. It was understood that the content of dilemma items determined shift in risky or cautious direction.

The dilemma items differed from one another on initial and shift scores. The item having initial score of 6.0 or below yielded risky shift; and the item having initial score of 6.8 and above yielded cautious shift. The median of shifts for risky items ranged from as low as 0.6 to as high as 1.6 and for cautious items from –0.1 to –0.6 (Cartwright, 1971). Some items yielded strong shifts and some weak shifts depending on their content.

Investigators from different cultures using both risky and cautious items replicated repeatedly both risky and cautious shifts respectively following group discussion and decision (Burnstein, Miller, Vinokur, Katz, & Crowley, 1971; Ferguson & Vidmar, 1971; Fraser, Gouge, & Billig, 1971; Stoner 1968). As an index of external validity, isomorphic shifts appeared in attitudes, judgements and perceptions (Pruitt, 1971a). Consequently, risky shift lost its novelty and heuristic provocativeness. This demanded a broader concept. Pruitt (1971a) coined a neutral term 'choice shift' to explain the findings. This connotation is occasionally appearing till today (Hinsz & Davis, 1984; Laughlin & Earley, 1982). The dilemma items are so much linked with the concept of risk that they need further clarification.

Risk and Choice Dilemma Items

Initially, Kogan and Wallach (1964) started their work on risk and conservatism using dilemma items to understand the cognitive processes of thinking and problem solving. Later on, when dilemma items were used to measure risk, it was seriously questioned (Blascovich, Veach, & Ginsburg, 1973).

The criterion tasks employed to measure risk in risky shift literature vary from CDQ to Tactical and Negotiation game (Streufert, 1968), Blackjack (Blascovich, Veach, & Ginsburg, 1973), Perdue Pegboard (Fortenberry & Smith, 1981), Duplex bet (Slovic & Lichtenstein, 1968), Light guess (Davis, Hoppe, & Hornseth, 1968), Hypothetical gamble (Coombs & Pruitt, 1960) and Race track bet (McCauley, Stitt, Woods, & Lipton, 1973). Sometimes risk is defined in terms of adverse effects or consequences (Fortenberry & Smith, 1981), sometimes in terms of expected value, probability preference, variance preference and so on (Coombs & Pruitt, 1960; Davis, Kerr, Sussmann, &

Rissman, 1974; Edwards, 1954; Johnson & Davis, 1972; Schoemaker, 1979; Slovic & Lichtenstein, 1968; Zajonc, Wolosin, & Wolosin, 1972). Even game and gambling situations are considered under risk. Here, risk is defined in terms of amount the subject bets (Blascovich & Ginsburg, 1978; Blascovich, Ginsburg, & Howe, 1975, 1976; Blascovich, Ginsburg, & Veach, 1975; Knox & Safford, 1976; McCauley, Stitt, Woods, & Lipton, 1973). In such situation, betting of first player without any reference strategy of others is equivalent to betting against complete uncertainty. These are also adult plays and subjects continue to play even if they lose. Thus, the measurement of risk vary from situation to situation (Fischhoff, Watson, & Hope, 1984). Therefore, defining risk is beset with numerous conceptual and practical difficulties.

It is well-known from statistical decision theory that risk is a component of uncertainty. If for a specific alternative, a specific outcome is not certain, but the probabilities of alternative outcomes are known or at least can be estimated subjectively, it is one of the situations under risk. Common sense usage considers risk as the compound measures of possible occurrence of an outcome with magnitude of its adverse effect. Even if these risk components are hypothetically incorporated in dilemma items, there are evidences that the dilemma items measure neither risk nor its desirability. First, following shifts towards risk, reliable shifts towards greater caution are also obtained on CDQ (items 5 and 12) and on other items (Burns, 1967; Fraser, Gouge, & Billig, 1971; Nordhoy, 1962; Myers, 1967; Rabow, Fowler, Bradford, Hofeller, & Shibuya, 1966; Stoner, 1968). Second, the 'shift effects' obtained on dilemma items are generalised across a variety of situations related to attitude, decision, judgement, person perception, negotiation, conformity behaviour and naturalistic observation of social conflict, group counselling and religious fellowship. These studies have used a variety of tasks. These tasks have any similarity neither with the dilemma items nor with the concept of risk (Myers, 1982; Myers & Lamm, 1976). It blusters the conception that the occurrence of shifts is specific to dilemma items only. Third, shifts towards high or low probability on dilemma items are found to fit a subjective expected utility model. It assumes that the individual does not value risk. Also, the content analysis of arguments generated privately as well as during discussion does not reveal much concern about the desirability of risk (Burnstein, Miller, Vinokur, Katz, & Crowley, 1971; Vinokur, 1971; Vinokur, Trope, & Burnstein,

1975). Fourth, after group discussion on dilemma items, group members do not perceive their posterior responses as more risky than their prior responses. Hence, risky shift is not a shift in subjective evaluation of risk (Kahan, 1975). Fifth, the dilemma items are neither interchangeable nor highly correlated among themselves to assess the variable risk. Each dilemma brings a new set of social value. One involves an engineer who must decide whether or not to change the job, another involves a research physicist who must decide whether to work on easy and short-term problems or on a very difficult and long-term problem, and so on. Lastly, the dilemma items are hypothetical in nature. The outcomes are ambiguous and difficult to realise after the decisions are made. Therefore, what the dilemma items measure cannot be conceptualised in terms of risk.

Meaning of Choice in Choice Dilemma Item

In each dilemma item, the subject recommends a probability level as an adviser for the success of uncertain alternative or else the certain alternative. It is assumed that the individual advice to the hypothetical person reflects his own decision. The items are semi-projective in nature. Second, on each item the response varies from individual to individual depending on his knowledge about the issue, his past experience with similar issues and his present socioeconomic status. Responses are configural in nature which take subject-item interaction into account (Scott, 1968, p.231). Each dilemma item records the subject's level of expectancy about the success of uncertain or certain alternative. The dilemma items are constructed in such a way that each item elicits predominantly the preference for low (generally called risky item) or high probability (generally called cautious item) in a specific culture. Lower probability is considered to be associated with greater risk and higher probability with greater conservatism.

Burns (1967) argues that, like Likert-type preference, selection of a very low probability of success indicates strong preference for the uncertain, risky alternative. On the other hand, selection of a very high probability of success indicates very strong preference for the certain, conservative alternative. In one study, subjects indicated on dilemma items to what extent they favoured the certain or uncertain alternatives on Likert scale (i.e., 'strongly recommend the uncertain alternative' through neutrality to 'strongly recommend the certain alternative'). The same subjects gave their options to same items with usual probabilities. Responses in these two forms yielded comparable findings on both initial and shift scores (Fraser, Gouge, & Billig, 1971). This supports the argument of Burns. The lower and higher probability choices are associated with intense preference towards uncertain and certain alternatives in Likert-type scale respectively on both initial and shift scores. The two forms measured the same variable, attitude towards certain or uncertain alternative described in each item and its shift.

Like decision, judgement involves the selection of a single alternative from a set of alternatives. The dilemma items measure attitudinal judgement because the subject's response to each item involves the selection of either uncertain or certain alternative with a particular valency. Although attitude is defined as a combination of cognitions, feelings and action tendencies, it is an affective (feeling) or evaluative response. The subject's response to each dilemma item similarly expresses the feeling about an alternative. Selection of lower probability means a higher expectancy of success of uncertain alternative, proportionately a favourable attitudinal judgement towards the uncertain alternative. This can be called conventionally as risky preference. Selection of higher probability means a lower expectancy of success of uncertain alternative and proportionately a favourable attitudinal judgement towards the certain alternative. This can be referred conventionally as cautious preference.

Conceptual Development of Polarisation Phenomenon: Origin, Definition and Difference

Facts do not organise themselves into concepts just by being looked at. Indeed, without the framework of concepts, there is no scientific development but only chaos. Therefore, clarification of key concepts is basic to any investigation. Initially, the findings obtained using CDQ were severely criticised (Blascovich, Veach, & Ginsburg, 1973; Cartwright, 1971; Smith, 1972). These findings induced wrongly many investigators to perceive the phenomenon from the perspective of risk and its shift. Second, the broader generality of the phenomenon was uncovered in risky shift experiments. As research has been continuing, knowledge is accumulating with evidence and the basic concept is maturing with support.

The concept of polarisation originated with the early work of Moscovici and Zavalloni (1969), Doise (1969), and Myers and Bishop

(1970). The French students initially having favourable attitude towards General de Gaulle policies and unfavourable attitude towards American foreign policy expressed even more favourable and unfavourable attitude towards the same issues respectively following discussion in small groups (Moscovici & Zavalloni, 1969). Similarly, Doise (1969) reported the enhancement of initial negative attitude following group discussion which French architectural students had towards their school. Myers and Bishop (1970), following a different methodology, composed groups of high, medium, and low prejudice high school subjects using a measure of racial attitudes. Group members then responded to new racial attitude items before and after discussion. Following discussion, the gap between high and low prejudice groups increased. Discussion enhanced prejudice in predominant initial direction of two groups. Immediately these observations were tagged to risky shift and choice shift phenomena. It was thought that the shift effects obtained on dilemma items would be better conceptualised as polarisation phenomenon. The risky and cautious items, initially eliciting low and high probability preferences, produced consistently shifts towards still lower and higher probabilities respectively following group discussion. This was also observed in different tasks in laboratory as well as in social reality (Myers, 1982; Myers & Lamm, 1976). At the same time, other supporting findings were available. For the items yielding large shift towards risk and caution, their initial means were on risky and cautious sides of the scale continuum respectively (Myers & Arenson, 1972; Teger & Pruitt, 1967). So what the findings on dilemma items demonstrated were a simpler instance of polarisation. It was the tendency of group discussion to enhance the dominant initial inclination.

Polarisation refers to an increase in extremity of average response of the subject population or the enhancement of the prevailing individual tendency (Myers & Lamm, 1976). This is similar to congruent change of opinion or attitude. For example, if individuals are mildly in favour of (or opposed to) a particular view, they favour (or oppose) it more strongly following discussion or comparison with others (see Fig. 1.1).

Polarisation phenomenon has three important characteristics. First, like a vector quantity in physical sciences, it is a psychological vector having both magnitude and direction. It projects the amount of shift in the valued direction on initial inclination. Second, its occurrence requires experimental treatment in laboratory or interaction with others in social reality. Third, the amount of polarisation depends upon the strength of initial inclination on an issue. More the strength of initial inclination, less will be the amount of yield in polarisation.

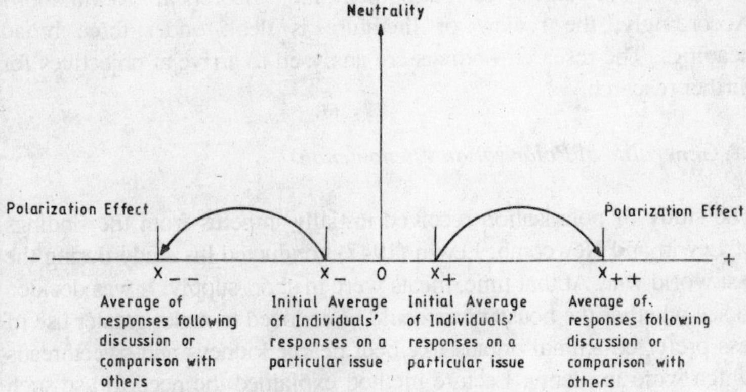

FIG. 1.1: **Individual Shifts to the Extreme Opinion in the Predominant Direction of his Initial Inclination Following Discussion or Comparison of Opinion with Others.**

Now evidences differentiate polarisation from its early nomenclature, extremisation (Lambert, 1969, 1971) and choice shift (Pruitt, 1971a). While polarisation refers to the individual level of shifts towards the earlier preferred pole, extremisation refers to the movement away from neutrality regardless of direction. Since extremisation occurs regardless of direction, it becomes easy to demonstrate. While polarisation is the enhancement of prevailing individual tendency, depolarisation is the decrement in it. In choice shift group is the unit of analysis and consensus among group members is the requirement. In polarisation individual is the unit of analysis. Individual decision-making followed by a brief period of group discussion is sufficient to produce polarisation (Hinsz & Davis, 1984).

Review of Literature and Objectives of Research

After having understood the historical development, the review of literature tries to answer three major questions. First, has the polarisation phenomenon derived using CDQ sufficient external validity and generalisation over other tasks? Second, is there a unified theoretical formulation to explain polarisation? Third, are there relationships between the variables supporting the theories and the magnitude of shifts to strengthen the theoretical formulation? Accordingly, the review of literature is dealt under three broad headings. The research findings are analysed to arrive at objectives for further research.

(a) *Generality of Polarisation Phenomenon*

The study of polarisation received initially impetus from the findings of Lewin and Newcomb. Lewin (1947) conducted his study during the last world war. At that time, meats were in short supply. It was decided to see whether the housewives could be induced to make greater use of less preferred animal organs like beef hearts, kidneys and sweetbreads which were in plenty. Lecture method explained the need to use such products – their nutritional value, how to overcome their odours, how to make them palatable and delicious dishes. In another condition, housewives in group discussed among themselves the same issue with the supply of information (as in lecture method) if required. A higher percentage of housewives changed their opinions following discussion (32%) than following lecture method (3%). Similarly, effective learning, problem solving, attitude change, increased productivity were observed following participative discussion (Barnlund, 1959; Coch & French, 1960; Lewin, 1947; McKeachie, 1968; Shaw, 1947). Polarisation phenomenon was observed following this paradigm. Literature is now well documented to demonstrate its external validity on attitude, jury decision, ethical decision, judgement, person perception, negotiation and risk-taking (Knox & Safford, 1976; Muehleman, Robinson, & Emerson, 1984; Myers, 1982; Myers & Lamm, 1976; Nagel & O'Driscoll, 1978).

The phenomenon is not only consistently observed in close house experiments but also in natural settings. Even if natural observations are argued to be immunised by many extraneous variables, they carry the force of apparent reality to validate the close house findings in laboratory. Judicious judgement of social realities in the tradition of Malinowski cannot keep natural observations away from causes and effects. Long back Newcomb (1943) observed attitude polarisation in social interaction. In Bennington college community, the students were from urban area and high income families. Their social attitudes were mostly conservative. Members of the teaching staff were liberal and they encouraged students to take active part in social and political problems. As the students passed from freshmen to seniors, some of them shifted their social attitudes from low liberalism to liberalism to identify with the college norm. The students change during college summarised by Feldman and Newcomb (1969) reveals even clearer evidence of polarisation. "Initial differences among students in different colleges and in different curricula are accentuated or amplified as students progress through college. Instances of this same phenomenon also occur with respect to initial differences among students entering different types of residences" (p.209). Polarisations in social conflicts, group counsellings and religious fellowships are extensively observed in real life social situations (Myers, 1982).

Independent and non-conformist students from higher socio-economic families get entry into our advanced technological institutions like IITs through a nationwide test. They differ in their outlooks, attitudes and values. The culture of such institutions remains akin to that of western countries. As the students spend few years and progress in their studies, they change and polarise their attitudes towards independency, earning, sex and many others. The occurrence of polarisation is so frequent that our daily newspaper headlines contain issues like villagers polarise, students polarise, workers polarise, extremists polarise and so on. Problems in Punjab, Kashmir and claim for Jharkhand in Bihar are some of the examples of attitude and behaviour polarisation of the people in search for a separate identity based on caste, religion and community feelings. When the feelings receive support in the social system for political, economic, social and cultural reasons, they intensify and polarise. Even in some of the constituencies, the votes also polarise in favour of a candidate due to caste and community feelings. Experience says that in village committee if any development work related to pressing requirements of the villagers is proposed and discussed, it receives immediate support and the villagers polarise to start the work. There is no dearth of observations on polarisation in social reality. The prevailing enhancement of individual tendency against a wide range of tasks and situations in laboratory and in social reality provides sufficient external validity to polarisation phenomenon.

It can be recalled that the relevant findings on shift literature at first place generated from researches on dilemma items. It contributed much to the theory of polarisation in general and to the understanding of change in opinions, attitudes, judgements and decisions in particular. In spite of this, the internal validity of dilemma items is questioned. Like the demand characteristics of research situation (Orne, 1969) and experimenter bias (Rosenthal, 1966), the shifts on dilemma items are proved to be contingent upon the biased risk-oriented instructions to check the lowest probability (Clark & Willems, 1969; Willems & Clark, 1969). This conclusion of Clark and Willems (1969) is not tested further by other researchers. It is objectionable on certain grounds. It requires replication in a different culture because any meaningful conclusion must satisfy the requirements of reproducibility and cross-cultural validity. Second, as discussed earlier, the extensively used dilemma items are concerned with neither risk nor the desirability of risk. Indeed, the risky and cautious dilemma items tap the attitudinal judgement towards the uncertain and certain alternatives respectively. This also needs empirical verification. With this conceptual backdrop, the first objective is proposed with twin purposes to test: (a) the contingency between instructional bias and shift, and (b) the measurement of attitudinal judgement by dilemma items. This methodological work will partly gauge the use of dilemma items in shift literature and partly clarify the meaning of dilemma items.

(b) *Theories of Polarisation*

Many theories in early work of polarisation have turned out to be inadequate owing to their repeated failures. Therefore, a brief discussion is made about the abandoned theories and a detailed discussion is made in which active researches are persuaded now. Second, most of the studies in this context have included choice dilemma findings. These findings in early stage of research contributed to the development of theoretical knowledge.

Diffusion of Responsibility

The oldest theory, 'diffusion responsibility' assumes that the individual's responsibility about the negative consequences of a risky decision is shared in group. Therefore, the decision in group becomes riskier than the decision made alone. The failure of dilemma items to capture risk, the inability of the theory to explain cautious shift, the development of emotional bonds in laboratory groups to share responsibility, the persistence of shift for a longer time (Johnston,

1968; Wallach, Kogan, & Bem, 1962) and the observation of shifts by hearing discussion (Kogan & Wallach, 1967b; Lamm, 1967) were responsible for its rejection.

Familiarisation

Familiarisation theory (Bateson, 1966) suggests that when the individual familiarises with the issue on subsequent occasions, it reinforces him to endorse a stronger decision. This is because of the general reduction in uncertainty about the issue. In testing the theory, shifts observed after further familiarisation with the issue remained quite comparable to the shifts obtained after group discussion (Bateson, 1966; Flanders & Thistlethwaite, 1967). Later on, consistent failure to replicate this effect (Bell & Jamieson, 1970; Stokes, 1971; Teger, Pruitt, St. Jean, & Haaland, 1970) made it hard to extricate the theory.

Leadership

Extreme position on an issue induces greater confidence and commitment (Burns, 1967; Burnstein & Katz, 1971; Burnstein, Vinokur, & Pichevin, 1974; Clausen, 1965; Stroebe & Fraser, 1971). It leads to greater influenciability of the individual (or leader) during discussion. As a result, others in group are swayed towards him that yields shifts (Burnstein, 1969; Clausen, 1965). However, shifts observed following familiarisation, passive listening of discussion and exposure to argument samples (Burnstein, Vinokur, & Trope, 1973) cast doubt on this theory.

Transfer of Control

Rettig (1966, 1972, 1979) using ethical and unethical judgement situations has mentioned that risky shift occurs because the individual transfers the control over the outcome to the group. Such transfer increases the stress on gain values and leads to more risk-taking in group. The individual conformity to the group norm depends upon trust and perceived competency of the co-group members (Sinha & Yousuf, 1972; Verma & Sinha, 1981). However, the theory fails to explain cautious shift. It incorporates the process which is outlined in normative influence (Deutsch & Gerard, 1955).

Commitment

Moscovici and Zavalloni (1969) mention that higher the effort put in forming an opinion, greater is the commitment to that opinion. The individual does not analyse effortfully the pros and cons of his opinion until he receives similar or contrary opinion. The initial opinion of the individual on the issue, therefore, remains broad and tentative. Group interaction provides the opportunity to evaluate critically his opinion against the opinion of others. The issue becomes more meaningful and clear. The value attached to the issue, which had less prominence, becomes more salient. He becomes committed to a specific choice which was not the case prior to group interaction. The authors found further intensification of initial opinion following group discussion and consensus. The observation of shifts without group interaction and with passive supply of argument samples charge the theory with inefficiency.

Social Decision Scheme (SDS)

SDS combines the individuals' initial preferences to predict the group decision. The important variables that account for group shifts are the distribution of initial preferences and group decision. There are nine possible social decision schemes (Davis, 1973; Davis, Kerr, Sussmann, & Rissman, 1974; Laughlin, Kerr, Davis, Halff, & Marciniak, 1975). A study (Laughlin & Earley, 1982) notes that the most risky and most cautious items (that strongly shift towards risk and caution respectively) are closer to the intellective end of group task continuum. SDS best fits to them is 'truth-supported wins' (risk-supported and conservative-supported wins on risky and cautious items respectively). Truth-supported wins predict the shift towards the correct option, if one member proposes it and he is supported by at least another group member. The moderate or less extreme items are closer to the judgemental end of group task continuum. SDS best fits to them is 'majority-wins'. If majority of group members are initially on the risk side of the scale continuum and thereby skewed towards risk, the predicted group shift will be towards more risk in accordance with 'majority-wins'. The converse applies to cautious shift.

Many studies indicate that the shift is not a statistical artifact. It is internalised but not a temporary group product. It persists for at least six weeks (Johnston, 1968; Wallach, Kogan, & Bem, 1962). SDS has only applicability when group decision and consensus are made obligatory to demonstrate choice shift (Hinsz & Davis, 1984). Skewness of initial distribution of preferences is not a mediator to shifts. On the items yielding risky shift, the positive and negative skewed groups have numbered almost equal (Vinokur, 1969). This contradicts majority-wins decision scheme. Dyads yielding shifts are also contradictory to skewness hypothesis (Swap & Miller, 1969). After all, SDS is a concomitant rather than a process to explain shifts.

Diffusion of responsibility, leadership, transfer of control and commitment theories try to explain shifts by the influence of group members. The process by which responsibility spreads, the extreme member influences others, the individual transfers control to the group and increases commitment to the valued position are through group interaction and informational influence. Familiarisation theory alone explains the shifts by self-generation of information through rethinking on the issue. A consensus prevails that these theories are no longer viable to explain shifts. These theories directly or indirectly escort the process of normative (affective) influence or informational (cognitive) influence (Deutsch & Gerard, 1955). Two independent theories exist for these two processes. They are social comparison and persuasive argumentation. They are pitted against each other. Their history of controversies are more or less similar to the stark contrast of attitude change theories in Festinger (1957) and Hovland (1954) tradition. Each one claims to be a primary, active contributor to explain shifts and views the other one as a secondary, passive outgrowth of the primary one. The social comparison theorists contend that persuasive arguments facilitate the shifts motivated by social comparisons (Sanders & Baron, 1977). The persuasive argument theorists argue that social comparisons are neither necessary nor sufficient to produce response polarisation. They deal "with relatively remote processes which may lead to polarisation on occasion, when they are mediated by persuasive argumentation" (Burnstein & Vinokur, 1977).

Evidences gathered so far in support of persuasive argument theory (PAT) and social comparison theory (SCT) are simply too massive. In PAT, the individual changes his opinion because of the access to additional persuasive arguments. In SCT, the individual being exposed to discrepant opinions of others, shifts his opinion to match with others. Literature proposes that PAT and SCT are not mutually exclusive rather they are complementary. The underlying process in PAT and SCT is basically one and the same.

Researches on polarisation may wax and wane periodically. On theoretical front, what men believe, how their minds and hearts can be changed cast an open challenge. Therefore, these two process theories which explain polarisation in opinions, attitudes, values and decisions deserve elaboration.

Persuasive Argument Theory (PAT)

PAT is a cognitive theory of information processing in collective decision-making (Burnstein, 1982; Burnstein & Schul, 1983; Burnstein & Vinokur, 1975, 1977; Burnstein, Vinokur, & Trope, 1973; Madsen, 1978; Vinokur & Burnstein, 1974, 1978a). It states : if two finite, exhaustive set of alternatives (say *X* and *Y*) are available, the individual in evaluating the alternatives, retrieves the ideas, images, and thoughts from memory. The ideas, images and thoughts in memory are organised into a pool of arguments favouring each alternative. The arguments vary in accessibility (the probability of coming to mind), direction (pro-*X* or pro-*Y*) and persuasiveness. When the pool of arguments favours one alternative over the other, the magnitude and direction of initial response reflect this preponderance. Polarisation of response occurs towards the alternative that elicits more persuasive arguments during group discussion and/or rethinking. Generally, the risky and cautious items are so constructed that they predominantly elicit pro-risk and pro-caution arguments respectively during initial session, group discussion, and rethinking. For this, the polarisation on risky and cautious items occurs in pre-inclined directions of further risk and caution respectively following group discussion. In neutral items, the pool of arguments in favour of risk and caution just evenly balance. Therefore, they neither favour any direction initially nor yield polarisation.

If all group members have initially thought of same arguments, no group member would gain any new arguments from group discussion. The higher the difference of argument samples from one individual to another before discussion, the lower occurs the overlap of argument samples among the individuals in group. Consequently, individuals in group gain access to a variety of arguments during discussion and yield more polarisation. Second, polarisation maximises if the initially thought arguments do not exhaust the larger pool of arguments available to the individual. When the individual rethinks on the issue, he finds many persuasive arguments that did not come to his mind earlier. Polarisation occurs when the individual gains access to additional persuasive arguments during discussion or rethinking.

Let us cite an example to explain PAT. Consider a situation having two alternatives, *X* (risky alternative) and *Y* (cautious alternative) in which culturally given pool contains four pro-*X* arguments of *a, b, c, d* and four pro-*Y* arguments of *i, j, k, l*. Several distinct outcomes would be expected depending on the distribution of arguments among individuals. For example, if all the three discussants have initially thought of same arguments favouring *X* than *Y*, prior attitude favouring *X* would be identical and discussion among them will produce no shift towards *X*. On the other hand, if initially the first individual has thought of *a, b* and *i*; second individual of *c* and *i*; and third individual of *d* and *i*, discussion among them will produce marked polarisation towards *X* because the different pro-*X* arguments will be made available to each discussant. However, polarisation towards *Y* would be expected following group discussion if initially the first individual has thought of *a, i,* and *j*; second individual of *a* and *k*; and third individual of *a* and *l*. If the disseminated arguments during discussion favour one alternative predominately, polarisation occurs in the direction of that alternative.

PAT makes polarisation contingent not only upon argument pool but also upon characteristics of arguments. The persuasiveness of an argument depends upon its (a) novelty, and (b) validity. Novelty is rather a pivotal property. If two arguments are equally valid, the one that is more novel, will be more persuasive than the other (Vinokur & Burnstein, 1978b). If arguments received during discussion are known to the individual (non-novel), the shift in his position will not occur (Kaplan, 1977). Novelty also connects well with validity. Both valid and novel arguments are perceived as more persuasive than either valid but non-novel arguments or non-valid but novel arguments (Vinokur & Burnstein, 1978b). A married couple favouring the use of contraceptives will favour them strongly if they are exposed to novel and valid persuasive arguments in their favour. Similarly, Bishop and Myers (1974) using a mathematical model confirmed that the amount of shifts is determined by (a) the direction of arguments, (b) their cogency, and (c) novelty. The force of an argument decreases if it lacks cogency and novelty.

Before discussion some individuals' argument pools contain a few arguments that are generally available to the average individual. Very few individuals' argument pools include a large number of arguments.

They contain few persuasive arguments that are generally non-available to the average individual before group discussion. This restricted availability of few persuasive arguments prior to discussion is assumed to be a necessary condition for polarisation. When the few persuasive arguments are disseminated to all group members during discussion, polarisation occurs.

Persuasive arguments are intrinsically cogent, novel and valid. They deny easy refutation. Once these few are made available to all group members through discussion, by virtue of their own merits, they come to mind more frequently than other arguments. Their frequent re-filtering in mind stimulates rethinking and cognitive elaboration upon them. They activate the large network of congruent arguments already available in memory (before discussion). Thereby, some new arguments self-generate through cognitive mediation. They also persuade to change.

Now, it is clearly understood that group members generate arguments that go beyond the direct availability of arguments in discussion. Rethinking, active comprehension and elaboration on persuasive arguments generate new information that influence shifts. The work on attitude, thinking and memory is germane here. It is observed that opinion change is poorly related to the passive learning of the explicit content of arguments (Greenwald, 1968) and is strongly influenced by the ideational embellishment that occurs either in (a) comprehending arguments (Brock, 1967; Cacioppo & Petty, 1979; Cacioppo, Petty, & Morris, 1983; Eagly, 1974; Eagly & Warren, 1976; Keating & Brock, 1974; McGuire, 1964, 1969, 1972; Petty & Cacioppo, 1977; Petty, Wells, & Brock, 1976), or (b) engaging in issue-relevant thinking (Burnstein & Vinokur, 1975; Tesser, 1976, 1978; Tesser & Conlee, 1975). More the thinking and elaboration on substantive features of persuasive communications, more it yields reformulated information and changes opinion or attitude (Chaiken, 1980). In the studies of Tesser and his associates, the magnitude of polarisation is also shown to vary positively with (a) the amount of information available to the individual about the issue, (b) the extent of time he spends in thinking about the issue, and negatively with (c) the extent to which he is distracted from thinking about the issue. Similarly, when subjects are made familiar with the issue on subsequent occasions and allowed to think about the issue, polarisation occurs (Bateson, 1966; Flanders & Thistlethwaite, 1967). If the individual has a longer time to think and generate arguments before indicating his initial preference, he will exhaust the larger pool of arguments. Rethinking would not bring new arguments and would keep the posterior preference unchanged. In both thinking and familiarisation procedures, polarisation occurs when less time is given to the subjects to think about their initial preferences than about their posterior preferences. More the thinking on an issue after stating initial preference, more ideas and information self-generate through cognitive mediation and thereby larger polarisation results. In social confrontations of debate and discussion; thinking, comprehension and active elaboration on information of others occur so quickly that they bring some self-generated new information when people think of their next contributions. The work on creative thinking, concept formation and transfer of training validates that human beings think and elaborate the available information and thereby self-generate new information congruent with them. The self-generated information and activities are even more influential to bring about change than the learning of information and activities. Piaget's support for intellectual development of the child through active play, Rogers's non-directive therapy for the patients to cure themselves, and Freire's (1977) critical consciousness stage to change one's own behaviour are just a few examples to justify the greater impact of self-generated information.

The arguments are encoded at the semantic level. The work on semantic memory and spread of processing (reported in Burnstein, 1982, pp.114-115) indicates that the retention of an argument depends upon how elaborate and widespread is the processing of that argument at the level of encoding. The spread of processing also implies the establishment of implicative links or paths between the (new) communicated arguments and the (old) prior arguments available to the individual (before discussion). The more congruent the two sets of arguments, the more exists the implicative path between the two. When the path is activated by gaining access to an idea in one, it links to the idea in other. Thereby, some associative new arguments come to mind.

The persuasiveness of an argument depends on (a) how much it lends itself to elaborate processing during encoding (or the number of arguments in memory with which it makes contact), (b) the degree of congruency with the larger network of arguments already available in memory, and (c) how far it activates the path to retrieve new arguments from memory. Relating to the characteristics of persuasiveness, more novel the argument, more it will lend itself to rethinking and elaborate processing. More valid the argument, more it will become congruent with the prior existing arguments (before discussion) in memory. The additional availability of novel and valid persuasive arguments following group discussion initiates more rethinking and elaborate processing upon them and link with the larger network of prior arguments already available in memory. Thereby, some inaccessible arguments are brought to mind that were not retrieved otherwise.

In summary, the extent of polarisation depends upon : (a) the number of arguments that predominantly favour one alternative over the other, (b) the individual's access to new arguments favouring his initial preference during discussion, (c) the persuasiveness of arguments, and (d) the self-generation of arguments. Similar theory of information integration has also been proposed by Anderson and Graesser (1976), Bishop and Myers (1974), Kaplan (1977), and Kaplan and Miller (1977).

Supportive Evidence

There are massive evidences in favour of PAT (see Burnstein, 1982; Isenberg, 1986; Madsen, 1978; Myers, 1982; Myers & Lamm, 1976). They support three hypotheses. (a) The initial (pre-test) preponderance of pro and con arguments correlates with the extent of polarisation. (b) Given the persuasive arguments, appropriate direction and magnitude of shifts can be yielded. (c) SCT is neither necessary nor sufficient. The comparison-induced shifts are due to integration of additional persuasive information.

The last proposition being a charge against SCT requires elaboration. In one study, subjects after responding to choice dilemma items, learned about the position of others (1 or 5) and the arguments (5 or 25) for these positions. These two factors – position of others and the arguments for them – were orthogonally manipulated in a 2 X 2 factorial design so that individuals in one condition received few position (1) of others but many arguments (25); in another condition many positions (5) but few arguments (5), and so forth. Shift towards further risk and caution increased with the increase in number of arguments but not with the increase in number of positions. Further examination of the data revealed a comparatively modest but noticeable shift when arguments available to the subjects were minimal (5) but comparison positions were maximal (5). This weak but atypical shift did not deny comparison explanations. The authors conjectured that knowing the position of others stimulated the subject to rethink and self-generate additional arguments to justify why others advocated for different positions than him. This self-generation of arguments through cognitive mediation to justify others' positions might have influenced the subject to revise and shift his own position (Burnstein, Vinokur, & Trope, 1973). As a further confirmatory test to this interpretation, in another experiment, subjects in one condition after giving their initial responses to dilemma items learned about the position of others. Then they were encouraged to think further about the issues and list arguments which came to their minds. In second condition, similarly subjects learned about the position of others and immediately after learning, they were given an irrelevant filler task that distracted from thinking further about the issues. The third condition was identical with the first except that the subjects received no information about the position of others. The first condition with comparison facilitated the self-generation of arguments, the second condition with comparison blocked the self-generation of arguments, and the third condition did like first except the availability of comparison positions. Polarisation occurred only in the first condition. Only knowledge of discrepant positions of others was not sufficient for polarisation. This knowledge was only relevant to the extent the individual thought and self-generated arguments to justify positions of others that revised his own initial position (Burnstein & Vinokur, 1975). Polarisation did not occur when the cognitive processes to rethink and self-generate arguments were blocked (condition II) and the comparison positions were unavailable (condition III). Knowledge of positions of others leads a person to rethink and self-generate arguments others might have had for their positions. Ordinarily, the self-generated arguments would not have come to mind without the knowledge of the discrepant position of others. After comparison and rethinking, the self-generated arguments function in the same way as the group members access to new persuasive arguments during discussion. In comparison process, the self-generated arguments persuade us to change and thus polarisation occurs. But the comparison theorists do not agree with this explanation (Sanders & Baron, 1977).

Social Comparison Theory (SCT)

SCT has many versions Brown's (1965) version of cultural value theory mentions that people are motivated to present and to perceive themselves favourably in socially desirable direction. Before knowing the norm of others, each one guesses the norm of others to be at or below his own option. When individuals talk together in a group, the actual distribution of opinions on the issue is made known and the norm of others is disclosed. By comparison, those who find their options below this norm change their options in the direction of that norm. It results in polarisation. Those who find their initial options at or above the norm of others feel no such compulsion to change because their initial options are already in socially desirable direction.

In western society, risk on certain issues and caution on others are socially valued. Group discussion on the issue disseminates information about the options of others and thereby provides information specifying and supporting the socially desirable norm. Arguments received during group discussion have no relevance to this theory. Later on, other variations of value theory such as cultural value (Hong, 1978), item specific value (Stoner, 1968) and self-anchoring theory (Brown, 1974), emerged.

Ability comparison version (Jellison & Arkin, 1977; Jellison & Riskind, 1970), deriving propositions from Festinger's social comparison theory (1954), supports the Brown's value theory. It holds that risk is a value. It is an index of one's ability. The level of risk one chooses indicates the level of ability he has. Festinger (1954, p.125) stated that with the evaluation of opinions, when the individual compares himself with others, the discrepancy produces "uncomplicated pressure toward uniformity" but with abilities there is an "unidirectional push to do better and better . . . (which) cease acting on a person if he is just slightly better than others." Since the individual wants to be slightly higher in ability, he defines others as less risky (or having lower ability) than himself. In group context, after learning the norm of others in risk continuum and finding himself at or below the group average, he increases his level of risk (or ability) to excel others. It produces risky shift. Those who find their initial positions above the norm of others, the motivation ceases to act on them because they are better in ability than others.

The risky dilemma items bear upon abilities of the central person. The items that evoke characteristics opposed to abilities of the central person yield conservative shift (Jellison & Riskind, 1970).

In pluralistic ignorance version (Levinger & Schneider, 1969; Schroeder, 1973), the individual faced with an issue of taking decision feels a conflict between an 'ideal preference' what he internally values and 'the norm of others' what he thinks to be realistic and reasonable. As a compromise, the individual's initial preference lies between these two. Pluralistic ignorance exists because of lack of accurate information about the norm of others. The average individual, by comparing his preference with others in group, discovers that the norm of others on the same issue is closer to his ideal preference. Upon making a second decision, the individual in group shifts closer to his ideal preference. This brings polarisation.

Like pluralistic ignorance, in release version (Pruitt, 1969, 1971a, 1971b), the individual initial position on an issue reflects a compromise between an 'ego-idealised extreme preference' and an 'assumed social norm of moderation'. The former one implies the individual to present and perceive himself more favourably in socially desirable direction. The latter one implies the individual to conform the wider social norm of moderation and not to be looked by others as 'too far out on a limb'. The moderates, by comparing their positions with others in group, discover that someone (the model) endorses their initial ideal preferences more strongly than they did. It releases them from the assumed social constraints which held them back to take extreme opinions. Finding an extreme model in group gives courage to their convictions. The model is imitated by moderates in group and polarisation occurs. This theory is also quite consistent with leadership theory and conformity behaviour. Moderates are swayed towards the extreme individual (leader). They conform to the choice of extreme individual in group to act out their internal preferences.

As research findings were evaluated, emphasis was drifted to a bandwagon version (Brown, 1974; Myers, 1978; Myers, Bruggink, Kersting, & Schlosser, 1980; Myers, Wojcicki, & Aardema, 1977). People are motivated to perceive and present themselves to be better embodiment of certain socially desirable behaviour than others. At the same time, they want to be perceived as somewhat different and distinct from others in socially valued direction (Fromkin, 1970, 1972). When people initially give ratings on certain socially desirable dimensions, they evaluate themselves more favourably than the assumed others. When directly or indirectly they infer the true norm of others on the same issue, the initial moderates try to improve them, climb up to keep themselves in desirable direction than others. This results in polarisation.

The early personality theories (Fromm, 1941; Horney, 1937; Maslow, 1962) and the empirical evidences add credence to this version. Individual has a need for separate identity or need for uniqueness. He is not identical with but similar to others. At the same time, he is somehow desirably distinct from others. When a sizeable discrepancy exists between what the individual does in accordance with societal reference group (perceived self) and what he internally wants to do (ideal self), the psychological balance breaks down. He experiences a series of distressful emotions – anxiety, insecurity, self-role incongruency and others (Sharan, Prasad, & Suar, 1989). Therefore, after knowing the real norm of others, people want to be desirably distinct from others in the socially valued direction.

Unfortunately, there is some variation among different versions of SCT so far as the selection of initial choice and comparison target are concerned. The comparison target motivates to shift. In value and bandwagon versions, the individual initial choice reflects the desirable social behaviour equal to or slightly higher than the norm of assumed others. Discovery of the realistic and desirable social norm of others in group (comparison target) permits the initial moderates in group to avoid the earlier undesirable behaviour and to improve the desirable social behaviour. Thereby, polarisation occurs. In ability version, the extent of initial risk level reflects upon the individual ability. After learning the realistic norm of others (comparison target) in group interaction, the initial moderates are motivated to outshine the others in ability that yields polarisation. In pluralistic ignorance and release versions, the individual initial choice is a compromising point between the internalised admired preference and an assumed social norm of moderation (although in pluralistic ignorance version, the social norm is not assumed to be moderate, the date pertaining to the perception of others confirm this proposition). In group interaction, the initial moderates find the realistic norm of others (comparison target in pluralistic ignorance version) or the extreme preference of someone in group (comparison target in release version) closer to their initial ideal preferences that they initially valued but suppressed. It legitimises their desire to act out their initial valued preferences. Except these, the basic formulations in different versions of SCT are superimposed on each other to a larger extent.

Supportive Evidence

From the different versions of SCT, four major hypotheses emerge to support the theory. (a) Those who deviate in socially desirable direction are evaluated positively. (b) The individual before subjection to reality underestimates the assumed norm of others, and (c) overestimates his ideal preference than that of his own in the desirable social direction. (d) Polarisation occurs by exposing the subject to the response of others who are similar to him on the opinion or attitude in question.

Those who take valued preferences on dilemma items are less susceptible to conformity pressure. They are evaluated positively on different dimensions of self by others in group (Baron, Monson, & Baron, 1973; Baron & Roper, 1976; Jellison & Riskind, 1970; Madaras & Bem, 1968). In polarisation research, after responding to choice dilemma items, individuals are asked to go over the items and guess how their peers would respond. Then they are asked to go over the items third time and indicate what responses they would admire most. Generally on risky and cautious items, risk and caution are socially valued. It is reported that the individual underestimates the assumed normative preference of his peers and overestimates his ideal preference than his own in socially valued direction (Myers, 1973, 1982; Myers & Lamm, 1976). This finding also extends to other behaviour. In decision-making, people tend to overestimate the possible occurrence of favourable events to them and underestimate those that are unfavourable (Lindsay & Norman, 1974, p. 545). In many heuristics and biases from 'halo effect' in interpersonal perception to 'gambler's fallacy' in decision-making (Schoemaker, 1980, pp. 39-41), the individual overestimates the 'judgement' of favourable events and underestimates the 'judgement' of unfavourable events. Similarly, the individual in possession of socially desirable characteristics overevaluates himself in comparison to his peers. People perceive themselves more favourably in their attitude towards church than others (Myers, Wojcicki, & Aardema, 1977). Most of the businessmen perceive themselves to be more ethical than the average businessman (Baumhart, 1968; Brenner & Molander, 1977). Many people perceive their views to be less racially prejudiced than the norm of their peers and neighbours (Fields & Schuman, 1976; Lenihan, 1965; O'Gorman & Garry, 1976). This self-perception is inflated and distorted; the average person is not better than the average person. In favour of third hypothesis, many studies have reported that the ideal self is higher than the perceived self (Sharan, 1977). Walter-Mittyness is a similar self presentation. The frictional character, Walter Mitty in James Thurber's short story being engaged in cautious behaviour described himself as engaged in exciting risky adventures. Similarly, on risky items, subjects chose cautious decisions but viewed them as risky decisions (Pruitt, 1969). In a five stage strategic game, at the end of every stage, people pictured themselves as having been less risky in past than they would be in future. However, their level of actual risk-taking and the perception of past risk-taking did not change from stage to stage. Not only people described their current behaviour as riskier than it actually was but they described their future behaviour to be riskier than their past behaviour (Higbee, 1971). Past is history, present is reality and future is mystery. Certainly, there are fewer reality constraints on what is said about future than about past or present. While supports exist, contradictions are also there in favour of the first three hypotheses.

Studies employing SCT have observed polarisation in perceptual and verbal tasks by exposing the subject to the response of others (Isenberg, 1986; Myers, 1982; Myers & Lamm, 1976). In laboratory as well as naturalistic observations of blackjack playing, the individual increase or decrease in risk and conservative levels depended upon the norms of risk and conservatism of their co-actors in group. Learning the bet of others produced individual shift in socially valued direction and the opportunity for full discussion did not increase this effect (Blascovich & Ginsburg, 1974, 1978; Blascovich, Ginsburg, & Howe, 1976; Blascovich, Ginsburg, & Veach, 1975; Blascovich, Veach, & Ginsburg, 1973). In ability version, the authors associated ability and skill with risk. As the level of risk increased for others, they were rated more favourably on adjectives relevant to ability and skill. Risky shift occurred after observing the norm of others because the individual wanted to appear more able and skillful than others (Jellison & Arkin, 1977; Jellison & Riskind, 1970; Madaras & Bem, 1968). It was also argued that group members who perceived themselves as similar in ability with others polarised to greater risk following comparison or group discussion. Subjects responded individually to risky dilemma items and rated themselves on overall 'talent, creativity and ability' and then assigned to conditions. In group discussion condition, subjects discussed the items in group and then gave their responses privately. In information exchange condition, subjects were exposed to positions of their group members and then gave their responses privately. In information-exchange-of-position-and-ability condition, subjects were exposed to each other's positions in group as in the earlier one and showed their self-ratings of ability in group. Highest polarisation occurred in the last condition followed by group discussion and information exchange conditions. After the experiment, subjects in the information-exchange-of-position-and-ability condition perceived their co-group members as similar in overall talent, creativity and ability. Thus, perceived similarities of abilities produced more polarisation (Goethals & Zanna, 1979).

In jury problems and dilemma items, subjects were exposed to the complete percentage distribution of others' responses (comparison target in release version) while others were to their peer group average on each item (comparison target in other versions). Mere exposure to the peer group norm was sufficient to yield polarisation as the exposure to the full percentage distribution of others' responses (Myers, 1978). Even when subjects learned the judgement of few others rather than a large distribution of others' responses, their judgement also polarised. Exposure to small distribution of opinions or attitudes of others was sufficient to motivate the person to line up his self-presentation similarly with others (Myers, Bruggink, Kersting, & Schlosser, 1980). In another attitude survey, subjects in one condition, without pre-test, were directly exposed to the complete percentage distribution of responses of one hundred subjects. In another condition, subjects were exposed to the average response of the same one hundred subjects. The post-exposure average responses in two conditions were compared with the baseline average of same one hundred subjects (average of comparison stimuli) and with the average of another control group. Subjects in both conditions shifted significantly from average of the control group. In addition, subjects in percentage exposure condition shifted significantly from the baseline average. Both the exposure conditions were necessary but yielded small polarisation effect beyond the baseline of observed responses (Myers, Wojcicki, & Aardema, 1977). In testing pluralistic ignorance version, subjects were exposed to the norm of others (as in other versions) whereas in testing release version they were exposed to the extreme model in the percentage distribution of others' responses. The low salient difference in manipulation of comparison information between two conditions did not give superiority to release version or pluralistic ignorance version. Still the yield in polarisation was small because of passive manipulation of comparison targets. In early studies, face-to-face exchange of comparison information yielded more polarisation (Clark & Willems, 1969; Teger & Pruitt, 1967). However, in reality, even today in a tribal village what the headman does, others just follow. In impulsive mob or crowd, the behaviour of the 'trigger person' or the 'single extreme individual' liberates the entire mob who at a moment share the common impulse. These support the release version. In group context, if the emerging group norm matches with what the individual internally wants to do, he acts in closer accord to his ideal inclination. The intensification of eating, drinking and jiving behaviour in group support the pluralistic ignorance version. On the whole, in different versions of SCT, the individual by comparing himself with the norm of others, lines up his self-presentation or differentiates himself from the norm of others in right direction and, to some extent, that yields polarisation.

Evaluation of Two Theories

The evaluation of many studies has confirmed the combined theoretical role of persuasive argumentation and social comparison to produce polarisation. But the former process yields more shifts than the later (Isenberg, 1986). Another recent literature has clearly pointed out that even in comparison process, people actively process information (Burnstein, 1982). This explanation is well evident in comparison-poor verbal tasks. Discussion on this point is made earlier in describing the support for PAT. In one study cited earlier, perceived similarities of abilities among group members in information-exchange-of-position-and-ability condition produced more shift on risky items (Goethals & Zanna, 1979). Perhaps, the individual's exposure to positions and ability-ratings of others in group helped in self-generation of more arguments to justify the high risk levels of high ability raters (multiple reference cue to self-generate arguments). This self-generated arguments being persuasive induced change.

The comparison theorists argue that a necessary pre-requisite to cognitive change is the presence of a psychological state of imbalance or inconsistency. Therefore, subjects in group are exposed to the position of others on certain issues that are mostly incompatible with their own positions. In many verbal tasks as cited earlier, the average individual being exposed to discrepant positions of others might have had self-generated persuasive arguments to justify positions of others that revised his own position and caused polarisation. In studies of attitude and value change, subjects are supplied with manipulated information about attitudes and values of others. The intention is to make them consciously aware of the states of inconsistency that exist within their attitudes and values. After that, a time interval was given and post-test measurement was taken that demonstrated shift in the manipulated direction. In this process, the change of attitude towards black (Hopkins, 1973), political value (Hamid & Flay, 1974), equality value (Gurbe, 1982a; Penner, 1971), self-controlled value (Conroy, Katkin, & Barnette, 1973) and others are obtained (cf. Gurbe, 1982b; Rokeach, 1971). Even change in individual terminal values is made through computer feedback of information containing the value ratings of other reference groups (Rokeach, 1975). Comparison served the function for processing and integrating information to justify one's conception of self as competent and moral human being quite like his reference groups. These self-generated information caused change in the manipulated direction.

In argument-poor perceptual tasks, even if it is counter-intuitive to postulate the effects of informational influence in comparison-induced shifts, it does happen. For example, the above cited blackjack playing is a sparse argument generation situation. After learning the bet of others, the subject might quickly self-generated few persuasive arguments to justify the amount of bet and the excellency of co-group members that influenced his amount of bet in the group. This possibility cannot be refuted. Some literature strongly supporting SCT also requires scrutiny. In a moving light task like autokinetic judgement, when subjects were told that larger estimates were indicative of positive valued traits ('larger estimates of movement indicate intellectual and academic promise'), subjects gave larger estimates after they learned others' estimates. When large estimates were not linked with positive valued traits prior to learning of others' estimates, it did not produce such shifts (Baron & Roper, 1976). The authors interpreted this as comparison-induced shifts indicative of a desire for valued positions. In fact, the actual movement of light in the dark room was ambiguous. Moreover, the instructions might have prompted the subjects to self-generate arguments to maintain positive self-images (such as intelligent people tend to give larger estimates, some of my peers are intelligent and being alike, I should not make smaller estimates and so on) for which polarisation occurred. In another study, two persons judged at a time the attractive and unattractive faces on slides. The second person always viewed and rated the slide after hearing the response from the first person. The second person rarely duplicated the judgement of the first person and most frequently reported the attractive faces as more attractive and unattractive faces as more unattractive (unpublished, Myers, 1982, p.153). At the surface level, this is a poor-argument situation and comparison-induced polarisation. The author could not completely rule out the possibility of argument generation through cognitive mediation. Two seconds or so lapsed between hearing of response from the first person and delivery of reply by the second person. This duration might have stimulated the second person to think of few persuasive arguments which the first person might have had to justify that judgement. Subjects' attitudes towards the subliminally presented stimuli became significantly more positive with repeated exposures, even when subjects were unaware that exposures had occurred. Similar attitude change was produced by subliminal exposure to photographs of actual persons (Bornstein, Leone, & Galley, 1987). Perhaps, repeated exposures helped in self-generation of information subconsciously which influenced the change.

In Asch's (1956) line judgement tasks, all members in group except one naive subject preinstructed to give incorrect responses unanimously on certain trials about the equality of comparison lines (say 6.25", 8.00", 6.75") with the standard line (say 8.00"). The naive subject was manoeuvred into sitting at the end of the table. Of the total number of judgements given by the naive subjects in groups, 37 per cent conformed to those of unanimous majority. Control subjects judging alone virtually made no errors. Knowing that the naive subject's disagreement with the unanimous majority would be made public and the monopolisation of attention by the single preference induced wrongly the naive subject to process information in favour of the option of unanimous majority. In Sherif's (1935) study of autokinetic effect, each isolated subject was asked by the experimenter to observe the apparent movement of a tiny point of light in a dark room. In reality, the light was not moving at all. Following a series of observations, each subject settled down and estimated his own average distance about the movement of light. The distance differed from each other considerably. The opinions of the subjects converged around a norm, concerning the movement of light, when they heard each other's reports and worked together in group. In such a unstructured situation, the estimation of the isolated subjects was influenced by the instructions of the experimenter. The individuals' estimates were further adjusted in group situation hearing the different judgement of group members. The instructions of the experimenter and different judgement of group members processed wrongly the information of the individuals in group to agree on a norm describing the movement of light.

In most of the perceptual tasks, frequently incorrect verbal instructions are contrived or deceptions are committed before or after the perceptual observations. In most cases, the task itself is ambiguous. As a result, the delivery of verbal instructions and information from others easily tilt the perceptual observations and biases the cognitive processing to generate arguments in favour of verbal instructions and information of others. Shifts occur in the direction of verbal instructions and information of others. Whatever may be the zany manipulations in perceptual tasks, it is difficult to imagine comparison-induced shifts without the cognitive processing of task-irrelevant information and the self-generation of information.

One proposition is clearly evident from this discussion. Perhaps, there is no comparison-induced polarisation without informational influence. Therefore, the second objective of the study is to test whether informational influence is the basis of polarisation in two theories. This will attempt to link the theories and settle down the controversies.

(c) *Factors Influencing Polarisation*

Attitude studies have involved the manipulation of source variables (expertise, trustworthiness, sex, religion), message variables (discrepancy, order effects, fear appeals, logicality) and audience variables (intelligence, self-esteem, cognitive complexity, ego involvement) to observe their impact on attitude change (see Fishbein & Ajzen, 1972, 1975; Himmelfarb & Eagly, 197; McGuire, 1969; Triandis, 1971). Since polarisation is more or less similar to congruent change of attitude, the source, message and audience variables are likely to influence polarisation. In laboratory formed group, it is difficult to differentiate the source and audience variables. Therefore, the variables influencing polarisation can be conceptualised at individual, message and group levels.

It was observed that extremity of individual response on risky items had poor relationship with certain attitude and personality dimensions (Kogan & Wallach, 1964; Rim,1964a, 1964b, 1965a, 1965b, 1966a, 1966b, 1966c). Subjects high in need for approval did not polarise to more risk than the subjects low in need for approval. The former subjects were more likely to present themselves in socially desirable direction than the latter (Lamm, Schaude, & Trommsdorff, 1971). The high machiavellian subjects also did not differ in the extent of polarisation from the low machiavellian subjects although the former were more manipulative and less emotional than the latter (Lamm & Myers, 1976). On the other hand, both field dependent and independent groups demonstrated polarisation towards further risk following discussion (Wallach, Kogan, & Burt, 1967). Anxious subjects polarised towards more risk than defensive subjects (Kogan & Wallach, 1967a). It was also mentioned earlier that the extremity of responses on risky items directly varied with the individual perception of his ability (Jellison & Arkin, 1977; Jellison & Riskind, 1970). Subjects high in self-esteem yielded more polarisation (Lamm, Trommsdorff, & Rost-Schaude, 1972). However, the traits like need for approval, machiavellianism, field dependence, defensiveness having direct bearing on image-maintenance strategy of SCT could not yield supportive results except self-esteem.

In message characteristics, novelty and validity of arguments are shown to influence shifts (Bishop & Myers, 1974; Vinokur & Burnstein, 1978b). After group interaction, those who polarised towards further risk attributed this tendency to the group of which they were members (Wallach, Kogan, & Burt, 1967), to the trust, competency, ability and self-evaluation of group members (Doise, 1969; Goethals & Zanna, 1979; Sinha & Yousuf, 1972; Verma & Sinha, 1981). Of course, at the message and group levels, these variables have influenced polarisation. To understand the theoretical formulations, other variables having direct bearing on PAT and SCT can be related to polarisation. Therefore, the third objective is to study the variables influencing polarisation keeping two theoretical proposals intact. This will enrich the knowledge about polarisation in general and will strengthen the understanding of the second objective in particular. In accordance with the three objectives, three experiments are conducted successively using dilemma items.

Method and Sample

Scientific inquiry in social sciences can be made under two conditions: (i) natural and, (ii) experimental. The real world phenomena are so complex that they need experimental verification. Keeping the nature of problems in mind, three experiments have been conducted in class-room setting as conducted earlier in polarisation research (e.g., Doise, 1969; Moscovici & Zavalloni, 1969).

It is often mentioned that (a) experiments demonstrate the obvious, (b) experiments are artificial, (c) laboratory contexts are oversimplified and (d) hypothesis testing leads to myopia (Weick, 1967). Experimentalists are well aware of the legitimate pitfalls. Still they operationalise variables, manipulate and control variables to bear upon mundane realism. At the same time, they assure the internal, external, statistical-conclusion and construct validity of the experiments (Cook & Campbell, 1976). Internal validity concerns the reasoning process that relates effects to hypothesised causes. External validity concerns the extent to which experimental results generalise to larger population (such as general public, workers, professionals), to other time periods and to other settings. Statistical-conclusion validity deals with the validity of quantitative judgements and proper application of statistics in relating causes to effects. Finally, construct validity refers to the correctness of connecting experimental treatments and outcomes with the theoretical constructs and abstractions. In spite of this, misconceptions about experimentation exist among those who are trained in other traditions of scientific inquiry and theory testing.

In three experiments, a total of 625 male and female students (270 + 267 + 88 = 625 Ss) from post-graduate departments of Sambalpur University, Jyoti Vihar, Orissa participated as subjects. Prior to each experiment, the students in classroom were requested through a teacher of the same department to appear on the scheduled date, time and place in their respective department. Those who volunteered to participate as per the schedule served as subjects. Hence, the sampling procedure is incidental non-random. There is practical difficulty in selecting random sample from the volunteers.

In each experiment, either the first year or the second year post-graduate students participated. Knowing the strength of males and females in each department, the departments were selected for different conditions of each experiment to reach a pre-estimated sample target. Out of the total subjects for a condition, those who could not be adjusted against different group size were eliminated. Those who could not reappear in subsequent sessions of a condition were also eliminated from the analysis. The subject loss was 2 per cent approximately.

Data Analysis

The *t*-test, product-moment correlation, one-way analysis of variance, multiple correlation and simple least square regression equation are used to analyse the data. The computer programmes were developed for statistical analysis. However, for the last two statistical methods, the system packages were used.

One may question the use of bi-variate and multi-variate statistical methods in data analyses. All the researches in this field except a few have used these statistics assuming the normal distribution of obtained scores on dilemma items and other variables. Parametric statistics are used accordingly.

Limitations

The polarisation phenomenon studied with the help of dilemma items are of similar complexity to the judgement situations the individual faces in reality. Unfortunately, all the judgement situations are hypothetical in nature that may limit the external validity of research findings. Since we are interested in the process of change or polarisation rather than the change in reality, the hypothetical versus real situations may not be troublesome. Second, in polarisation literature, the difference between pre-test and post-test scores is taken as the index of change or shift. Even if the difference score is inappropriate measure of change (Cronbach & Furby, 1970), it is conventionally followed here. Third, to tap the situational variables associated with polarisation, single or double item questions are developed and used. The questions are so straightforward that their reliability and validity are taken for granted but can be objected. Some other minor limitations of the work are also here and there. However, they are not detrimental to this kind of research.

2

DO RISK-ORIENTED INSTRUCTIONS INFLUENCE SHIFTS AND DILEMMA ITEMS MEASURE ATTITUDINAL JUDGEMENT?

This study is an attempt to test the first objective discussed in review of literature : (a) whether the shifts obtained on dilemma items are dependent upon instructions; and (b) whether the dilemma items measure the attitudinal judgement.

Risk-oriented Instructions and Shift

The dependence of shifts on instructions was confirmed by, Clark and Willems (1969). In their study, 200 subjects were distributed equally in four conditions : non-verbal comparison of opinion, face to face active discussion, passive listening of discussion, and test-retest control condition. Six risky dilemma items were used. In each condition, half of the fifty subjects — 5 five-person groups — received usual instructions in the questionnaire. This was typically called the risk-oriented instructions – to check the lowest probability of success they would consider acceptable to make it worthwhile for the central person to take the uncertain alternative. The other half received the same items with neutral instructions. The risk-oriented instructions contained the phrase 'lowest probability' which was missing in neutral instructions. The risk-oriented and neutral instructions remained identical to the subjects during pre-test, experimental manipulation and post-test sessions. When the items contained the risk-oriented instructions, the pre-test responses followed by group discussion and comparison with others yielded significant shifts towards further risk. Under neutral instructions, subjects did not yield significant shifts in any of the conditions. It was concluded that the risk-oriented instructions cued shifts in the direction of further risk while the neutral instructions did not. On further probe, the pre-test average scores of the subjects on four conditions under two different instructions were almost identical. But subjects under neutral instructions having similar pre-test scores did not show further shifts following group discussion and comparison. This observation identified the location of instructional bias in group processes. The authors concluded that the directional expectation to check the lowest probability was legitimised through group processes of discussion and comparison. Under neutral instructions, the exclusion of the word 'lowest' could not orient the group members during discussion and comparison to shift their preferences towards lower probability or further risk.

Though the findings appear to be impressive, they rest on certain objections. First, only risky items have been used in the above study. Many studies taking the cautious items and using the same risk-oriented instructions 'to check the lowest probability' have obtained shifts towards the higher probability or further caution following group discussion or social comparison. If directional expectancy 'to check the lowest probability' is legitimised in group processes, then how the risky and cautious items with same instructions have yielded shifts in two opposite directions, one towards lower probability and other towards higher probability. Second, as discussed earlier, the shift effect is not a content bound phenomenon specific to the dilemma items. It has sufficient external validity in the areas of attitude, jury decision, judgement, person perception, negotiation, conformity, moral reasoning, and instrumental risk-taking (see Myers, 1982; Myers & Lamm, 1976). These studies have yielded shifts, time and again using a variety of instrumental and verbal as well as hypothetical and real tasks. These tasks have no similarity with dilemma items or with instructions. Third, in study of Clark and Willems, each experimental condition under risk-oriented or neutral instructions has included only twenty-five subjects – 5 five-person groups. The number of subjects in each condition under each set of instructions (N = 25) lags behind the desired target of standard experiments. The authentic studies of Burnstein, Myers, and Vinokur (e.g., Burnstein & Vinokur, 1973; Myers, 1978) in this area have employed minimum 40 to 60 subjects in each condition comprising 10 to 15 groups. These rationalities cast doubts on strict contingency between risk-oriented instructions and shifts.

Few empirical evidences also question the validity of risk-oriented instructions. In study of Burnstein, Miller, Vinokur, Katz, and Crowley (1971) subjects after having stated their initial preferences on dilemma items, discussed about outcome utilities and then responded on the probability scale they had not discussed. Shifts occurred on risky and cautious items in the absence of an opportunity for discussion to incorporate the risk-oriented instructions. Myers, Bach, and Schreiber (1974) taking three risky items instructed subjects to discuss on each item whether the protagonist should attempt the risk. Each item was presented without the probability scale and risk-oriented instructions. The post-discussion average score on dilemma items shifted in the direction of further risk when compared to the initial average of a control group. Here, the instructions given during discussion favouring risk might have influenced the subsequent probability preferences. To rule out this possibility, subjects in another condition were directly exposed to the percentage distribution of initial responses by control subjects. The exposure percentages did not contain any risk-oriented instructions. The comparison of post-exposure average score with control group initial average yielded significant shift. Given these findings, the risk-oriented instructions to legitimise shifts in its direction through group processes of discussion or comparison is hardly compelling.

Other studies have also yielded shifts on dilemma items under neutral instructions. In study of Fraser, Gouge, and Billig (1971) subjects gave their responses to each of the dilemma items on Likert-type scale indicating their uncertain or certain preferences. The same subjects gave responses to the same items on probability scale containing the usual risk-oriented instructions. Both forms yielded comparable findings on initial and shift scores. The Likert-type options and probability responses correlated significantly. On risky items, uncertain preferences on Likert-type scale correlated significantly with lower probabilities and on cautious items, certain preferences with higher probabilities. Attaching similar seven-point Likert-type scale to dilemma items, Singleton (1979) obtained risky and cautious shifts on risky and cautious items respectively. Myers and Bishop (1971) engaged students in discussion of imaginary, non-risky dilemma items. The items contained responses in Likert-type neutral scale. Group discussion enhanced significantly the predominant pro or con initial tendency. On all accounts, the logical contradictions and empirical evidences argue that neither the shifts are contingent on instructional bias nor the bias is located in group processes. Therefore, the first purpose is to test whether the instructional bias determines shifts on risky, neutral and cautious items.

Dilemma Item and Attitudinal Judgement Measurement

The above studies (Fraser, Gouge, & Billig, 1971; Singleton, 1979) as well as the discussion in the introductory chapter hold a clear proposition that the risky and cautious items measure the attitudinal judgement towards uncertain and certain alternatives respectively. If attitudinal judgement is measured by the dilemma items, then the subjects' responses on probability scale to usual dilemma items with or without risk-oriented instructions will correlate significantly with their responses to same items on Likert-type scale. This will ascertain the convergent validity of usual dilemma items as an expression of attitudinal judgement. Convergent validity is the degree of agreement among multiple measures of the same variable or item. For example, if there are three methods of measurement (m_j, where j = 1 to 3) of three items or three categories of items (x_i, where i = 1 to 3), the convergent validity (*CV*) of the items will be a 3 x 3 matrix of correlations as follows:

$$CV = \begin{array}{c|ccc|c} m_1 & m_1x_1 \cdot m_2x_1 & m_1x_1 \cdot m_3x_1 & m_2x_1 \cdot m_3x_1 & x_1 \\ m_2 & m_1x_2 \cdot m_2x_2 & m_1x_2 \cdot m_3x_2 & m_2x_2 \cdot m_3x_2 & x_2 \\ m_3 & m_1x_3 \cdot m_2x_3 & m_1x_3 \cdot m_3x_3 & m_2x_3 \cdot m_3x_3 & x_3 \end{array}$$

Hence, the second purpose is to test whether the risky, neutral and cautious dilemma items with risk-oriented and neutral instructions measure the attitudinal judgement.

Since group interaction and intensification of initial inclination are common to choice shift and polarisation, the distinction between them have often been obscured. Choice shift is the difference between pre-discussion responses of groups and actual group decisions on the issue (group to group transfer). Polarisation is the change in individuals' pre- to post-discussion responses (individual to individual transfer). Second, while choice shift requires group decision and convergence of choices, individual decision followed by group discussion is sufficient to produce polarisation. Third, since polarisation is the individual-level change, persuasive argument and social comparison theories are better suited to explain it. Since choice shift is the group-level change, social decision schemes are better suited to predict the group decision from the initial distribution of choices (Hinsz & Davis, 1984).

A design which randomly assigns subjects to individual-group-individual for three successive decisions allows both within-subjects and between-subjects assessment of choice shift and polarisation (Laughlin & Earley, 1982, p.273). Even if there is a random assignment of subjects, the design remains akin to within-subjects design because the same subjects are used in successive decisions. If three successive decisions are taken at the level of individual- group-individual, and the group decisions are subtracted from the pre-test responses of the same groups, it will be a within-subjects measure of choice shift. If the post-treatment individual decisions are subtracted from the same individual pre-treatment decisions, it will be a within-subjects measure of polarisation. Accordingly, this is followed to incorporate both within-measures of choice shift and polarisation in a single design. When shifts were proved to be contingent upon instructional bias, at that time, there was no difference between choice shift and polarisation. Even if we are interested in polarisation, this study addresses itself to both the phenomena.

Keeping all these essence in mind, three parallel forms of dilemma items differing in instructions and response formats are developed. The items in one contain the so-called risk-oriented instructions and is called percentage form (PEF). The items in other two forms contain the neutral instructions. They are called probability form (PRF) and attitudinal judgement form (AJF). In the group discussion and decision condition (GDC), the three forms are given to three groups of subjects following the above design to test the role of instructional bias in choice shift and polarisation. This condition has been taken because it has yielded more shifts in a past study (Wallach & Kogan, 1965). In another, successive presentation condition (SPC), three forms are presented to the same subjects at the interval of fifteen days to test whether the dilemma items measure the attitudinal judgement. However, no control condition is taken against GDC. But this should not be considered as a serious drawback of the study because it is a preliminary methodological work to scrutinise the role of instructional bias in a different culture. If the instructional bias proves to be the sole contributor to shift, the research with dilemma items will not proceed further. Along with this, clarification of the meaning of dilemma items is considered to be a necessary step towards further research.

Method

Sample

A total of 270 male and female students in the age group of nineteen to twenty-six (Male = 161, Av. age = 21.142; Female = 109, Av. age = 20.679) from post-graduate departments of Sambalpur University, Jyoti Vihar, Orissa participated as subjects in this study. Prior to their participation, the students in class room were requested to cooperate in a study related to the understanding of human behaviour in social situations. Nothing about the actual experiment was communicated.

The subjects participated as individuals and in groups of three to four persons. The subjects were homogeneous in age and education. In group interaction session, the groups were homogeneous in sex. Twelve to thirty subjects participated in each session. Each session under group discussion and decision condition (GDC) lasted for about one and a half hours. In successive presentation condition (SPC), each session took about forty minutes.

In GDC, against AJF, 11 male and 3 female three-person groups, 2 male and 4 female four-person groups and against PRF, 10 male and 6 female three-person groups, 3 male and 1 female four-person groups participated. Agaianst PEF, 7 male and 8 female three-person groups, 2 male and 3 female four-person groups participated. Against three forms the subjects constituted a total of 112 males and 83 females comprising 60 groups (20 groups against each form). In SPC, 49 males and 26 females participated (Table 2.1).

TABLE 2.1: Sample Characteristics

Condition	Form	Sex	Group		Total Subjects	Av. Age	Education
			3-person	4-person			
GDC	AJF	M	11(33)	2(8)	41	21.121	Post-graduate (2nd yr.)
		F	3(9)	4(16)	25	20.828	—do-
	PRF	M	10(30)	3(12)	42	21.023	—do-
		F	6(18)	1(4)	22	20.409	—do-
	PEF	M	7(21)	2(8)	29	20.793	—do-
		F	8(24)	3(12)	36	20.843	—do-
SPC	AJF;PRF;	M	—	—	49	21.469	—do-
	PEF	F	—	—	26	20.538	—do-
Total		M	—	—	161	21.141	
		F	—	—	109	20.679	

Note: Number of individuals is given in the parentheses.

Materials

(a) *Choice Dilemma Item*

Nine choice dilemma items were chosen so as to include five risky items, one neutral item, and three cautious items. The items were collected from many sources and assembled in the questionnaire labelled 'opinion questionnaire'. The content, source and expected direction of shift of each item are summarised below:

1. An engineer must decide whether to join a new company with attractive salary and other benefits or stick to the lifetime job with moderate salary and liberal pension benefits (Kogan & Wallach, 1964 : risky).
2. An old accountant must decide whether to go for a delicate heart operation the success of which cannot be guaranteed or to carry on with heart ailment that will disrupt his strongest life habits (Kogan & Wallach, 1964 : neutral).
3. A first class post-graduate in chemistry must choose whether to attend a prestigious university where it is difficult to receive the Ph.D degree or to attend a lower prestigious university where it is almost certain to receive the Ph.D. degree (Kogan & Wallach, 1964 : risky).
4. The captain of a football team on the last game with its rival team must decide whether to settle for a tie score or try a complicated, risky play that would bring either victory or defeat (Kogan & Wallach, 1964 : risky).
5. Two known partners having controversies contacted a well-known relative and arrived at the conclusion that the happiness in marriage, though possible, would not be assured. They must decide whether to marry (Kogan & Wallach, 1964 : cautious).
6. A research physicist must decide whether to work on a long-term, difficult research problem which would bring high scientific honours or to work on a series of easy, short-term problems of lesser scientific importance where solutions are almost certain (Kogan & Wallach, 1964 : risky).
7. A man on a vacation trip at the airport experiencing severe abdominal pains must decide whether to disrupt his vacation plans in order to be examined in a hospital or to board the plane for an overseas flight (Stoner, 1968 : cautious).

8. A couple without any child must decide whether to allow a complicated pregnancy to continue with danger to wife's life or to terminate the pregnancy without any hope to have a child in future (Stoner, 1968 : cautious).
9. A writer having creative talents must choose whether to write a significant novel to boost his literary career or to continue the writing of short stories to just earn a comfortable living (Myers, 1982 : risky).

In the original choice dilemma questionnaire (Kogan & Wallach, 1964), although the items dealing with delicate heart operation and marriage decision were risky items, later on many studies proved the former to be a neutral item and the latter to be a cautious item (e.g., Vinokur, 1971). In adopting the items to our culture, some minor changes have been made. The central figure in each item is given explicitly Indian nationality by changing the abstract names to some popular Indian names. The item describing a college senior in chemistry eager to do Ph.D. is changed to a first class post-graduate in chemistry because in Indian universities the national tests leading to doctoral research in science prescribe first class degree as the minimum qualification. In the item dealing with marriage decision, the professional advice from a marriage counsellor is replaced by the advice from a well-known relative because the profession of marriage counselling is non-existent in India. Three parallel forms of the nine items are developed.

(i) *Attitudinal Judgement Form (AJF)*

In AJF, each item was accompanied by the following instructions. "Imagine that you are advising the central person. Please put a tick mark against the statement that best expresses your advice." Responses below each item were given on a seven-point Likert-type scale from strongly recommend the uncertain, risky alternative (score = 1) through neutrality (score = 4) to strongly recommend the certain, cautious alternative (score = 7).

(ii) *Percentage Form (PEF)*

PEF was the extensively used form of dilemma items. Each item was accompanied by the following instructions: "Imagine that you are advising the central person. Please tick the lowest percentage of chances that you would consider acceptable to make it worthwhile for the central person to choose the uncertain alternative." The response descriptions incorporated chances (with the phrase 'at least') from 10 per cent (score = 1), to 90 per cent (score = 9), for the selection of uncertain alternative and an option to reject the uncertain alternative irrespective of chances (score = 10). Only odd probabilities of responses were mentioned in original version. Responses below each item were given on a continuous scale transferring the probabilities into percentages. This was done to obtain better approximation of subjects' responses. A choice is measured as the percentage of chance chosen by the subject. Lower score is associated with higher acceptance of uncertain alternative and higher score with greater acceptance of certain alternative.

(iii) *Probability Form (PRF)*

PRF was similar to PEF with two major exceptions. Responses below each item were given in probabilities. Second, neither the word 'lowest' nor the phrase 'at least' were attached to the instructions. The instructions read: "Imagine that you are advising the central person. Please tick the probability you would consider acceptable for the central person to choose the uncertain alternative." The response descriptions incorporated probabilities from 1 in 10 (score = 1), to 9 in 10 (score = 9), for the selection of uncertain alternative and an option to reject the uncertain alternative irrespective of probabilities (score = 10).

PEF incorporated the so-called demand characteristics of the instructions with the words 'lowest' and 'at least'. AJF and PRF contained the neutral instructions. The instructions and response formats differed from one form to another. The positions of the items were randomly placed in different forms. The response descriptions below each item were given in alternate sequence from one item to another.

As the measure of homogeneity of items or internal consistency, the pre-test score on each of the risky and each of the cautious items correlated significantly with the total score of risky items and the total score of cautious items respectively against three forms in GDC. The item concerned with an engineer was generally considered as a risky item. The score of this item could not correlate significantly with the total score of risky items. It correlated significantly with the total score of cautious items. On further check, the initial score of the item also elicited cautious orientation in all forms. Therefore, the item was considered as a cautious item. When this item score was added to the total score of cautious items, it correlated significantly with the total score of cautious items. Each risky item score did not correlate frequently with scores of other risky items. The cautious items behaved similarly. The neutral item score sometimes correlated with the individual risky item score and the total score of risky items (Appendix II). Thus, each of the risky and cautious items had high internal consistency but poor inter-item relationship.

(b) *Demographic Variables*

In the last part of each form under the heading 'personal data', each subject was asked to register his name, age, sex, and education to keep a record of sample characteristics and to match the questionnaire of each subject in different phases of a condition.

Procedure

(a) *Pre-test (GDC)*

In GDC, the subjects were given the questionnaire called 'opinion questionnaire'. It contained standard instructions, an examplar, and nine dilemma items. They were given five minutes time to read the instructions carefully and ask about the difficulty, if any, before proceeding to give their responses. Then the experimenter explained the instructions and answered questions raised by the subjects. When subjects completed giving responses, the questionnaires were collected.

(b) *Experimental Manipulation (GDC)*

The subjects were immediately instructed to form homogeneous sex groups of three or four persons among themselves. Each subject in group was handed over a fresh opinion questionnaire containing the same dilemma items as in pre-test with the following instructions (see Moscovici & Zavalloni, 1969; Vinokur, 1971):

"In front of you is the same opinion questionnaire that filled out before. The former one was given to you in order to familiarise you with all the situations, and also to enable you to state your personal opinion on each situation.

However, in everyday life, whenever there are problems, people are likely to discuss them with others and they often arrive at a common decision. Similarly, we are interested in your discussing each situation in the questionnaire in your group and arriving at a common decision on each.

The discussion of the situations in the group may bring about different opinions and reasons for them. However, these differences of opinion can be bridged if the problem is re-read carefully and judged rationally.

Since we are interested in discussion, now you can start to discuss each situation one after another in your group and decide unanimously on each. After discussion, when the group reaches its decision on a particular situation, each of you mark it on your own questionnaire so that a record of your group decision can be kept."

After all subjects had gone through the instructions, clarifications were made by the experimenter. The subjects were also told to discuss each item for maximum five minutes. Within that period, if the group failed to reach a unanimous decision on that item, they were instructed to mark the response where they had reached and to switch over to the next item. On completion of discussion in all groups, the questionnaires were collected and subjects were requested to return to their original positions.

(c) *Final Personal Decision (GDC)*

Each subject was provided with the opinion questionnaire with the following instructions:

"Attached are additional copies of the same situations. Refer to each of these now and indicate your ***own present personal decision.***

In some cases you may feel that the group decision was the best one which could have been made and you will mark it as your own present personal decision. In other cases, you may disagree with the group decision in which case you will mark different option as your own decision at present. Please do not feel bound by what you marked before. What is important is that you consider each situation seriously and carefully and choose what you consider your best decision now. Please complete this part without having any discussion with others."

On completion, the questionnaires were collected. In GDC, each form containing the dilemma items and different instructions was given three times. The instructions were kept identical against three forms during group discussion and decision, and post-treatment sessions. The items in each form were placed randomly in the questionnaire in different phases of GDC to check against the carry over effect of memory.

(d) *Successive Presentation Condition (SPC)*

In SPC, the three different forms were given to same subjects successively at the interval of fifteen days. In the first phase, subjects were given AJF. The remaining procedures were identical to the pre-test session of GDC till the filled-in questionnaires were collected. Subjects reassembled on request in class room after fifteen days as scheduled for the second phase. They were given two blank sheets of paper along with verbal instructions and clarifications. They were requested to register their names and write backwardly from 5,000 as quickly as possible for seven minutes. This was a buffer task designed to brush off their earlier memory. All were requested to start `on and stop getting signal 'start' and 'stop'. After collecting the two sheets of paper, each subject was handed over PEF to fill in as followed in the first phase. Once again, when the subjects reassembled for third phase after fifteen days, they were requested to write backwardly from 9,000 for seven minutes. Then the subjects were given PRF to fill in as done earlier.

In SPC, each form included the general instructions, an examplar, and nine dilemma items. Each form differed from others in instructions and response formats.

On completion of each condition, subjects were debriefed, answered and thanked by the experimenter.

Results and Discussion

(a) *Response Shift*

The average consensus score of groups on each item is subtracted from the average pre-test decision score to index the within-subjects measure of choice shift in GDC. The average post-treatment score of individuals is subtracted from the average pre-treatment score to obtain within-subjects measure of polarisation. The shifts towards lower score indicate the increased preference for uncertain alternative or risky shift. Just the opposite indicates cautious shift.

The results reveal very significant choice shift and polarisation on total risky and total cautious items in three forms. The neutral item in AJF only elicits risky inclination in pre-test. It does not yield significant shift in any form. The group decisions and the individual post-treatment decisions become more risky on risky items and more cautious on cautious items than their earlier decisions (Table 2.2).

As noted in Indian context, the shift at the level of individual item needs mention. In item-specific shift, a contradiction exists. The risky item dealing with an engineer to join an attractive job in a new company with uncertain future or stick to the old, lifetime job with moderate salary elicits cautious initial inclination and further shift in the same direction. The choice shift and polarisation on this item approach significance only in PEF. Such peculiarity in change of risky item characteristics is not surprising as the culture differs (Carlson & Davis, 1971). In India, generally job security is weighted heavily because of high unemployment. There is age bar for every job. Hardly an engineer after five or six years of secure job will join a company with uncertain future and risk his career. Indeed, out of a total of four risky and four cautious items, one risky item and one cautious item in AJF, two risky items and three cautious items in PRF and one risky item and three cautious items in PEF fail to demonstrate significant choice shift. Similarly, polarisation does not occur on one cautious item in AJF, one risky item and two cautious items in PRF and two cautious items in PEF. All the insignificant shifts on risky and cautious items remain in expected directions of further risk and further conservatism respectively. Thus, the resultant shifts are somehow weak at the level of individual item but are larger and reliable at the level of total risky and total cautious items.

The magnitude of initial choice and the shift towards risk or caution depend upon the content of each dilemma item. When one alternative becomes more attractive and meaningful than the other, the initial choice and the shift on the item reflect predominantly that attractiveness. Each item differs from other items in the magnitude of initial average and the yield in shift. The content of the neutral item equally favours both alternatives and make them equally attractive and meaningful to the subjects. That is why, it neither elicits any predominant initial tendency nor yields any significant shift in any form.

TABLE 2.2: Choice Shift and Polarisation on Dilemma Items in GDC

Judgement Situation	Form	Mean				*t*-value		Choice Shift–Polarisation
		Pre-test (PT)		Discussion	Post-test	Choice shift	Polarisation	
		PT(G)	PT(I)	DC(G)	PO(I)	PT(G)-DC(G)	PT(I)-PO(I)	DC(G)-PO(I)
University	AJF	1.825	1.788	1.212	1.273	2.597*	2.338*	–0.338
Enrolment	PRF	5.408	5.438	3.800	3.828	2.404*	3.389**	–0.038
	PEF	5.475	5.492	4.300	4.154	2.052	3.168**	0.211
Playing	AJF	3.196	3.136	2.246	2.258	3.167**	2.889**	–0.023
Strategy	PRF	6.012	5.984	4.800	4.969	2.171*	2.601*	–0.245
	PEF	5.433	5.400	4.242	4.200	2.094*	2.521*	0.051
Project	AJF	2.625	2.652	1.983	2.091	1.800	2.105*	–0.279
Work	PRF	6.121	6.141	5.650	5.688	0.927	1.316	–0.064
	PEF	5.625	5.554	4.283	4.015	2.611*	4.017***	0.383
Novel	AJF	3.183	3.212	2.075	2.227	2.806*	3.182**	–0.321
Writing	PRF	5.025	5.016	4.300	4.328	1.608	2.091*	–0.056
	PEF	5.392	5.323	4.250	4.385	2.151*	2.459*	–0.200
Average of	AJF	2.707	2.697	1.879	1.962	5.275***	5.176***	–0.393
Risky	PRF	5.641	5.645	4.638	4.703	2.945**	4.170***	–0.172
items	PEF	5.481	5.442	4.269	4.188	2.988**	4.550***	0.165
Operation	AJF	2.446	2.424	2.200	2.076	0.907	1.883	0.278
(Neutral	PRF	6.246	6.234	6.325	6.141	–0.162	0.198	0.226
item)	PEF	6.438	6.338	5.750	5.431	1.090	1.762	0.360
Job	AJF	4.629	4.712	5.200	5.288	–1.310	–1.717	–0.141
	PRF	7.462	7.438	8.067	7.844	–1.663	–1.311	0.384
	PEF	7.208	7.262	8.071	7.938	–2.802*	–2.076*	0.235
Marriage	AJF	4.212	4.273	5.363	5.212	–2.659*	–3.133**	0.260
	PRF	7.375	7.281	7.817	7.813	–0.972	–1.778	0.007
	PEF	6.604	6.600	7.279	7.123	–1.661	–1.485	0.261
Boarding	AJF	5.463	5.561	6.150	6.197	–2.615*	–2.370*	–0.108
Plane	PRF	6.896	6.844	7.750	7.656	–1.918	–2.086*	0.131
	PEF	6.654	6.646	8.088	8.077	–2.029	–3.043**	0.015
Pregnancy	AJF	5.529	5.545	6.350	6.121	–2.681*	–2.926**	0.508
	PRF	7.667	7.578	8.317	8.156	–2.116*	–2.392*	0.382
	PEF	7.883	7.892	8.671	8.677	–1.342	–1.903	–0.010
Average of	AJF	4.958	5.023	5.766	5.705	–5.032***	–4.642***	0.229
Cautious	PRF	7.350	7.285	8.000	7.867	–2.853*	–3.162**	0.380
items	PEF	7.087	7.100	8.027	7.954	–3.373**	–4.001***	0.196

* $p < .05$ (two tailed).
** $p < .01$ (two tailed).
*** $p < .001$ (two tailed).

G and I in parentheses stand for group and individual respectively. For each item or each set of items the number of groups is 20 but the number of individuals in AJF, PRF, and PEF is 66, 64, and 65 respectively.

On both choice shift and polarisation in all forms, the item that initially elicits the predominant inclination for uncertain alternative (or lower probability) shifts towards still stronger preference for uncertain alternative. Just the reverse happens on the item that initially elicits the predominant preference for certain alternative (or higher probability).

The pre-test scores on each of the items are averaged across groups and individuals to obtain within-subjects measure of both choice shift and polarisation. On each item, the pre-test average score of groups and that of individuals almost match each other. Therefore, the mean difference between group decisions and post-treatment individual decisions on any item can be considered as the difference between choice shift and polarisation. On each of the items and on each set of items, such differences are far from significance. The amount of choice shift and that of polarisation on any item in any form almost match each other. In spite of this, polarisation occurs, on more number of items, at more stringent levels of statistical significance than choice shift. In estimation of correlated *t*-values, more degrees of freedom are associated with the individual-level analysis in polarisation in comparison to the group-level analysis in choice shift. In choice shift, the degrees of freedom are almost one-third of the degrees of freedom in polarisation.

(b) *Instructional Bias*

Let us now examine the results in light of the findings of Clark and Willems (1969). The results refute the strict contingency between risk-oriented instructions and resultant shifts with some reservations. The risky and cautious sets of items in both AJF and PRF accompanying the neutral instructions yield significant choice shift and polarisation. Similarly, the items in PEF containing the so-called demand characteristics of the instructions yield significant shifts. In face of these evidences, there is no logic to believe that the shifts will be drastically suppressed and completely nullified with the elimination of risk-oriented instructions. However, the average shifts on risky and cautious sets of items in AJF containing the neutral instructions more or less match with the average shifts on same items in PEF (Fig. 2.1). PEF is more parallel to PRF. Only the items in PEF contain additionally the risk-oriented instructions. The risky and cautious sets of items in PEF yield slightly more shifts than the same items in PRF. This slight increase in shifts on usual dilemma items in PEF is an evidence of slight contamination of shift effects by risk-oriented instructions.

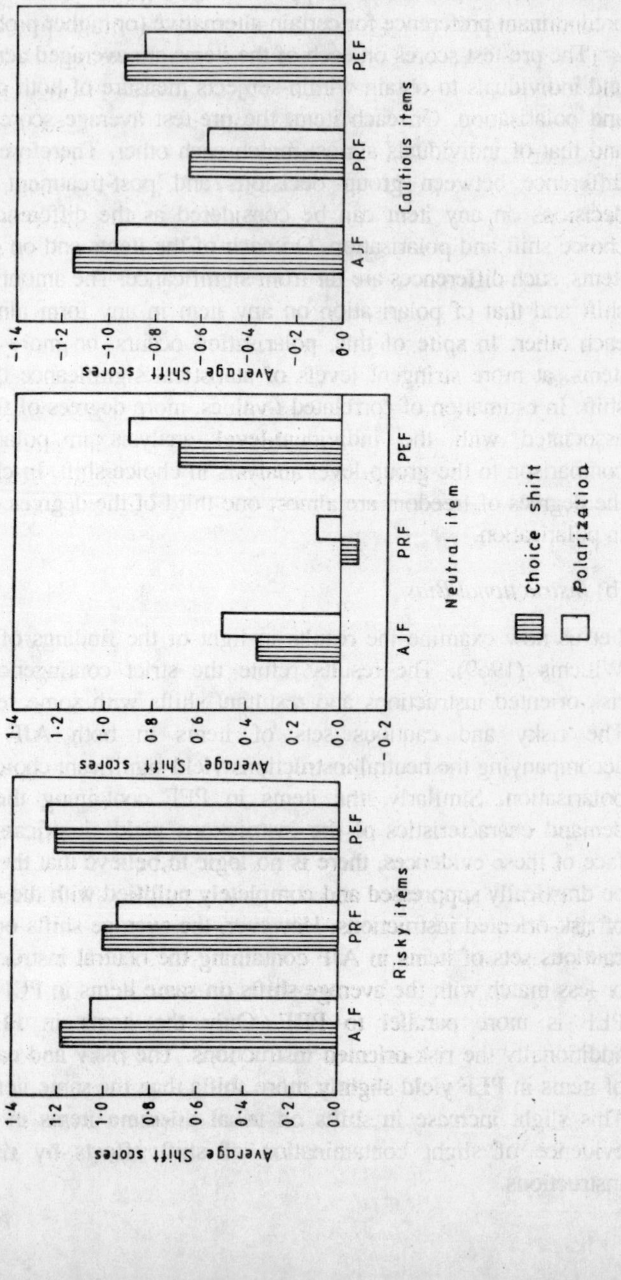

FIG. 2.1: Average Shifts on Risky, Neutral, and Cautious Items in Three Forms (the average shifts on 7-point scale in AJF are transferred to 10-point scale for comparison with other two forms).

The instructional effect is minimum and its exclusion is in no way an inhibitor to the yield of significant shifts. Still, it is of academic interest to identify the locus of this minimum effect as clearly as possible. If the variation in instructions is primarily a psychometric phenomenon, in GDC subjects' pre-test responses should predominantly show the effect. If the effect is located somewhere in group processes and in shift *per se*, that is, if the effect is completely a socio-psychological phenomenon, then only the shift scores should show the effect and not the pre-test scores. The items in PRF do not incorporate the words 'lowest' and 'at least'. The average pre-test scores on risky and cautious sets of items in PRF increase by 0.16 and 0.26 at the group level and 0.20 and 0.19 at the individual level respectively in comparison to the average pre-test scores on same items in PEF (Table 2.2). The average shifts on risky and cautious sets of items in PRF decrease almost by the same amount than the shifts on same items in PEF. Therefore, the effect of risk-oriented instructions is predominantly a psychometric one and is located in initial distribution of scores. Being psychometric one, its effect spreads partly to group decisions and post-treatment individual decisions. Without risk-oriented instructions, the scores on items increase mainly during pre-test decisions and partly during group decisions and post-treatment individual decisions. Thereby, the shifts on risky items decrease. Conversely, the shifts on cautious items do not increase. This is because the pre-test scores on cautious items have already increased. Moreover, at best the cautious items can shift to a limit. The reverse argument applies to the items which include the words 'lowest' and 'at least' in instructions.

In GDC, the pre-test average scores on items in PEF and in PRF are obtained from two different groups of subjects. It is also appropriate to compare the same subjects' score on items in two different forms. In SPC, the same subjects gave their responses to same items in three forms successively. In this within comparison, the average scores on risky, neutral and cautious items in PRF accompanying neutral instructions increase slightly than the average scores on same items in PEF. The trend is prominent in within-subjects comparison of SPC than in between-subjects comparison of GDC (Fig. 2.2). It further validates that the minimum effect of instructional bias on usual dilemma items is psychometric in nature.

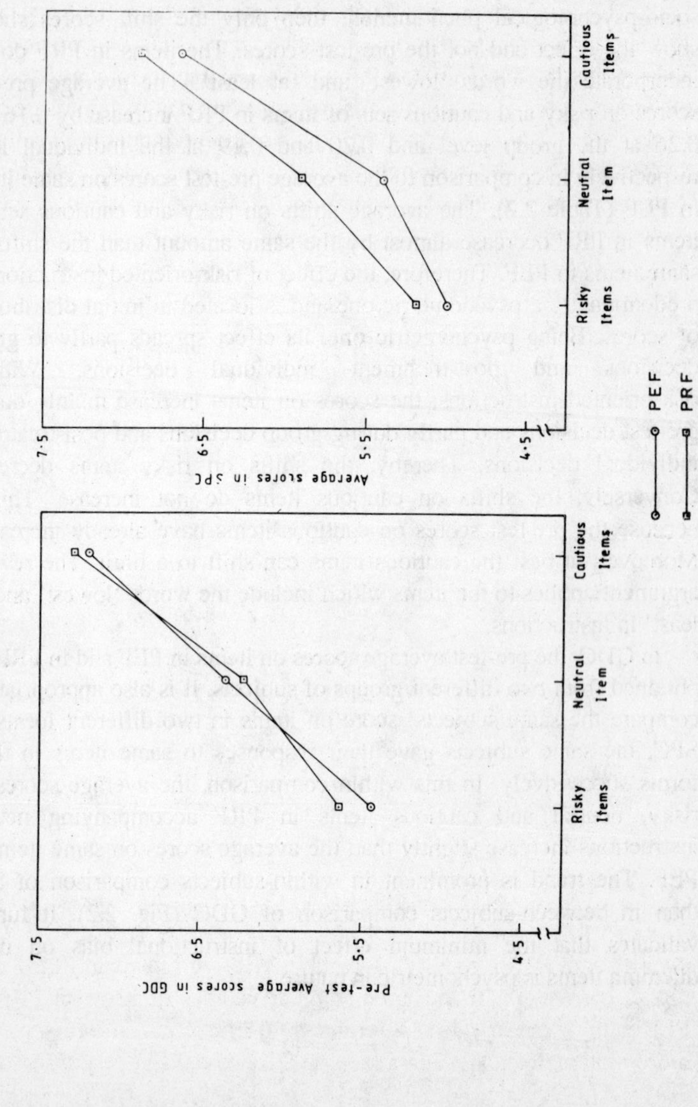

FIG. 2.2: Average Scores on Risky, Neutral, and Cautious Items in PRF and PEF.

(c) *Attitudinal Judgement Measurement*

SPC records some interesting findings. The scores on each item and on total risky and cautious items in AJF correlate positively with the scores on same items in other two forms (Table 2.3). Only the neutral item fails to show such relationship because it elicits preferences favouring the uncertain alternative in AJF only (Av. score = 2.400). Except this deviation, the correlations demonstrate the convergent validity of items in three forms. It leads to conclude that the usual risky and, cautious items with or without risk-oriented instructions measure the attitudinal judgement towards the uncertain and certain alternatives respectively. On risky items, the low probability equalises itself with the stronger uncertain preference in Likert-type scale. On cautious items, the high probability equalises itself with the stronger certain preference in Likert-type scale.

TABLE 2.3: Convergent Validity of Dilemma Items in Three Forms

Items[a]	Correlation		
	AJF and PRF	AJF and PEF	PRF and PEF
1.	0.265*	0.241*	0.739***
2.	0.257*	0.251*	0.696***
3.	0.239*	0.298**	0.596***
4.	0.249*	0.407***	0.777***
Total score of Risky items	0.252*	0.273*	0.815***
5. (Neutral item)	0.134	0.168	0.418***
6.	0.266*	0.262*	0.584***
7.	0.398***	0.227*	0.543***
8.	0.240*	0.234*	0.527***
9.	0.357**	0.330**	0.537***
Total score of Cautious items	0.377***	0.359**	0.723***

* $p < .05$ (two tailed).
** $p < .01$ (two tailed).
*** $p < .001$ (two tailed).
a Serial number of items corresponds to the items in Table 2.2.

The convergent validity of items in PRF with items in PEF records higher correlations than the convergent validity of items in PRF and PEF with items in AJF. In former case, the items in two forms are more similar than in latter cases. In PRF and PEF, responses below each item are given in numerical probabilities. Only the words 'lowest' and 'at least' remain present in one form and absent in another. In latter cases, the convergent validity of items in PRF and PEF with same items in AJF decreases. Below each item in AJF, responses remain on a seven-point Likert-type scale in comparison to responses on a ten-point probability scale in other two forms. Therefore, the response variability in AJF decreases in comparison to other two forms in establishing correlations. A particular response in Likert-type scale is not likely to coincide with the expression of a particular numerical probability. Rather, a particular verbal expression falls within a range of probabilities. For example, strongly recommend the uncertain alternative on an item in AJF may fall within 10 per cent to 30 per cent chance that the uncertain alternative will be successful (Beyth-Marom, 1982).

(d) *Other Findings*

A few other findings can also be noted. In GDC. we also correlate the initial mean for each of the nine items with the amount of choice shift and polarisation each item yields. If intensification of initial inclination is common to choice shift and polarisation, the item for which there is a clearly preferred predominant initial tendency will elicit greater choice shift and polarisation than the item having initial mean near the neutral point.

The initial mean of an item correlates with and predicts the average shift that item yields in three forms (Fig. 2.3). Earlier studies also obtained similar relationship between the initial item means and the mean shifts for dilemma items (Teger & Pruitt, 1967; Myers & Arenson, 1972).

In regression equations, the psychological midpoint of the scale does not correspond to the mathematical midpoint of the scale. Even if in AJF, the mathematical midpoint of responses on each item is well defined in Likert-type response (score = 4.0), the regression lines locate the psychological midpoints slightly below the mathematical midpoints at 3.75 for choice shift and at 3.85 for polarisation. The item having the initial mean at the psychological midpoint yields no shift. In other two forms, the psychological midpoints remain above the mathematical midpoints, near to 6.5 for both choice shift and polarisation. When the initial mean on an item remains below the psychological midpoint of the response scale, it yields risky shift; when it remains above the psychological midpoint, conservative shift results.

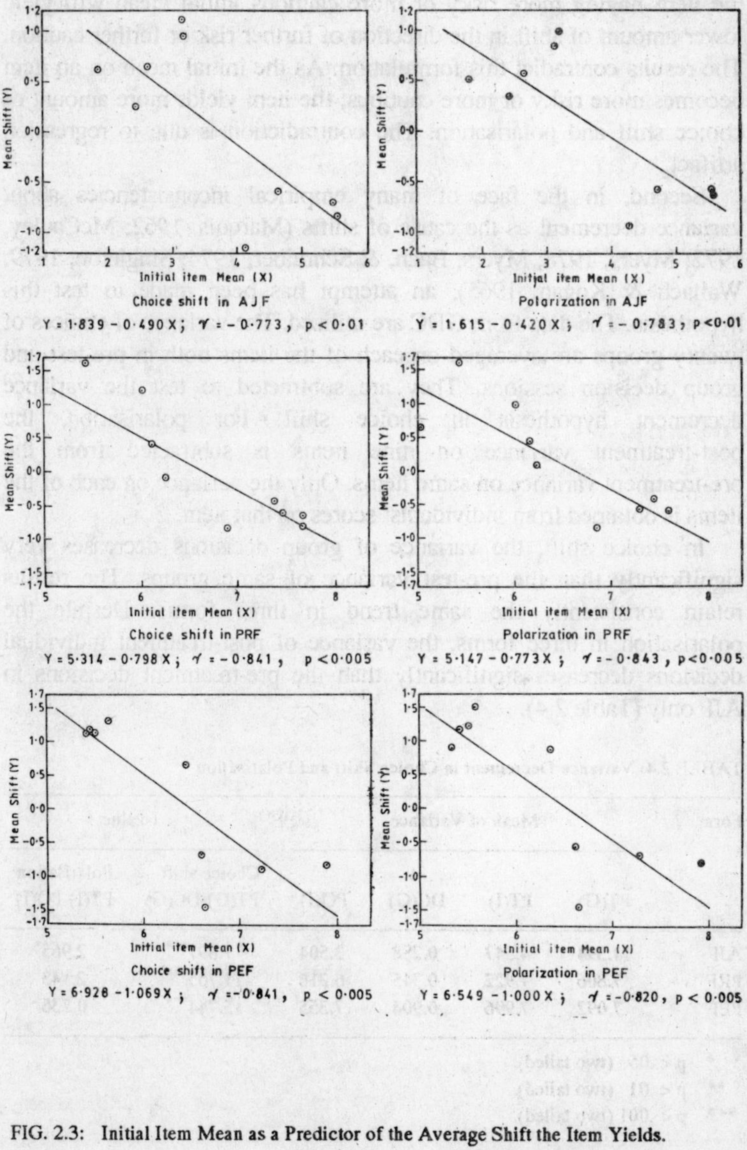

FIG. 2.3: Initial Item Mean as a Predictor of the Average Shift the Item Yields.

Generally, the risky subjects on risky items and the cautious subjects on cautious items in pre-test yield less shifts in the direction of further risk and further caution respectively (Ferguson & Vidmar, 1971). This can be generalised to the level of items. It can be said that the item having more risky or more cautious initial mean will yield lower amount of shift in the direction of further risk or further caution. The results contradict this formulation. As the initial mean on an item becomes more risky or more cautious, the item yields more amount of choice shift and polarisation. The contradiction is due to regression artifact.

Second, in the face of many empirical inconsistencies about variance decrement as the cause of shifts (Marquis, 1962; McCauley, 1972; Myers, 1978; Myers, Bach, & Schreiber, 1974; Singleton, 1979; Wallach & Kogan, 1965), an attempt has been made to test this hypothesis. The data from GDC are utilised. The variance of choices of twenty groups are averaged on each of the items both in pre-test and group decision sessions. They are subtracted to test the variance decrement hypothesis in choice shift. For polarisation, the post-treatment variance on nine items is subtracted from the pre-treatment variance on same items. Only the variance on each of the items is obtained from individuals' scores on that item.

In choice shift, the variance of group decisions decreases very significantly than the pre-test variance of same groups. The results retain consistently the same trend in three forms. Despite the polarisation in three forms, the variance of post-treatment individual decisions decreases significantly than the pre-treatment decisions in AJF only (Table 2.4).

TABLE 2.4: **Variance Decrement in Choice Shift and Polarisation**

Form	Mean of Variance				t-value	
					Choice shift	Polarisation
	PT(G)	PT(I)	DC(G)	PO(I)	PT(G)-DC(G)	PT(I)-PO(I)
AJF	4.394	4.547	0.288	3.504	7.897***	2.965*
PRF	7.806	7.922	0.345	6.316	11.765***	2.143
PEF	7.092	7.996	0.904	7.355	15.744***	0.736

* $p < .05$ (two tailed).
** $p < .01$ (two tailed).
*** $p < .001$ (two tailed).

In choice shift, the group decision on each item results in convergence of choices among group members. During group decision, the conformity pressure of majority operates on deviant minority to comply the emerging group norm (Kiesler & Kiesler, 1969). The variance of choices on any item during a group decision and consensus approaches zero. Therefore, the variability of group decisions decreases very sharply than the pre-test variability. In polarisation, if variance decrement has any role, it is not so pronounced as it is in choice shift. Variance decrement is a typical concomitant to polarisation but not a necessary cause of polarisation.

Third, we question : whether the shifts on dilemma items occur in between-subjects comparison. It is often mentioned that the within-subjects comparison is an essential requirement for the occurrence of shifts on dilemma items (Castore, 1972).

After having obtained the item-specific shifts, the individual's scores on three categories of items in SPC are compared with the group decisions and post-test individual decisions on same items in GDC. This is distinctly a between-subjects comparison.

The risky and cautious sets of items record significant choice shift and polarisation in three forms. The neutral item yields no shift in any form as observed earlier. Only the risky set of items in PRF enlists deviations (Table 2.5). The choice shift and polarisation on risky set of items do not approach significance at the conventional level ($P < .05$). They approach significance at a liberal level ($p < .10$). By and large, choice shift and polarisation occur in between-subjects design (Davis, Kerr, Sussmann, & Rissman, 1974; Gaskell, Thomas, & Farr, 1973; Myers & Bach, 1974; Myers, Bach, & Schreiber, 1974) but they decrease on usual risky set of items accompanying neutral instructions.

Conclusions

The conceptual and methodological differences of this study from the study of Clark and Willems (1969) are easily apparent. At the conceptual level, in spite of the risky items, this study has used risky, neutral, and cautious items in three forms. Two forms accompanying neutral instructions have been used in comparison to their one form. The aim is to cross-validate the findings in three forms. From methodological point of view, in each form more number of subjects are used in comparison to their study. However, only one condition is taken to test the role of instructional bias in comparison to their four conditions.

TABLE 2.5: Choice Shift and Polarisation in Between-subjects Design

Item set	Form	Mean in SPC(I)	Choice shift SPC(I)-DC(G)	Polarisation SPC(I)-PO(I)	t-value[a] SPC(I)-DC(G)	t-value[a] SPC(I)-PO(I)
Risky	AJF	2.747	0.868	0.785	3.574***	4.992***
	PRF	5.180	0.542	0.477	1.662	1.831
	PEF	4.990	0.721	0.802	1.998*	2.700**
Neutral	AJF	2.400	0.200	0.324	0.452	1.086
	PRF	5.893	–0.432	–0.248	–0.563	–0.459
	PEF	5.387	–0.363	–0.044	–0.497	–0.082
Cautious	AJF	4.753	–1.013	–0.952	–3.799***	–5.351***
	PRF	6.910	–1.090	–0.957	–2.631**	–3.617***
	PEF	6.650	–1.377	–1.304	–3.431***	–4.857***

* $p < .05$ (two tailed).
** $p < .01$ (two tailed).
*** $p < .001$ (two tailed).
a Number of subjects in SPC = 75; Number of groups during discussion and consensus = 20.

The results pose limits upon the conclusions of Clark and Willems (1969). The risky and cautious sets of items irrespective of instructions in three forms yield significant choice shift and polarisation in within-subjects comparison. It refutes the strict contingency between risk-oriented instructions and shifts. On close observation, the usual risky and cautious items accompanying neutral instructions yield lesser average shifts than the usual dilemma items accompanying risk-oriented instructions. The risk-oriented instructions somehow influence the shifts. The elimination of the risk-oriented instructions reduces the yield in shifts on usual dilemma items. Hence, the observed shifts on conventionally used dilemma items are tainted slightly with the demand characteristics of instructions.

The possibility of systematic bias is forever present in social psychological research. It is even difficult to find out an experiment without some sort of bias (Carlsmith, Ellsworth, & Aronson, 1976, p. 301). If one scrutinises the instructional bias from the point of relevance, its exclusion from the instructions exerts hardly any influence on significant yield in shifts. However, the complete absence of bias in usual dilemma items cannot be accepted. The usual risky and cautious sets of items non-accompanying risk-oriented instructions yield reduced but significant shifts in within-subjects comparison. The bias influences marginally the dependent variable. Disagreeing to the findings of Clark and Willems (1969), the locus of this minimum instructional bias is found to be located in initial distribution of scores. This is further confirmed by comparison of average scores on risky, neutral, and cautious items in SPC. The bias is psychometric in nature. Clear reasoning hits upon one factor as the cause of this bias. This is acquiescence set – to act according to the instructions.

The usual risky and cautious items irrespective of instructions measure the attitudinal judgement towards the uncertain and certain alternatives respectively. That is why in SPC, the risky and cautious item scores in AJF correlate significantly and positively with the same item scores in PRF and PEF. The usual risky and cautious dilemma items are so constructed that they predominantly elicit the low and high probability preferences respectively. On usual risky items, when the probability of success with or without risk-oriented instructions decreases, it directly taps the uncertain preference verbatim in Likert-type scale. On usual cautious items, when the probability of success increases, it directly taps the certain preference strongly in Likert-type scale. Therefore, the usual risky and cautious items measure the attitudinal judgement. This agrees with the intuitions and findings of others (Burns, 1967; Cartwright, 1971; Fraser, Gouge, & Billig, 1971).

On the basis of findings, one may argue liberally that the observed shifts on usual dilemma items are not completely free from instructional bias. No such argument can be pleaded when they are used in AJF. Each of the items in AJF accompanies neutral instructions and response descriptions on Likert-type scale. In spite of this, the risky and cautious sets of items in AJF yield robust shifts consistently in both within and between subjects comparison. The items in AJF yield comparable shifts to the same items in PEF and larger shifts than the same items in PRF.

The use of dilemma items in AJF guarantees many advantages. First, it cannot be argued that the resultant shifts on dilemma items in AJF are contaminated by instructional bias. Second, each of the items in AJF contains a well-defined neutral point. The direction of initial preference and shift favouring risky or cautious alternative can be detected precisely than the response to an usual dilemma item that describes the choice as relatively risky or relatively cautious. Third, the responses below each item on Likert-type scale will be easy to understand. It will be easier for the subjects to choose Likert-type responses than numerical probabilities for the success of uncertain alternative on each item. Fourth, the use of dilemma items in AJF will be compatible with traditional attitude change studies. On all accounts, this study recommends the use of dilemma items in AJF. Unfortunately, only a few researchers have used the dilemma items in AJF (Fraser, Gouge, & Billig, 1971; Singleton. 1979).

Irrespective of instructions and response formats, the initial mean on an item captures the mean amount of shift that item yields. The predominant tendency on an item intensifies following group decision and post-test individual decision. The variability of preferences at the level of group decreases following choice shift because group consensus is the obligatory requirement in choice shift. Variability of subjects' preferences may decrease occasionally following polarisation but it cannot fully account for the occurrence of polarisation. Although choice shift and polarisation occur in between-subjects design, they decrease on usual risky set of items accompanying neutral instructions.

It is reported that the individual opinion change is greater when subjects are instructed to discuss an item to arrive at a group consensus than when groups are simply asked to have the discussion on the same item (Pennington, Haravey & Bass, 1958). In dilemma items, greatest shifts have observed under experimental condition of discussion followed by group consensus; moderate to small shifts under experimental condition of discussion without any consensus; and finally, small or no shifts under the condition of consensus without discussion (Teger & Pruitt, 1967; Wallach & Kogan, 1965). The amount of choice shift following group consensus more or less matches with that of polarisation on any item in any form. Thus, the difference between choice shift and polarisation appears to be shaky. Choice shift on the basis of group level analysis and consensus requirement claims to differentiate itself from polarisation. When intensification of initial inclination is common to both choice shift and polarisation, this suggests a concentration on polarisation phenomenon for testing hypotheses in shift literature.

3

IS INFORMATIONAL INFLUENCE THE BASIS OF POLARISATION? : A Test of Two Competing Theories

A theory refers to a set of interrelated concepts organised into a generalised principle to predict or explain an empirical phenomenon. With the conceptual spirit of this and the second objective discussed earlier, this study is an attempt to analyse the concepts of persuasive argument theory (PAT) and social comparison theory (SCT) to test whether informational influence is the basis of polarisation.

Concepts of PAT

The behavioural decision theory is applied to dilemma items for predicting preferences (Burnstein, Miller, Vinokur, Katz & Crowley, 1971; Vinokur, 1971; Vinokur, Trope, & Burnstein, 1975). There are three propositions of the theory : (a) an individual prefers an alternative (from a set of alternatives) with a subjective probability, (b) the subjective probability depends on the evaluation of outcome utilities attached to alternatives, and (c) the outcome utilities combine by decision rules to predict the individual preference so as to maximise the subjective expected utility (SEU) for him.

It was suggested in previous chapter to use the dilemma items in attitudinal judgement form (AJF) for its advantages over the usual dilemma items. Now, we can discuss how the application of SEU model can be extended to dilemma items in AJF.

Each original dilemma item incorporates two alternative courses of action : (a) an uncertain alternative with success and failure outcomes, and (b) a certain alternative with a sure outcome. The subject is instructed to choose the lowest probability for the success of uncertain alternative or else to choose the certain alternative. Let U_s and U_f designate the utilities of success outcome and failure outcome of the uncertain alternative. Let U_c designate the utility of sure outcome of the certain alternative (hence its probability of occurrence is 1.0). Let p and q designate respectively the probabilities of success and failure outcome of the uncertain alternative, so that $p+q = 1.0$ and $q = 1.0 - p$.

SEU is the multiplicative function of the subjective probability of each possible outcome with its utility summed over all the products. Thus, SEU for uncertain, risky alternative (SEU_R) will be :

$$SEU_R = pU_s + qU_f = pU_s + (1-p)U_f$$
$$= p(U_s - U_f) + U_f$$

SEU for certain, cautious alternative (SEU_c) will be :

$$SEU_c = 1 \cdot U_c = U_c$$

The choice of uncertain alternative for the individual will follow when:

$$SEU_R \geq SEU_c$$

or $p(U_s - U_f) + U_f \geq U_c$

or $p(U_s - U_f) \geq U_c - U_f$.

Consequently, the individual chosen level of probability (p) for the success of uncertain alternative will be :

$$p \geq (U_c - U_f)/(U_s - U_f) \qquad (1)$$

Cartwright (1971, p. 369) suggested that U_s, U_f and U_c are concerned with outcomes. The dominant values for risk and caution on risky and cautious items become salient during group discussion and bring more arguments in their favour. Responses shift towards further risk and further caution (Brown, 1965). The utilities inherent in taking risky and cautious actions should be added to the outcome utilities of uncertain and certain alternatives respectively. When the arguments were content analysed for risky, neutral and cautious items together, 70 per cent of the arguments generated in private and 72 per cent of the arguments emitted in discussion were concerned with evaluating three outcome utilities (U_s, U_f and U_c). Very few percentage of the arguments focused on utilities of actions, explicit action recommendations and outcome action probabilities. Further, step-wise multiple regression analysis confirmed the significant contribution of three outcome utilities to predict preferences (Vinokur, Trope, & Burnstein, 1975). Therefore, the action utilities are not important to SEU model for predicting preferences. The evaluation of outcome utilities is important.

It was confirmed in earlier chapter that the responses on usual dilemma items in probability scale varied directly with responses on same items in Likert-type scale. Higher probability for success of uncertain alternative equalises itself with the stronger preference for certain alternative in Likert-type scale. Lower probability equalises with the stronger preference for uncertain alternative.

Therefore, $P \propto R$ (subject's response to a dilemma item in Likert-type scale)

$$\text{Eqn. 1} \Rightarrow R \geq (U_c - U_f)/(U_s - U_f) \qquad (2)$$

Let $\bar{R}$ be the final quantitative expression for the utilities' ratio as judged by the subject. Then

$$\bar{R} = (U_c - U_f)/(U_s - U_f) \qquad (3)$$

If R and $\bar{R}$ are not measured on the same unit scale, then $R \propto \bar{R}$. In other words, $\bar{R}$ and R will relate directly and $\bar{R}$ will serve as a predictor of R.

There are several implications of this extended model. First, $\bar{R}$ is not determined by the utility of any single outcome rather by the ratio of outcome utilities as specified in eqn. 3. Second, an increase in utilities of success (U_s) and/or failure (U_f) of uncertain alternative or a decrease in utility of certain alternative (U_c) will result in lower utilities' ratio ($\bar{R}$). Conversely, an increase in U_c or a decrease in U_s and/or U_f will result in higher $\bar{R}$. Lower will be $\bar{R}$ for lower R (or for higher uncertain preference) and higher will be $\bar{R}$ for higher R (or for higher certain preference). It implies high correlation between $\bar{R}$ and R and the utilities' ratio to predict the individual preference on a dilemma item.

In testing PAT, polarisation is observed on usual dilemma items following group discussion. Group discussion provides a medium where the persuasive arguments, available to a few individuals before discussion, are made available to all group members. Polarisation towards further risk occurs when group discussion contains substantially a greater proportion of pro-risk to pro-caution arguments.

Polarisation towards further caution occurs when group discussion contains a greater proportion of pro-caution to pro-risk arguments (Ebbesen & Bowers, 1974; Silverthorne, 1971; Vinokur & Burnstein, 1974). Studies using SEU model to explain polarisation have demonstrated that the arguments disseminated during discussion, revise the outcome utilities, utilities' ratio and in turn predict the individual preference (Burnstein, Miller, Vinokur, Katz, & Crowley, 1971; Vinokur, 1971). The arguments generated in private and received during discussion are concerned with changing the outcome utilities so as to make the uncertain preference highly attractive on risky items and the certain preference highly attractive on cautious items (Vinokur, Trope, & Burnstein, 1975). Thus, the availability of persuasive arguments revises the relative evaluation of outcome utilities (i.e., utilities' ratio) and the utilities' ratio predicts the preference following SEU model.

In traditional polarisation research, subjects give their responses to dilemma items following which certain experimental manipulations (e.g., group discussion, position comparison) are made. Then the same subjects give their final responses to same dilemma items. The posterior preferences change following experimental manipulations. Subjects favour strongly the uncertain alternative on risky items and the certain alternative on cautious items. If additional access to persuasive arguments causes polarisation, given the data before and after experimental manipulations, important explanations for polarisation can be conjectured.

First, the pre- and post-test ratios of utilities ($\bar{R}_1$, $\bar{R}_2$) will vary directly and predict the pre- and post-test preferences (R_1, R_2) on dilemma items respectively. Second, there has to be a change in preference in the direction of change in utilities' ratio. In other words, following shift towards the uncertain alternative on risky items, post-test utilities' ratio will decrease than that of the pre-test. The converse will occur following shift towards the certain alternative on cautious items. The magnitude of shifts in utilities' ratio will vary directly and predict the magnitude of shifts in preference. Third, an utility or a combination of utilities will change following shifts in preference. The evaluation of U_s and/or U_f will increase or the evaluation of U_c will decrease in post-test to account for risky shift on risky items. The evaluation of U_c will increase or the evaluation of U_s and/or U_f will decrease in post-test for conservative shift on cautious items.

Another variable that relates to PAT is the certainty and confidence one expresses in his preference. The extent of certainty and confidence is the introspective conviction regarding the correctness of preference. The information processing theory mentions that the individual faced with a stimulus situation searches for information in order to reduce the uncertainty about the stimulus situation (Fowler, 1965). Putting it otherwise, increase in certainty of the stimulus situation depends upon the availability of information. Leadership theory describes simultaneously that people who hold extreme preferences are more confident and committed to their preferences. By virtue of this, they exercise more influence during group discussion to sway others to their side that results in shifts (Burns, 1967; Burnstein, 1969). Thus, high certainty and confidence are associated with the extremity in preference and availability of many persuasive arguments. It helps in exercising greater influence during discussion. Probably for this reason, shifts appeared in groups where high risk members were high in confidence and disappeared in groups where high risk members were low in confidence (Clausen, 1965).

Certainty and confidence is found to be natural concomitant of an extreme preference (Burnstein & Katz, 1971; Burnstein, Vinokur, and Pichevin, 1974; Clausen, 1965; Stroebe & Fraser, 1971). Positive correlation is shown to exist between the two. When extremity in preference varies directly with certainty and confidence, it implies that the individual possesses many persuasive arguments supporting his preference. Also, highly certain and confident choices are perceived as more persuasive, admirable and sincere as the risky and cautious choices on risky and cautious items respectively (Burnstein, Vinokur, & Pichevin, 1974). Very few among the subjects who were initially more certain in their positions yielded to group pressure. The reverse happened to those who were initially less certain in their positions (Coleman, Blake, & Mouton, 1958). The former subjects initially held large number of persuasive arguments about the correctness of their positions than the latter. Hence, the extent of certainty and confidence relates directly to the availability of persuasive arguments and extremity in preference.

If additional access to persuasive arguments causes polarisation, the certainty and confidence will increase in polarised preferences in comparison to prior preferences. Second, the extent of certainty and confidence will vary directly with preferences. Third, as the extent of certainty and confidence in initial preferences will increase, the shifts in preference will decrease. Fourth, the increase in certainty and confidence from pre- to post-test will vary directly with shifts in preference.

Concepts of SCT

SCT popularly explains the image-maintenance strategy in two ways by taking the relative deviation of (a) self from assumed others (self > assumed others), and (b) self from ideal preference (ideal/admired > self). These postulated differences motivate the individual to shift.

The risky and cautious items elicit risky and cautious preferences respectively and they are valued. Initially, the individual guesses himself to be more risky and more cautious than his assumed peers on risky and cautious items respectively. He keeps his ideal preferences more in valued directions than his own preferences (Myers, 1982). The self-others discrepancy reflects (a) an attempt to present oneself favourably in socially desirable direction to receive social sanction, and (b) a defensive manoeuvre that he is in no way less competent than his peers possessing the cherished social value. PAT gives a different explanation (Burnstein, Vinokur, & Pichevin, 1974). The preference for self exceeds the preference for assumed others because the individual is more certain and confident about his own preference than about others. The self-ideal discrepancy in SCT reflects the adherence to desirable behaviour, what the individual internally values and appreciates than his own perceived behaviour. In PAT, the extremity in ideal preference indicates the well-founded solution to a problem involving choice. The individual holds sufficient persuasive arguments for his ideal preference.

There are many compelling logic in favour of self-ideal than self-others discrepancy to predict shifts. Occasionally, when subjects initially underestimated their assumed peers, risky shift increased (Clark, Crockett, & Archer, 1971). In other studies, the initial underestimation of assumed peers did not predict the subsequent risky shift (Myers, Wong, & Murdoch, 1971; Pruitt & Teger, 1967). There was no differential yield in shifts following discussion between the groups of subjects underestimating and overestimating their assumed peers (Lamm, Trommsdorff, & Rost-Schaude, 1972). Perhaps, the underestimation of assumed peers does not motivate to shift (Cartwright, 1971). In contrast, when high self-ideal discrepancy and low self-ideal discrepancy groups discussed the dilemma items, the former evidenced more shifts than the latter (Lamm, Schaude, & Trommsdorff, 1971). Besides this, given the non-obvious character of the item that does not elicit a predominant valued preference, what the individual internally values will be a better indicator of socially desirable behaviour than what he recommends for his assumed peers. Second, the reporting of ideal preference is free from reality constraints. What the individual values internally cannot be checked empirically. Third, the self-ideal discrepancy is less affected by order of measurement (self then ideal or ideal then self preference measurement) than the self-others discrepancy (Myers, 1974). Thus, the self-ideal discrepancy seems to be a more viable motivator for shifts than the self-others discrepancy.

The pluralistic ignorance (Levinger & Schneider, 1969; Schroeder, 1973) and release (Pruitt, 1969, 1971a, 1971b) versions of SCT mention that the individual initial preference reflects a compromising point between his internal valued (or ideal) preference and an assumed social norm of moderation. The moderates in group during comparison discover that the average group norm on each item is closer to their initial ideal preferences (pluralistic ignorance) or some one (model) in group embodies their internal valued preference more strongly than they initially did (release version). It convinces the moderates to move closer to their initial ideal preferences which they suppressed earlier. It results in shifts. Therefore, following social comparison posterior self preferences will more or less approximate to initial ideal preferences on items. The initial self-ideal discrepancies will relate directly to shifts in preference. PAT predicts shifts in preference following the additional access to persuasive arguments. Therefore, following additional access to persuasive arguments, ideal preferences will be more well-founded and become more extreme than earlier. Second, both pre- and post-test self preferences will vary positively with pre- and post-test ideal preferences respectively. Self preferences grounded on persuasive arguments availability will make the ideal preferences well-founded. Shifts in ideal preference from pre- to post-test will vary directly with shifts in self-preference.

In SCT, the individual undergoes through a process of evaluation. He compares his own opinion with others. He asks himself "Is what I have just said or done consistent with the way I would like to think of myself and the way I want others to perceive me"? If the answers are in affirmative, it is bound to induce an affective state of self-satisfaction. If they are in negative, it is bound to induce an affective state of self-dissatisfaction. In other words, if the individual compares his response with others and finds his position discrepant from others on an issue, he experiences dissatisfaction. If he finds similarity with others, he experiences satisfaction. These affective states can be presumed to have motivational qualities. On one hand, self-satisfaction being a positive state can reinforce the individual to keep his opinion intact. On the other hand, self-dissatisfaction being a negative dissonance state can induce the individual to change. The change occurring out of self-dissatisfaction cannot be arbitrary in nature. The change will occur in the direction that will reduce self-dissatisfaction and will be ultimately consistent with desirable social behaviour and positive self-presentation.

The awareness of discrepancies leading to change and awareness of consistencies leading to stability of opinion are stated in SCT (Brown, 1965; Pruitt, 1969, 1971a, 1971b) and belief organisation theory (Rokeach, 1973, 1979a). In belief organisation theory using a comparison process called 'self confrontation technique', attitudes, values and behaviour are changed successfully through manipulated arousal of dissatisfaction with certain target attitudes and values (Grube, 1982b; Rokeach, 1973, 1979a, 1979b). In polarisation research no study has been conducted in this direction. In belief organisation theory or in SCT, subjects finding discrepancies and experiencing dissatisfaction shift their preferences to match with the norm of others. Hence, satisfaction will increase on polarised preferences. Second, in Brown's (1965) value theory, moderate preferences are more valued than extreme preferences. Hence, after comparison subjects will feel satisfied if their initial preferences were moderate in valued directions of items. Otherwise, they will feel dissatisfied and change towards moderate preferences that will increase satisfaction. Third, dissatisfaction with initial preferences will vary directly with shifts in preference. PAT holds a different explanation. The awareness about the norm of others on each item will be disclosed during group discussion. Those who found many additional persuasive arguments that were initially not available to them in holding their preferences will experience dissatisfaction. They will change their initial preferences in the direction of additional availability of arguments that will increase satisfaction with changed preferences. More satisfaction will be associated with the increasing uncertain and certain preferences on risky and cautious items. More the satisfaction with initial preferences, lower will be the yield in shifts. Shifts in satisfaction from pre- to post-test preferences will vary directly with shifts in preference.

To test these objectives, three conditions are taken : persuasive argument (PA) condition to facilitate information dissemination, social comparison (SC) condition to facilitate position comparison and still another, control (CO) condition to generate the base level data for comparison with the above two conditions. A limited number of dilemma items is used in attitudinal judgement form to measure attitudes towards the uncertain and certain alternatives.

Method

Sample

A total of 267 students in the age-group of nineteen to twenty-six (Male = 144, Av. age = 20.882; Female = 123, Av. age = 20.472) from post-graduate departments of Sambalpur University, Jyoti Vihar, Orissa participated as subjects in this study. Prior to their participation, subjects were informed in class room to cooperate in a study relating to the development of a questionnaire for measuring human relations in group. Nothing about the actual experiment was communicated.

The subjects were run in individual and groups of three, four and five persons. The age (19-26), educational level and homogeneous sex-groupings (during group interaction) of the subjects were controlled (Table 3.1).

TABLE 3.1: **Sample Characteristics**

Condition	Sex	Group			Total subjects	Average Age	Education
		3-person	4-person	5-person			
PA	M	5 (15)	4 (16)	3 (15)	46	20.696	PG (1st year)
	F	4 (12)	4 (16)	3 (15)	43	20.419	-do-
SC	M	6 (18)	4 (16)	3 (15)	49	21.122	-do-
	F	3 (09)	4 (16)	3 (15)	40	20.500	-do-
CO	M	6 (18)	4 (16)	3 (15)	49	20.816	-do-
	F	3 (09)	4 (16)	3 (15)	40	20.500	-do-
Total	M	17 (51)	12 (48)	9 (45)	144	20.882	
	F	10 (30)	12 (48)	9 (45)	123	20.472	

Number of individuals is given in the parentheses.

Fifteen to thirty subjects participated in each session. Each experimental session under different conditions took about one hour and thirty minutes. In many sessions, males outnumbered the females. There were 3 male and 3 female five-person groups, 4 male and 4 female four-person groups in each condition. Along with this, in PA condition there were 5 male and 4 female three-person groups and in both SC and CO conditions there were 6 male and 3 female three-person groups. Each condition comprising 89 subjects constituted a total number of 23 groups.

Materials

(a) *Attitudinal Judgement Measurement*

Four choice dilemma items were chosen from the earlier study to include two risky and two cautious items. The risky items involved the decision of (a) a post-graduate student in chemistry to do Ph.D. from a prestigious or a non-prestigious university, and (b) a research physicist to work on a difficult, long-term problem or a series of easy, short-term problems. The cautious items involved the decision of (a) a person experiencing abdominal pains at the airport to go for medical check-up or to go for an overseas flight, and (b) a couple without child to terminate a complicated pregnancy or allow it to continue with danger to wife's life. Contents of items were same as in the earlier study to suit Indian context.

The following instructions were given below each item to measure attitudinal judgement towards the uncertain or certain alternative. "Imagine that you are advising the central person. Please put a tick mark against the statement that best expresses your advice." The responses were given on an eleven-point Likert-type scale from 'very strongly recommend the uncertain alternative (score = 1)' through neutrality (score = 6) to 'very strongly recommend the certain alternative (Score = 11)'. On each of the items, lower score associated with the preference for uncertain alternative and higher score with certain alternative. To obtain finer response, eleven-point response scale has been preferred to seven-point scale used earlier. The response descriptions favouring uncertain and certain alternatives were given alternately from one item to another.

The earlier study observed high internal consistency of these items. Hence, the average scores on two risky items and two cautious items in both pre- and post-tests indexed the preference for uncertain alternative and certain alternative respectively (see Bishop & Myers, 1974; Burnstein & Vinokur, 1973; Burnstein, Vinokur, & Trope, 1973; Vidmar & Burdeny, 1971). The positive difference between pre- and post-test scores indicates shifts towards uncertain alternative and the negative difference indicates shifts towards certain alternative.

(b) *Assessment of Outcome Utilities and Utilities' Ratio*

Utility is the subjective appraisal and evaluation of an outcome. Each outcome utility was assessed independently on four bipolar adjectives. Each bipolar adjective was presented in a seven-point semantic differential scale. For example, below the item concerning a post-graduate in chemistry to choose between prestigious University *X* and non-prestigious University *Y* to do Ph.D., the following scale was given:

(1) Goes to University *X* and receives the degree (U_s) :

	Very	Moderately	Slightly	Neither	Slightly	Moderately	Very	
desirable	...	...	...	...	...	...	...	undesirable
bad	...	...	...	...	...	...	...	good
beneficial	...	...	...	...	...	...	...	harmful
punishing	...	...	...	...	...	...	...	rewarding

The same adjectives were used to evaluate the other two outcomes : (2) Goes to University *X* and does not receive the degree (U_f), and (3) Goes to University *Y* and receives the degree (U_c). The four bipolar adjectives had high loading on evaluative factor of semantic differential scale (Osgood, Suci, & Tannenbaum, 1957) and had been used previously (Vinokur, 1971) to evaluate the outcome utilities. The positions of positive and negative anchors were reversed from one outcome utility to another to make it difficult for the subject to respond in 'a consistent fashion. In evaluation of U_f, the anchors were undesirable-desirable, good-bad, harmful-beneficial and rewarding-punishing. Above the bipolar adjectives, the Likert-type responses filled up the seven spaces in semantic differential scale for better clarity (Bagozzi, 1981). Depending upon the subject's response from extreme positive end of a bipolar adjective (very desirable, very good etc.; score = 7) through neutrality (score = 4) to extreme negative end of a bipolar adjective (very undesirable, very bad etc.; score = 1), the score was assigned accordingly.

The outcome utility scores obtained on two risky and two cautious items were averaged to get a single estimation of each utility for each set of items. The utilities' ratio was computed for each set of items from the average scores of different outcome utilities. The negative difference between pre- and post-test scores indicates the increase in an outcome utility and utilities' ratio. The positive difference indicates the reverse.

(c) *Measurement of Certainty and Confidence*

On each item the subject was asked : 'how sure are you of your response to this situation?' The response descriptions were given on a five-point unidirectional scale ranging from 'very sure (score = 5)' to 'not sure at all (score = 1)'. Confidence was measured similarly in earlier studies (Brim, 1955; Kogan & Wallach, 1964). The certainty and confidence scores obtained on two risky and two cautious items were averaged to index a single estimation of certainty and confidence for each set of items. The negative difference between pre- and post-test scores indicates the increase in certainty and confidence.

(d) *Admired/Ideal Response*

The subject was asked to go through each item once again and indicate the response for which he had the highest regard (Lamm, Trommsdorff, & Rost-Schaude, 1972, p. 259). The ideal preference was scored and estimated in the same fashion as the self-preference on the both sets of items. Positive and negative self-ideal discrepancy scores on risky and cautious sets of items respectively indicate the extremity of ideal preference than the self-preference in valued directions of items.

(e) *Satisfaction/Dissatisfaction with Preference*

The subject was asked to indicate the level of satisfaction/ dissatisfaction with his initial response to each of the items following experimental manipulations. The subject was also asked to report the satisfaction/dissatisfaction with his post-test response (Grube, 1982b).

The response descriptions were given on a seven-point Likert-type scale from 'highly satisfied (score = 7)' through neutrality (score = 4) to 'highly dissatisfied (score = 1)'. The satisfaction/dissatisfaction scores obtained on two risky and two cautious items were averaged to get a single index of satisfaction/dissatisfaction with each set of preferences. The negative difference between satisfaction with pre- and post-test preferences indicates increase in satisfaction.

(f) *Demographic Variable*

In the last part of the questionnaire under the heading 'personal data', each subject was asked to report his name, age, sex and education to obtain demographic information as well as to match the questionnaire of each subject in pre- and post-test sessions.

Procedure

(a) *Pre-test*

The subjects were distributed the 'opinion questionnaire' containing the standard instructions and examplars. They were given seven minutes time to read the instructions. Then the experimenter explained the instructions and answered questions raised by the subjects. It was emphasised that they should read the items carefully and answer them sincerely. Subjects filled out the questionnaires at their own pace. On completion, the questionnaires were collected in persuasive argument (PA) and control (CO) conditions.

(b) *Experimental Manipulation*

The subjects were instructed to form homogeneous sex groups. Males and females were adjusted in groups depending upon the number of subjects who appeared in a particular session. Following this, experimental manipulations were made in different conditions.

In PA condition, each subject in group was distributed a fresh questionnaire containing the four dilemma items in the same order as in pre-test with the following instructions.

"Attached are the descriptions of the same situations that you have considered before. In real life, whenever people face such situations, they are likely to discuss them with others. Similarly, now having formed the group, you discuss each situation in the questionnaire. In each situation, two alternatives are available to the central person. *You discuss among yourselves which alternative is to be preferred and to what extent for the central person.*

For each situation, you may argue among yourselves as effectively as possible to justify a suitable stand for the central person. By the way, the discussion of each situation will facilitate you to receive different opinions, ideas and reasons from others that you had not considered before as well as to give your opinions, ideas and reasons to others. In fact, consider each situation carefully in the light of information gained during the course of discussion to specify which alternative and to what extent is to be preferred for the central person. Perhaps, during the course of discussion, you will arrive at a common decision. However, if you cannot, do not worry.

Please do not write anything in the questionnaire whether you want to change your response or not, because you will be provided another opportunity to give your response to each situation after group discussion. Now you can start discussing each situation one after another in your group. Please ask if there is any difficulty."

After the subjects went through the instructions, clarifications were made by the experimenter. It was also made clear that the discussion on each item would last for seven minutes maximum. If the discussion for an item was not completed within that time, they were mentioned to switch over to the next item. On completion of discussion in all groups, the questionnaires were collected.

In social comparison (SC) condition, each subject having the pre-test questionnaire in group was handed over a fresh questionnaire containing the four dilemma items as in PA condition with the following instructions.

"Given here are the descriptions of the same situations that you have considered before. In real life, whenever people face such situations, they are likely to search for the opinions of others to know what opinions they prefer. Similarly, now having formed the group, you can know and compare your opinion with those of other group members. *To do this, for each situation copy your own recommendations for the central person in the given questionnaire and pass it on to others in a clock-wise fashion until you receive your own questionnaire again.*

In this way, others can know your recommendation for each situation. You can also know what statement others have recommended for each situation which may be different from or identical with yours. *After receiving the questionnaire from others, do not discuss or make any comments, you should simply see what others have recommended for each situation.*

After seeing the recommendation of others in your group, do not worry whether you want to change your response or not, because you will be provided another opportunity to give your response to each situation. Now copy in the given questionnaire your own recommendations from the first questionnaire and pass it on to others. Please ask if there is any difficulty."

After the subjects went through the instructions, clarifications were made by the experimenter. They were also told to pile up their pre-test questionnaires on the table after copying their own recommendations in the fresh questionnaire and then only to pass on the fresh questionnaire to others. The pre-test questionnaires were collected. On completion of comparison, the fresh questionnaires were collected.

In CO condition, a cancellation test was given to each subject in the group as a filler task with the following instructions.

"Please do not open the next page until told to do so. This is a test to measure your speed. In the next pages, you will find alphabets from A to Z arranged in rows and columns. You have to cancel the vowels (A, E, I, O, U) in each row and on completion have to cancel again the letters B, D, J, N, T and Z in each column until told to stop."

The instructions were clarified further and then the signal was given to 'start'. After ten minutes the 'stop' signal was given and the cancellation sheets were collected.

Following the experimental manipulation in each condition, subjects were instructed to take new questionnaires kept on the table and to report their satisfaction/dissatisfaction with their initial responses to dilemma items. After all had responded, the questionnaires were collected and subjects were requested to return to their original positions.

(c) *Post-test*

Each subject was provided with a new questionnaire. The dilemma items and related questions were given in reverse order to check the carry over effect of memory from pre- to post-test session. The following instructions were attached.

"The questionnaire in the next pages asks to report your present personal feelings by giving responses to similar situations, to the level of certainty and satisfaction with your present response to each situation, to the estimation of possible outcomes and lastly your response to each situation for which you have the highest regard.

During discussion (after seeing the recommendations of others), perhaps you have considered new facets of the situations which have caused you to change your responses to the situations, to the related questions and to the estimation of outcomes or, perhaps these have remained the same. If you feel that the group discussion (seeing the recommendations of others) has enriched your opinions, ideas and reasons for each situation, then you will incorporate these while you mark your responses. Otherwise, you may keep your responses the same as before. However, while marking your responses, do not feel bound by what you marked earlier. *What is important is that you consider each situation, the related questions and the estimation of outcomes seriously and carefully and mark at the appropriate place what you consider your best responses for each aspect of the questionnaire.* Go ahead and complete this part."

The portions in parentheses were in the instructions of SC condition. In addition to first paragraph, last three sentences were in the instructions of CO condition.

After the subjects read the instructions, necessary clarifications were made. It was also stressed not to leave any portion of the questionnaire blank. On completion, the questionnaires were collected. Finally, the subjects were debriefed, answered and thanked by the experimenter.

Results and Discussion

(a) *Shift in Preference*

Subjects have stated their responses before and after experimental manipulations. Risky set of items elicits responses favouring the uncertain alternative and cautious set of items elicits responses favouring the certain alternative in pre-test session. Responses polarise (or shift) following group discussion in PA condition and position comparison in SC condition. The subjects prefer more strongly the uncertain alternative on risky set of items and the certain alternative on cautious set of items. This replicates the often-reported shift effects. Responses do not polarise on both sets of items following the cancellation exercise in CO condition (Table 3.2).

TABLE 3.2: Shifts in Preference in Different Conditions

Condition	Item set	Mean			t-value ($R_1 - R_2$)		
		Pre-test (R_1)	Post-test (R_2)	Shift ($R_1 - R_2$)	Within[a] condition	Between condition[b]	
						SC	CO
PA	Risky	3.725	2.646	1.079	6.026***	3.149**	5.099***
	Cautious	8.157	9.449	–1.292	–6.036***	–3.619***	–5.632***
SC	Risky	3.781	3.438	0.343	2.281*	0.000	2.040*
	Cautious	8.236	8.607	–0.371	–2.695**	0.000	–2.356*
CO	Risky	3.708	3.781	–0.073	–0.530	–2.040*	0.000
	Cautious	8.079	8.062	0.017	0.186	2.356*	0.000

* $p < .05$ (two tailed).
** $p < .01$ (two tailed).
*** $p < .001$ (two tailed).
a t-values are correlated mean differences.
b t-values are uncorrelated mean differences for homogeneity or heterogeneity of variance.

The pre-test average response on each set of items is very close across the conditions. Despite this, each condition differs significantly from others on observed shifts. Each set of items in PA condition yields significantly more shift in comparison to SC condition. Similarly, each set of items in SC condition notes larger absolute shift than in CO condition. Therefore, shifts in different conditions are due to differential treatments. The group discussion in PA condition disseminated actively the few persuasive arguments to group members in initial valued directions of items that yielded largest shifts. The comparison of positions among group members in SC condition yielded significant shifts. However, such shifts were lesser than the shifts in PA condition. In CO condition, subjects after pre-test were given immediately a filler task which neither disseminated arguments nor facilitated comparisons. Further familiarisation with the items following cancellation exercise did not intensify the initial risky or cautious tendency.

Both argumentation and comparison produce polarisation. But the effect of the former tends to be larger than the latter (Isenberg, 1986). Few early studies studies have noted weak shift effects following social comparison (Burnstein & Vinokur, 1977; Myers, 1982). There in comparison process, subjects after pre-test are exposed to the average norm of others or to the percentage distribution of others in response units on each item. Here the subjects are exposed to preferences of others in face-to-face manner. The yield in shifts does not rule out the possibility of comparison process in inducing polarisation. If both PAT and SCT are immediate rival to each other for occurrence of shifts, on the basis of results, argumentation process claims an edge over comparison process.

(b) *Utilities' Ratio, Outcome Utility and SEU Model*

(i) *Variation of Utilities' Ratio with Preference*

The results are consistent with the predictions of SEU model (Table 3.3). The pre- and post-test ratios of utilities correlate positively with pre- and post-test preferences. Risky items elicit inclination towards the uncertain alternative (lower score) and cautious items towards the certain alternative (higher score). On risky set of items, the utilities' ratio decreases for intense uncertain preference and on cautious set of items, it increases for certain preference. However, these correlations are higher than those obtained in earlier studies (Burnstein, Miller, Vinokur, Katz, & Crowley, 1971; Vinokur, 1971). The earlier studies used the usual dilemma items. There the response to each item in probability scale was mixed with the success of uncertain alternative (e.g., 'the central person should choose the uncertain alternative if the chances are at least 1 in 10 that the uncertain alternative will succeed'). Here the response to each item in Likert-type scale keeps itself independent of any outcome.

The utilities' ratio predicts excellently the individual preference in pre- and post-tests. The least square regression graphs confirm this clearly (Fig. 3.1). On risky set of items, the persuasive arguments available to the subjects during pre- and post-tests have favoured predominantly the utilities of uncertain alternative (U_s, U_f) in comparison to the utility of certain alternative (U_c). Consequently, the utilities' ratio has decreased as the strength of uncertain preference has increased (lower score). On cautious set of items, the available arguments have focused on favourable evaluation of the utility of certain alternative in comparison to the utilities of uncertain alternative. The utilities' ratio has increased as the strength of certain preference has increased. This is quite consistent with item characteristics.

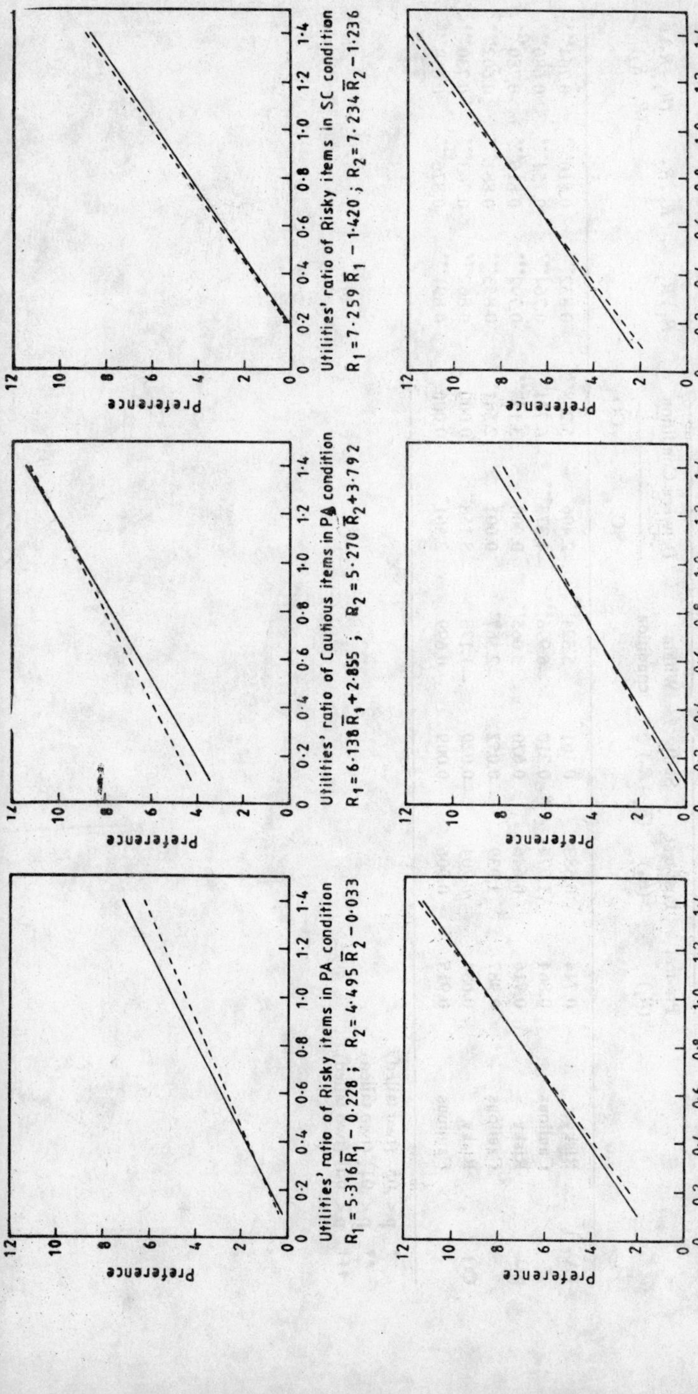

Utilities' ratio of Risky items in PA condition
$R_1 = 5{\cdot}316\,\overline{R}_1 - 0{\cdot}228$; $R_2 = 4{\cdot}495\,\overline{R}_2 - 0{\cdot}033$

Utilities' ratio of Cautious items in PA condition
$R_1 = 6{\cdot}138\,\overline{R}_1 + 2{\cdot}855$; $R_2 = 5{\cdot}270\,\overline{R}_2 + 3{\cdot}792$

Utilities' ratio of Risky items in SC condition
$R_1 = 7{\cdot}259\,\overline{R}_1 - 1{\cdot}420$; $R_2 = 7{\cdot}234\,\overline{R}_2 - 1{\cdot}236$

Utilities' ratio of Cautious items in SC condition
$R_1 = 6{\cdot}976\,\overline{R}_1 + 1{\cdot}350$; $R_2 = 7{\cdot}214\,\overline{R}_2 + 1{\cdot}113$

Utilities' ratio of Risky items in CO condition
$R_1 = 6{\cdot}364\,\overline{R}_1 - 0{\cdot}646$; $R_2 = 6{\cdot}035\,\overline{R}_2 - 0{\cdot}468$

Utilities' ratio of Cautious items in CO condition
$R_1 = 7{\cdot}079\,\overline{R}_1 + 1{\cdot}602$; $R_2 = 7{\cdot}303\,\overline{R}_2 + 1{\cdot}445$

——— Pre-test Preference (R_1) - - - - - Past-test Preference (R_2)

TABLE 3.3: Ratios of Utilities, their Shifts and Correlations with Preferences

Condition	Item set	Utilities Ratio			t-value ($\bar{R}_1 - \bar{R}_2$)			Correlation		
		Pre-test ($\bar{R}_1$)	Post-test ($\bar{R}_2$)	Shift ($\bar{R}_1 - \bar{R}_2$)	Within condition	Between Condition SC	Between Condition CO	$R_1 \cdot \bar{R}_1$	$\bar{R}_2 \cdot R_2$	$(R_1 - R_2)$ $(\bar{R}_1 - \bar{R}_2)$
PA	Risky	0.744	0.583	0.161	5.324***	2.406*	5.238***	0.832***	0.810***	0.764***
	Cautious	0.864	1.074	–0.210	–6.996***	–4.373***	–6.721***	0.764***	0.754***	0.680***
SC	Risky	0.716	0.646	0.070	3.065**	0.000	3.158**	0.792***	0.816***	0.780***
	Cautious	0.987	1.039	–0.052	–2.567*	0.001	–2.561*	0.853***	0.881***	0.602***
CO	Risky	0.684	0.704	–0.020	–1.173	–3.158**	0.000	0.862***	0.763***	0.730***
	Cautious	0.915	0.906	0.009	0.699	2.561*	0.000	0.891***	0.876***	0.658***

* $p < .05$ (two tailed).
** $p < .01$ (two tailed).
*** $p < .001$ (two tailed).

Although the regression lines are similar in nature for both sets of items, they reveal some interesting facts. On risky items, the higher utilities' ratio does not predict the stronger certain preference so sharply as the lower utilities' ratio predicts the intense uncertain preference. On cautious items, the lower utilities' ratio does not capture the intense uncertain preference so efficiently as the higher utilities' ratio captures the stronger certain preference. It is observable if the regression lines for one set of items are superimposed on another. This indicates that the available persuasive arguments to the average subject have evaluated relatively the outcome utilities (i.e., utilities' ratio) and determined his preference as per SEU model. He has valued the uncertain alternative on a risky item and the certain alternative on a cautious item because of the predominant availability of persuasive arguments in their favour.

(ii) *Change in Preference in the Direction of Change in Utilities' Ratio*

The post-test utilities' ratio decreases on risky set of items and increases on cautious set of items than the pre-test utilities' ratio in PA and SC conditions. In accordance with these shifts, the posterior scores on risky set of items decrease than the prior scores to account for risky shift. The reverse happens on cautious set of items to account for cautious shift. Thus, preferences change in the direction of shifts in utilities' ratio. In CO condition, the utilities' ratio does not change on two sets of items (Table 3.3). Accordingly, no such shifts in preference appear in this condition. This reveals that the subjects have gained access to some additional persuasive arguments favouring the pre-inclined valued alternatives on items following group discussion and position comparison. The arguments have changed the relative evaluation of outcome utilities in the direction of shifts in preference.

As stated earlier, the changed utilities' ratio captured the posterior preference. Even the same trend continued in CO condition without any significant shifts in utilities' ratio and shifts in preference. The relationship between the two variables in pre-test is carried over similarly to the post-test session on both sets of items in CO condition.

PA condition differs significantly from SC condition on the amount of change in utilities' ratio. The subjects in PA condition yield more change in utilities' ratio on each set of items than in SC condition. This specifies that the subjects have gained access to more additional persuasive arguments following discussion than following comparison.

(iii) *Shifts in Utilities' Ratio Predicting Shifts in Preference*

As a crucial predictor of SEU model, the amount of shifts in utilities' ratio correlates positively with the amount of shifts in preference (Table 3.3). On estimation of coefficient of determination, shifts in utilities' ratio explain 53 per cent to 60 per cent variability of shifts in preference on risky set of items and 36 per cent to 46 per cent variability on cautious set of items in different conditions. The regression graphs demonstrate clearly the linear trend between the two variables (Fig. 3.2). The same trend continues in CO condition without any shifts in utilities' ratio and shifts in preference. The trend in CO condition is due to regression artifact. Reasonably, the change in relative assessment of outcome utilities caused by the additional access to persuasive arguments determines the shifts in preference in PA and SC conditions. It is conclusive that the amount of additional access to persuasive arguments following discussion and comparison influences both shifts in utilities' ratio and shifts in preference proportionately.

(iv) *Change in Outcome Utilities*

The outcome utilities on both sets of items change in expected directions as per SEU model following discussion and comparison. Only on cautious set of items, the utility of success outcome increases meagerly in reverse direction following comparison (Table 3.4).

All changes in different utilities from pre- to post-test are not significant and the results show a complex pattern. The extent to which change in specific utilities contributes to the change in utilities' ratio varies from one set of items to another and from one condition to another. On risky set of items, the increase in utility of success (U_s) and utility of failure (U_f) outcomes following discussion contributes most to the decrease in utilities' ratio for that set of items. On same items, the increase in utility of failure (U_f) outcome alone following comparison contributes to the decrease in utilities' ratio. On cautious set of items in PA condition, the increase in evaluation of sure outcome (U_c) and decrease in evaluation of failure outcome (U_f) contribute to the increase in posterior utilities' ratio. On same items in SC condition, the increase in evaluation of sure outcome (U_c) alone contributes to the increase in posterior utilities' ratio. The CO condition keeps neither the direction of change in outcome utilities consistent with the reverse direction of insignificant shifts in preference nor the change significant

FIG. 3.2: Changes in Utilities' Ratio as the Predictor of Shifts in Preference.

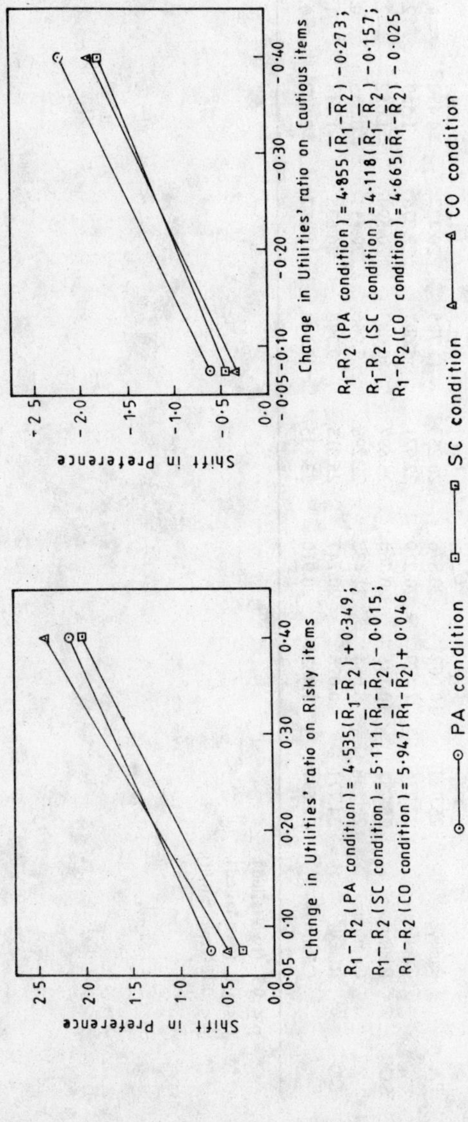

TABLE 3.4: Change in Outcome Utilities in Different Conditions

Condition	Item set	Outcome utility Mean						t-value (within condition)		
		Pre-test			Post-test			U_{s1} - U_{s2}	U_{f1} - U_{f2}	U_{c1} - U_{c2}
		U_{s1}	U_{f1}	U_{c1}	U_{s2}	U_{f2}	U_{c2}			
PA	Risky	25.017	10.062	20.876	26.253	11.725	20.427	–4.490***	–4.879***	1.303
	Cautious	22.736	7.489	20.219	22.921	6.607	23.376	1.569	2.613*	–8.090***
SC	Risky	25.281	10.185	20.764	25.697	10.983	20.590	–1.652	–2.331*	0.615
	Cautious	22.208	8.084	21.438	22.298	7.966	22.511	–0.385	0.479	–3.598***
CO	Risky	24.771	10.028	20.247	25.315	9.708	20.635	–1.714	1.079	–1.150
	Cautious	22.697	7.433	20.910	23.135	7.500	21.157	–2.603*	–0.252	–1.10

* $p < .05$ (two tailed).
** $p < .01$ (two tailed).
*** $p < .001$ (two tailed).

in outcome utilities except one. On cautious set of items, the utility of success outcome increases significantly following the cancellation exercise. In the absence of change in other outcome utilities and change in utilities' ratio, this can be attributed to chance variation.

Three conclusions emerge. First, there is no consistent informational influence that cuts across the conditions. The subjects have gained access to additional persuasive arguments following group discussion as well as following position comparison. The arguments have revised the evaluation of outcome utilities as per SEU model. Second, the locus of informational influence varies from one set of items to another. The additional persuasive arguments have concentrated invariably on consequences of failure at uncertain alternative on risky items and on consequences of certain alternative on cautious items. Third, the amount of informational influence varies between PA condition and SC condition. More number of outcome utilities have changed following discussion than following comparison. The average amount of change in any outcome utility on a particular set of items in PA condition is at least two times larger than the change in same utility in SC condition. Hence, the subjects have gained access to more additional persuasive arguments following group discussion rather than following position comparison.

The results support PAT and the extended SEU model. The persuasive arguments generated in private and gained access to following discussion or comparison are concerned with changing the relative evaluation of outcome utilities to make the uncertain preference more attractive on risky items and the certain preference more attractive on cautious items. The preferences also change in the direction of change in utilities' ratio following discussion and comparison. The changed utilities' ratio predicts the polarised preferences. The amount of shifts in utilities ratio captures directly the amount of shifts in preference. The additional access to persuasive arguments following discussion and comparison has not remained same for all the subjects. Generally, those who took lenient positions on items initially, they possessed a few persuasive arguments in favour of their positions. They have gained access to many persuasive arguments following discussion and comparison favouring the uncertain and certain preferences on risky and cautious items respectively. Consequently, they have yielded more changes in outcome utilities, utilities' ratio and preference as per SEU model. The reverse holds good for those who took initially stronger preferences in valued dirctions of items. This gives a clear support that the comparison-induced shifts are caused by informational influence. Moreover, the amount of change in outcome utilities, utilities' ratio and preference is more following discussion rather than following position comparison. This is because the subjects have received additional persuasive arguments directly and self-generated other arguments following group discussion. The subjects have only self-generated persuasive arguments following position comparison to justify the discrepant valued preferences of others (Burnstein & Vinokur, 1975; Burnstein, Vinokur, & Trope, 1973).

(c) *Certainty and Confidence in Preference*

(i) *Change in Certainty and Confidence*

The subjects feel more certain and confident in their polarised preferences than in their prior preferences in PA and SC conditions. Subjects have gained access to some additional persuasive arguments favouring the uncertain and certain alternative on risky and cautious items respectively following discussion and comparison. Therefore, the certainty and confidence has increased in polarised preferences. Although the amount of increase in certainty and confidence on each set of items in PA condition is larger than in SC condition, the difference between them does not approach significance. However, the average increase in certainty and confidence in PA condition is 1.8 times larger on risky set of items and 1.3 times larger on cautious set of items in comparison to the magnitude of increase in SC condition. The absolute increase in certainty and confidence on each set of items in PA and SC conditions exceeds significantly and frequently the insignificant amount of decrease in certainty and confidence in CO condition (Table 3.5). Somehow, more change in certainty and confidence in PA condition in comparison to SC condition indicates the subjects access to more persuasive arguments following group discussion rather than following position comparison.

(ii) *Variation of Certainty and Confidence with Preference*

If the individual takes an extreme valued preference, many persuasive arguments remain available to him favouring his position. He is likely to feel more certain and confident in his position. The results confirm this (Table 3.6). As the subject holds the stronger uncertain preference on risky set of items and the stronger certain preference on cautious set of items, his certainty and confidence in them also increases in both pre- and post-tests. This implies that the subject possesses many persuasive arguments for an extreme valued preference. CO condition notes very insignificant shifts in certainty and shifts in preference. In spite of this, the certainty and confidence increases with the increasing certain preference on cautious set of items in post-test session. This is because of the carry over of pre-test relationship between two variables to post-test session.

TABLE 3.5: Change in Certainty and Confidence in Different Conditions

Condi-tion	Item set	Certainty and Confidence Mean			*t*-value ($C_1 - C_2$)		
		Pre-test (C_1)	Post-test (C_2)	Change ($C_1 - C_2$)	Within condition	Between condition SC	Between condition CO
PA	Risky	4.022	4.298	–0.276	–3.516***	–1.198	–2.895**
	Cautious	4.000	4.365	–0.365	–5.054***	–0.875	–4.999***
SC	Risky	3.978	4.129	–0.151	–2.201*	0.000	–1.807
	Cautious	3.938	4.213	–0.275	–3.759***	0.000	–3.876***
CO	Risky	4.017	3.994	0.023	0.334	1.807	0.000
	Cautious	4.011	3.961	0.050	1.240	3.876***	0.000

* $p < .05$ (two tailed).
** $p < .01$ (two tailed).
*** $p < .001$ (two tailed).

TABLE 3.6: Correlations of Certainty and Confidence Scores with Preferences and Shifts in Preference

Condition	Item set	Correlation $C_1 . R_1$	$C_2 . R_2$	$C_1 (R_1 - R_2)$	$(C_1 - C_2)(R_1 - R_2)$
PA	Risky	–0.226*	–0.336**	–0.389***	–0.388***
	Cautious	0.227*	0.484***	0.212*	0.285**
SC	Risky	–0.294**	–0.286**	–0.254*	–0.222*
	Cautious	0.342**	0.357***	0.265*	0.246*
CO	Risky	–0.209*	–0.168	–0.191	–0.101
	Cautious	0.377***	0.415***	0.043	–0.011

* $p < .05$ (two tailed).
** $p < .01$ (two tailed).
*** $p < .001$ (two tailed).

The subjects who feel highly certain and confident in their pre-test preferences yield lower amount of shifts in preference. Also, the amount of increase in certainty and confidence from pre- to post-test varies directly with the amount of shifts in preference. These correlations remain consistently significant on both sets of items in PA and SC conditions. The subjects who held preferences in valued directions of items initially felt highly certain and confident in their positions. They possessed many persuasive arguments in favour of their positions. They have gained access to few additional persuasive arguments favouring their initial positions following discussion and comparison. Accordingly, they have yielded lower shifts in preference. The extent of access to persuasive arguments have influenced the amount of shifts in certainty and the amount of shifts in preference. Therefore, both the variables co-vary. These findings in PA and SC conditions support the explanations of PAT proposed earlier.

(d) *Self-Ideal Discrepancy*

(i) *Shift in Self and Ideal Preference*

In pre-test of all the conditions, ideal preferences become more risky on risky set of items and more cautious on cautious set of items than self preferences. This difference, retaining the said trend on risky set of items, fails to approach significance in SC condition only. By and large, what the individual internally values and appreciates remains in more socially desirable direction than his own self-presentation (Table 3.7).

In SC condition, posterior self preferences and ideal preferences do not differ significantly from prior ideal preferences. Indeed, the posterior self preferences move closer to initial ideal preferences in accordance with SCT. In CO condition, self preferences and ideal preferences remain unaltered in post-test session. As a result, post-test self preferences become significantly less risky and less cautious than initial ideal preferences on risky and cautious sets of items respectively. In PA condition, posterior self preferences and ideal preferences become significantly more extreme in valued directions of items than initial ideal preferences. The post-test self preferences do not move closer to initial ideal preferences. Surprisingly, this result is an apparent contradiction to pluralistic ignorance (Levinger & Schneider, 1969) and release (Pruitt, 1969, 1971a, 1971b) versions of

TABLE 3.7: Self-ideal Discrepancies and Shifts in Ideal Preference in Different Conditions

Condition	Item set	Ideal Preference Mean		Discrepancy Mean		*t*-value				
						Within Condition			Between Condition (I_1 - I_2)	
		Pre-test (I_1)	Post-test (I_2)	(R_1 - I_1)	(I_1 - I_2)	(R_1 - I_1)	(I_1 - R_2)	(I_1 - I_2)	SC	CO
PA	Risky	3.444	2.596	0.281	0.848	2.392*	4.255***	4.601***	2.703**	4.335**
	Cautious	8.697	9.427	–0.539	–0.730	–2.888**	–3.213**	–3.242**	–3.162**	–3.401**
SC	Risky	3.522	3.343	0.258	0.179	1.943	0.484	1.089	0.000	1.566
	Cautious	8.680	8.596	–0.444	0.084	–4.255***	0.553	0.676	0.000	–0.234
CO	Risky	3.365	3.528	0.343	–0.163	2.765**	–2.693**	–1.140	–1.556	0.000
	Cautious	8.567	8.444	–0.489	0.123	–2.916**	2.790**	1.121	–0.234	0.000

* $p < .05$ (two tailed).
** $p < .01$ (two tailed).
*** $p < .001$ (two tailed).

SCT. These findings support PAT. The subjects have received and self-generated additional arguments favouring the valued alternatives on items following group discussion. Therefore, posterior self preferences become significantly more extreme, and posterior ideal preferences become significantly more well-founded in valued directions of items than prior ideal preferences in PA condition. The self-generation of few additional arguments following comparison does not retain this trend in SC condition.

More access to additional persuasive arguments in PA condition have yielded more shifts in ideal preference. The magnitude of change in ideal preference on each set of items in PA condition is larger than the change in SC and CO conditions.

(ii) *Variation of Self Preference and Ideal Preference with Shift in Preference*

According to Brown's (1965) value theory, moderate preferences are more valued than extreme preferences on dilemma items. Ideal preferences are likely to remain close to the moderate self preferences. Contradicting this presumption of SCT, correlations between self preferences and ideal preferences retain almost one-to-one relationship across the conditions. Hence, ideal preferences do not move altogether towards the moderate self preferences. Depending upon the availability of persuasive arguments, as the self preferences increase in valued directions of items, ideal preferences become more extreme in same directions in both pre- and post-tests. The CO condition retains similar correlations in posterior session without any significant shifts in self preference and shifts in ideal preference. The pre-test relationship obtained between the two variables is carried over to the post-test session on two sets of items (Table 3.8). Second, initial self-ideal discrepancies vary positively with the amount of shifts in preference. The pre-test self-ideal discrepancy in SCT indicates the extent to which the individual aspires to display his internal valued preference. As the self-ideal discrepancy in pre-test decreases, the average subject yields smaller shift in his preference. PAT gives a different explanation for this finding. The extremity of ideal preference implies that the subject's solution to a problem involving choice is well-founded and he has sufficient reasons for his preference (Burnstein, Vinokur, & Pichevin, 1974). According to this, lower self-ideal discrepancy results in pre-test when self preference and ideal preference of the average subject remain in extreme valued direction of an item. The subject gains access to few additional persuasive arguments following discussion or comparison. Accordingly, he yields lower shift in his preference. In CO condition, without any shifts in self preference, this correlation becomes significant on risky set of items. This can be attributed to regression artifact. Further supporting PAT, the magnitude of shifts in ideal preference correlates positively and substantially with the magnitude of shifts in self preference. Even if the ideal preferences do not shift significantly following comparison, the correlations remain highly significant on both sets of items in SC condition as in PA condition. Both the variables also correlate significantly on two sets of items in CO condition despite their insignificant shifts. The correlations in this condition can be attributed to regression artifacts. However, following discussion and comparison, as the additional access to persuasive arguments increases, it makes proportionately the ideal preferences more well-founded than earlier in accordance with the magnitude of shifts in self preference. A look at the correlations specifices that the shifts in self preference are captured finely by the shifts in ideal preference than by the pre-test self-ideal discrepancies. In SCT, the initial self-ideal discrepancy motivates the individual to display his internal valued preference. This motivation reinforces him to shift his preference. This discrepancy is no more a good predictor for his shift in preference. The good predictor is the amount of shift in his ideal preference. This adds further credence to PAT.

TABLE 3.8: Correlations Among Self Preference, Ideal Preferences and Shifts in Preference

Condition	Item set	Correlation			
		$I_1 \cdot R_1$	$I_2 \cdot R_2$	$(R_1 - I_1)(R_1 - R_2)$	$(I_1 - I_2)(R_1 - R_2)$
PA	Risky	0.837***	0.916***	0.254*	0.762***
	Cautious	0.706***	0.938***	0.323*	0.707***
SC	Risky	0.824***	0.873***	0.248*	0.598***
	Cautious	0.927***	0.973***	0.430***	0.726***
CO	Risky	0.838***	0.862***	0.308**	0.445***
	Cautious	0.792***	0.827***	0.113	0.618***

* $p < .05$ (two tailed).
** $p < .01$ (two tailed).
*** $p < .001$ (two tailed).

Depending upon the extent of access to additional persuasive arguments following discussion and comparison, ideal preferences become well-founded favouring the valued alternatives on items. Ideal preferences shift proportionately in accordance with shifts in self preference. Second, larger shifts in ideal preference in PA condition than in SC condition confirm the subjects access to more additional persuasive arguments following discussion rather than following comparison.

(e) *Satisfaction with Preference*

(i) *Shift in Satisfaction*

After experimental manipulations, subjects were asked to express their feelings of satisfaction with pre-test preferences and then with post-test preferences. They are compared. Subjects feel more satisfied with their polarised preferences than with their prior preferences in PA and SC conditions. The increase in satisfaction, remaining in expected direction, does not approach significance on risky set of items in SC condition only. In CO condition, neither the satisfaction increases with post-test preferences nor the insignificant change in satisfaction remains consistently in expected directions (Table 3.9).

TABLE 3.9: Change in Satisfaction in Different Conditions

Condi-tion	Item set	Satisfaction Mean			t-value ($S_1 - S_2$)		
		Pre-test (S_1)	Post-test (S_2)	Change (S_1-S_2)	Within condition	Between condition SC	Between condition CO
PA	Risky	6.092	6.348	–0.256	–2.435*	–1.147	–2.276*
	Cautious	5.938	6.461	–0.523	–4.875***	–2.139*	–3.077**
SC	Risky	6.185	6.287	–0.101	–1.101	0.000	–1.006
	Cautious	6.017	6.225	–0.208	–2.058*	0.000	–0.835
CO	Risky	6.213	6.202	0.011	0.179	1.006	0.000
	Cautious	5.904	6.000	–0.096	–1.083	0.835	0.000

* $p < .05$ (two tailed).
** $p < .01$ (two tailed).
*** $p < .001$ (two tailed).

In pair-wise comparison of conditions, subjects yield larger shifts in satisfaction in PA condition than in SC and CO conditions. Even if

PA condition yields larger shifts in satisfaction than SC condition on risk set of items, the difference fails to approach significance. Despite this, the average increase in satisfaction on each set of items in PA condition is almost 2.5 times larger in magnitude than in SC condition. Although the absolute increase in satisfaction on each set of items in SC condition is much larger in comparison to the meager change in CO condition, the difference between them does not approach significance. The consistent and larger shifts in satisfaction in PA condition in comparison to SC condition cannot be explained by SCT. The access to more persuasive arguments following discussion rather than following comparison can account for this finding.

(ii) *Variation of Satisfaction with Preference*

The satisfaction increases linearly with the increasing valued preferences on items. This holds good for both pre- and post-test preferences. This indicates that as the availability of persuasive arguments increases, subjects feel more satisfied with their preferences. Despite any shifts in satisfaction and shifts in preference in CO condition, satisfaction increases linearly with the increasing valued preferences on items in post-test session. In this condition, the pre-test correlations are carried over to the post-test session (Table 3.10).

TABLE 3.10: Correlations of Satisfaction Scores with Preference and Shifts in Preference

Condition	Item set	Correlation			
		$S_1 \cdot R_1$	$S_2 \cdot R_2$	$S_1(R_1 - R_2)$	$(S_1 - S_2)(R_1 - R_2)$
PA	Risky	−0.379***	−0.412***	−0.376***	−0.350***
	Cautious	0.582***	0.349***	0.371***	0.364***
SC	Risky	−0.213*	−0.269*	−0.208*	−0.134
	Cautious	0.264*	0.214*	0.107	0.191
CO	Risky	−0.211*	−0.258*	0.038	0.071
	Cautious	0.341**	0.348***	−0.013	−0.118

* $p < .05$ (two tailed).
** $p < .01$ (two tailed).
*** $p < .001$ (two tailed).

Those who feel more satisfied with their initial preferences yield lower shifts in preference in PA and SC conditions with an exception. The correlation fails to approach significance on cautious set of items in SC condition. By and large, when the availability of persuasive arguments to the subjects following discussion or comparison matched with their earlier possession of arguments in holding preferences, it induced more satisfaction with initial preferences. These subjects possessed many persuasive arguments in favour of their preferences and held extreme preferences initially. They have gained access to a few additional persuasive arguments following discussion or comparison and have yielded lower amount of shifts in preference. Thus, satisfaction with initial preferences relates inversely to shifts in preference. The amount of shifts in satisfaction relates directly to the amount of shifts in preference in PA condition. These correlations on both sets of items, remaining in expected directions, do not approach significance in SC condition. The amount of increase in satisfaction depends upon (a) the additional access to persuasive arguments and upon (b) a facilitative interaction process (Vinokur, Burnstein, Sechrest, & Wortman, 1985) where the individual can give and receive information, see implications of his opinions etc. Neither of these two, however, worked actively during comparison. The meager shifts in satisfaction following comparison, therefore, fail to correlate with shifts in preference. This reason can also account for larger and more consistent shifts in satisfaction in PA condition in comparison to SC condition.

In interpreting the correlation, a word of caution is in force. Generally shift data are associated with statistical difficulty. Increasing uncertain and certain preferences are associated with lower and higher scores respectively. While risky shift yields positive difference, cautious shift yields negative difference. Moreover, the increase in utilities' ratio, certainty and satisfaction yields the negative score. A naive inspection of the direction of correlation will lead to erroneous interpretation.

By and large, the stringent concepts of SCT (self-ideal discrepancy, satisfaction) shift and vary in accordance with the assumptions of PAT in PA and SC conditions. The concepts of PAT (utilities' ratio, certainty) also change and vary in SC condition as well as in PA condition. This gives support to PAT. The processing and integration of persuasive arguments is the cause of polarisation (Burnstein, 1982). Second, shifts in preference increase with the corresponding shifts in utilities' ratio, increase in certainty and confidence, ideal preference and satisfaction. These variables are significantly and directly related among themselves in PA and SC conditions (Fig. 3.3). Only shifts in satisfaction fail to relate significantly with the shifts in few other variables in SC condition. The observation of shifts in satisfaction in SC condition substantiates the cause for such anomalies. The shifts in satisfaction are meager in magnitude in comparison to the shifts in other variables. Even the shifts in satisfaction on risky set of items are insignificant. The subjects self-generation of few persuasive arguments following comparison could not enhance satisfaction proportionately with the shifts in preference, shifts in utilities' ratio, shifts in ideal preference and shifts in certainty. In spite of these partial deviations, the overall pattern of results indicates that shifts in all these variables are influenced by a common process primarily. The amount of change in one variable brings the corresponding change in others. Taking the earlier findings into consideration, it is imperative to conclude that the shifts in all these variables are activated by the access to additional persuasive arguments.

(f) *Other Findings*

The data address some other questions. We question : whether the males and females yield differential amount of shifts. Ours is a male dominated society. Many restrictions are imposed upon females from early childhood. Generally, females are submissive, conformist and loyal. When the desirable norms on items are disclosed during discussion or comparison in group, the females are likely to conform more to the desirable norms and yield more shifts than the males.

The shifts of males and females are compared (Table 3.11). The females yield more shifts in preference than the males only on risky set of items in PA condition and on cautious set of items in SC condition. On risky set of items in CO condition while the males yield shift in risky direction, the females yield shift in cautious direction. As a result, the difference between them becomes significant. This difference is artificial. In remaining sets of items in different conditions, the males show, albeit insignificantly, a tendency of yielding more shifts than the females. The results provide poor support to image – maintenance strategy of SCT in absence of a consistent trend for more shifts among females than males (Wallach, Kogan, & Bem, 1962).

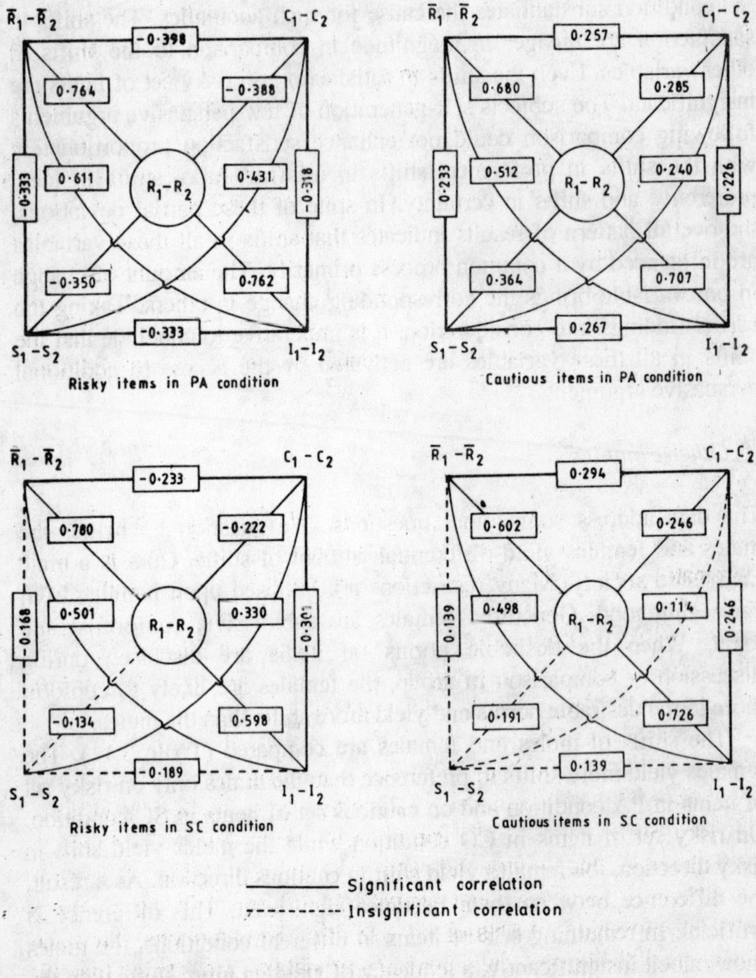

FIG. 3.3: Correlations among Shifts in Preference and Shifts in Conceptual Variables.

TABLE 3.11: Sex Difference in Shifts

Condition	Item set	Shifts in Preference Mean		t-value (M-F)
		Male (M)	Female (F)	
PA	Risky	0.739	1.442	–1.996*
	Cautious	–1.533	–1.035	–1.164
SC	Risky	0.467	0.225	0.800
	Cautious	–0.112	–0.687	2.121*
CO	Risky	0.214	–0.425	2.242*
	Cautious	–0.010	0.050	–0.310

* $p < .05$ (two tailed).

Second, we question : whether the shifts in preference increase in bigger groups. According to the conformity explanation of SCT, when the valued norm on each item is disclosed following discussion or comparison, the conformity pressure operates on deviant minority in group to comply the emerging group norm. This is also described in *P-O-X* unit of Heider's balance theory and in A-B-X model of Newcomb's interpersonal communication. In dyads, if two individuals hold different opinions on an item, the conformity pressure decreases on each other during group interaction. If four or five individuals discuss or compare their opinions in a group on an issue, the conformity pressure increases on deviant minority to conform the emerging group norm (passive conformity pressure). SCT also mentions that during group discussion persuasive talks direct towards the deviant minority who are 'farthest out' of the group norm (active conformity pressure). Bigger the size of the group, the conformity pressure increases on deviants during group interaction to yield shifts. Therefore, bigger groups are likely to yield more shifts in preference than smaller groups.

The shifts of the subjects in three-, four- and five-person groups are compared (Table 3.12). The amount of shifts in preference does not increase with increasing group size in PA and SC conditions. The difference becomes significant only on risky set of items in CO condition. On this set of items, while subjects in five-person groups yield cautious shift, subjects in three-person groups yield risky shift. This condition also did not yield significant shifts earlier. This difference is artificial. The conformity pressure of SCT operates neither through persuasion nor through social comparison to yield more shifts in bigger groups than in smaller groups (Myers & Arenson, 1972).

TABLE 3.12: Group Size and Shifts in Preference

Condi-tion	Item set	Shift Mean			MSOS		F[a]
		Group size			Between	Within	
		3-person	4-person	5-person			
PA	Risky	0.574	1.390	1.200	5.215	2.797	1.865
	Cautious	–1.444	–1.453	–0.983	2.158	4.123	0.523
SC	Risky	0.370	0.437	0.217	0.392	2.047	0.192
	Cautious	–0.278	–0.531	–0.283	0.643	1.709	0.376
CO	Risky	0.352	0.062	–0.600	6.896	1.570	4.394*
	Cautious	–0.018	0.016	0.050	0.033	0.746	0.045

* $p < .05$ (two tailed).
a *F*-ratios are against 2 and 86 df.

Third, wc question : whether heterogeneity in initial preferences of discussion and comparison groups influences shifts. Although heterogeneity in initial choices is shown to influence shifts (Bishop & Myers, 1974; Burns, 1967; Moscovici, Doise, & Dulong, 1972), sometimes poor support exists in favour of this hypothesis (Singleton, 1979). When group members differ highly in their initial preferences, there operates hardly any conformity pressure on each other during discussion or comparison to yield shifts. Similarly, when all group members hold similar initial preferences, the conformity pressure decreases on each other during group interaction. On the other hand, when the initial preferences of group members are moderately different from one another, the conformity pressure increases on deviants during discussion or comparison to yield shifts. Therefore, when the initial preferences of discussion or comparison groups are moderately heterogeneous, they are likely to yield more shifts than others.

The following formula is developed to measure heterogeneity in initial responses of groups.

$$G_H \text{ (Initial group heterogeneity)} = (\sum_{i=1}^{N-1} | X_i - X_{i1..N} | /C$$

where i = the number of individuals in group from 1 to N,
X_i = the pre-test preference of *i*th individual in group,
C = the total number of comparisons, $C = N(N\text{-}1)/2$.

If there are three individuals in a group, the total number of comparisons becomes 3; for four individuals in a group, it becomes 6 and so on. For example, in calculating the pre-test heterogeneity of a three-person group, the choice of the first individual is subtracted from the second and the third, and the choice of the second is subtracted from the third individual. All these differences are added irrespective of signs and divided by 3 (i.e., *C*) to obtain a standard measure of heterogeneity across comparisons.

The heterogeneity in initial responses of three-, four- and five-person groups is calculated. On the basis of heterogeneity scores, the groups are arranged in high, moderate and low heterogeneity cells. The groups in high, moderate and low heterogeneity cells do not yield differential amount of shifts on risky and cautious sets of items (Table 3.13). Only shifts in preference increase on cautious set of items in PA condition with increasing heterogeneity in initial preferences of groups. The heterogeneity in initial responses of discussion and comparison groups and their shifts are not related causally (McCauley, 1972; Singleton, 1979).

Fourth, we question : whether the initial preference of an individual determines his shift in preference. Initial preferences correlate positively and substantially with shifts in preference (Fig. 3.4). The correlations expressed in least square regression graphs indicate that the subjects' initial preferences are excellent predictor of their shifts. When subjects in pre-test prefer the uncertain alternative strongly on risky set of items, their shifts in direction of further risk decrease following experimental manipulations. In contrast, when subjects in pre-test prefer leniently the certain alternative on cautious set of items, their shifts in direction of further caution increase. But the graph trends for two sets of items are more sharp in PA condition than in SC condition. This is because the subjects have yielded more shifts in PA condition in comparison to SC condition. CO condition also retains significant correlations and similar graph trends like SC condition on both sets of items. In the absence of any significant shifts in CO condition, the trends are due to regression artifacts. The initial preferences determine inversely the shifts in preference following discussion or comparison.

The results are quite consistent with PAT. The subject who initially holds an extreme uncertain preference on a risky item or a certain preference on a cautious item, many persuasive arguments remain available to him in favour of his position. He gains access to a very few additional persuasive arguments favouring his initial position following discussion or comparison in group. Accordingly, he yields smaller

TABLE 3.13: Shifts in Preference of Initial High, Moderate and Low Heterogeneity Groups

Condi-tion	Item set	Shifts of heterogeneity Groups			MSOS		F
		High	Moderate	Low	Between	Within	
PA	Risky	1.024	1.456	0.630	1.281	1.088	1.178
	Cautious	–2.411	–1.102	–0.854	5.120	1.400	3.658*
SC	Risky	0.411	0.531	0.293	0.114	0.504	0.226
	Cautious	–0.542	–0.220	–0.359	0.194	0.490	0.395
CO	Risky	–0.285	0.035	0.223	0.489	0.685	0.714
	Cautious	–0.062	0.019	0.068	0.032	0.157	0.202

* $p < .05$ (two tailed).

amount of shift in preference. One who holds initially a non-valued position on a dilemma item yields larger shift in his preference. This interpretation supports an earlier finding of similar nature (Ferguson & Vidmar, 1971). The amount of additional access to persuasive arguments following discussion or comparison determines the individual shift in preference. This also supports the 'truth-supported wins' decision scheme (Laughlin & Earley, 1982). Probably, a correct answer exists for each item. During group discussion or position comparison when the correct answer is ascertained, the subject tries to fetch the correct option and shifts accordingly. One who holds the correct option initially does not shift.

Conclusions

One major conclusion emerges. Polarisation occurs because of informational influence. The persuasive arguments available to the subjects initially evaluate relatively the outcome utilities (i.e., utilities' ratio) following SEU model. They value the uncertain alternative on risky items and the certain alternative on cautious items. The certainty and confidence in and satisfaction with valued preferences increase. Ideal preferences become more extreme than self-preferences in valued directions of items. The subjects gain access to additional persuasive arguments following group discussion and position comparison. Thereby, the conceptual variables of two theories change. The subjects favour more strongly the uncertain alternative on risky items and the certain alternative on cautious items. The relative assessment of outcome utilities changes as per SEU model. The subjects feel more

FIG. 3.4: Initial Preferences as the Predictor of Shifts in Preference.

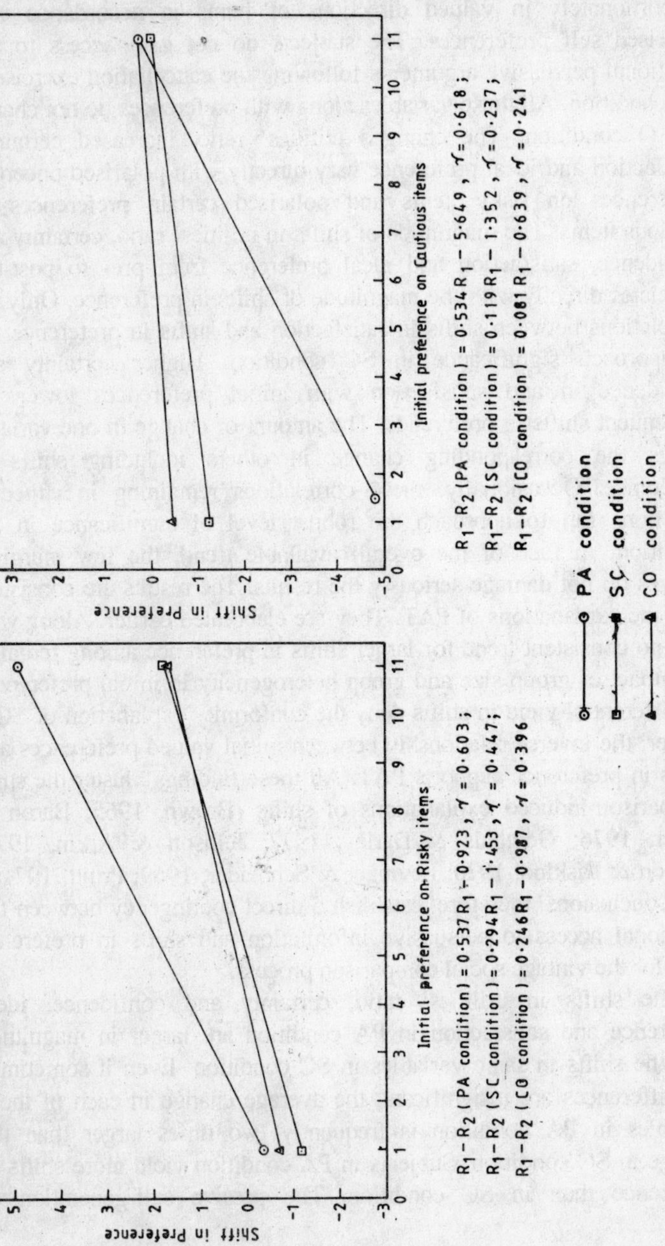

confident and satisfied with their polarised preferences than with their prior preferences. Ideal preferences become well-founded proportionately in valued directions of items in accordance with polarised self preferences. The subjects do not gain access to any additional persuasive arguments following the cancellation exercise in CO condition. All these variables along with preferences do not change in CO condition. The changed utilities' ratio, increased certainty, satisfaction and ideal preference vary directly with polarised uncertain preferences on risky items and polarised certain preferences on cautious items. The magnitude of shifts in utilities' ratio, certainty and confidence, satisfaction and ideal preference from pre- to post-test correlates directly with the magnitude of shifts in preference. Only the correlations between shifts in satisfaction and shifts in preference fail to approach significance in SC condition. Higher certainty and confidence in and satisfaction with initial preferences lower the subsequent shifts in preference. The amount of change in one variable brings the corresponding change in others including shifts in preference. Occasionally, these correlations remaining in expected directions fail to approach the robust level of significance in SC condition. In face of the overall available trend, the few marginal failures do not damage seriously the results. The results are consistent with the explanations of PAT. They are elaborated earlier. Along with this, no consistent trend for larger shifts in preference among females, no impact of group size and group heterogeneity in initial preferences on differential yield in shifts deny the conformity explanation of SCT. Rather, the inverse relationship between initial valued preferences and shifts in preference supports PAT. All these findings bluster the strict comparison-induced explanations of shifts (Brown, 1965; Baron & Roper, 1976; Goethals & Darley, 1977; Jellison & Arkin, 1977; Jellison & Riskind, 1970; Levinger & Schneider, 1969; Pruitt, 1971a). The conclusions, therefore, establish a direct contingency between the additional access to persuasive information and shifts in preference even for the vintage social comparison process.

The shifts in utilities' ratio, certainty and confidence, ideal preference and satisfaction in PA condition are larger in magnitude than the shifts in same variables in SC condition. Even if sometimes the differences are insignificant, the average change in each of these variables in PA condition is frequently two times larger than the change in SC condition. Subjects in PA condition yield more shifts in preference than in SC condition. The passive self-generation of persuasive information – without any background support and justification from others – following comparison has yielded weak shifts in conceptual variables and in preference. These findings confirm that the subjects have gained access to more additional persuasive information following discussion rather than following comparison. Certain inferential clues are available for such a conclusion. First, PA condition is an active informational influence condition. The persuasive arguments available to few individuals are disseminated to group members during discussion. The disseminated arguments have favoured predominantly the uncertain alternative on risky items and the certain alternative on cautious items (Ebbesen & Bowers, 1974; Silverthorne, 1971). The persuasive arguments are novel, valid or cogent (Bishop & Myers, 1974; Vinokur & Burnstein, 1978b). After reception, they are accepted and internalised. By virtue of their characteristics, they have come to mind more frequently than the other arguments. They have tried to link and activate the prior congruent arguments in memory. As a result of rethinking and cognitive elaboration upon them, some other persuasive arguments are self-generated through cognitive mediation further supporting the valued alternatives on items. The direct availability of arguments during discussion and the self-generation of other arguments following discussion have increased the subjects access to additional persuasive information. SC condition is not an active informational influence condition. Finding the discrepant positions of others during comparison in group, the individual has rethought, cognitively elaborated and self-generated few persuasive arguments through cognitive mediation to justify the discrepant positions of others (i.e., 'why have others taken different positions than him on the same issue?'). The self-generated arguments could not come to mind without the availability of discrepant positions of others (Burnstein & Vinokur, 1975; Burnstein, Vinokur, & Trope 1973). The self-generated arguments have acted in the same way as the direct availability of persuasive arguments during discussion. In PA condition, after active access to persuasive arguments following group discussion, the secondary process of rethinking, cognitive elaboration and self-generation of persuasive arguments takes place. This secondary process in PA condition accounts for the primary process in SC condition. Second, group discussion is more lively and duplicates the social reality of conversation and argumentation. It provides opportunity to work out the problems of dissonance by giving and receiving information in natural sequence. The repetition, rehearsal and argumentation in natural sequence enhance the power of arguments during group discussion. They remain absent in comparison of positions. Third, group discussion incorporates both verbal and non verbal communications (like touch, glance, vocal nuance, gesture, eye contact, facial expression etc.). The latter is no less important than the former in sharing the mental frame of others during interaction. In normal conversation, 65 per cent of the meaning is conveyed by non verbal cues and the remaining 35 per cent by words or verbal cues (reported in Knapp, 1972, p.12). No doubt, the non verbal messages are an important part of communication (Mehrabian, 1971). They are mostly sacrificed in comparison of positions. On all accounts, subjects have gained access to more additional persuasive information following group discussion rather than following position comparison.

Few studies have demonstrated polarisation in argument-poor tasks (Baron & Roper, 1976; Sanders & Baron, 1977) supporting SCT. Many studies have demonstrated polarisation in comparison-poor tasks (Burnstein & Vinokur, 1977; Isenberg, 1986; Vinokur & Burnstein, 1978a) supporting PAT. In argument-poor tasks like Asch's (1956) line judgement task and Sherif's (1935) autokinetic phenomenon, the decision tasks are couched in a set of information items. They consist an array of visual information and a set of verbal instructions defining the judgement to be made. The verbal information from majority of others as in Asch's experiment or from the experimenter as in Sherif's study remains contrary to the visual information. Second, the individual brings to the group a set of personal beliefs, feelings, attitudes and knowledge that are relevant to the decision to be made. These information are residue from past experiences. Frequently, the task itself is ambiguous as in Sherif's autokinetic phenomenon. The task-mediated information is insufficient and does not allow a definitive judgement. The individual depends heavily upon a set of verbal information provided by others in group and on a series of his personal information for making a judgement. The perceptual filterings describing the task reality are altered by these information. The entry of biased information into the cognitive field generates the problem of GIGO (garbage-in-garbage-out). The over-riding of verbal information from majority of others in group over the visual reality of task yields wrong output. The judgement, attitude and decision-making tasks are comparison-poor tasks. In these tasks, when three friends agree on an issue, they do not just agree by comparison of their opinions rather by rational justification. So what appears externally in first glance a comparison-induced polarisation is basically caused by information processing and integration (Burnstein, 1982). In comparison-poor verbal tasks of opinions, attitudes and values, polarisation is observed following social comparison. In these task, it is difficult to reject the self-generation of persuasive arguments following the exposure to comparison stimuli. Sometimes, opinions, attitudes and values are popularly pleaded to develop and change through conformity, identification, ritualism, source expertise, source credibility and source attractiveness. They support SCT. On depth inquiry, they can be simply traced back to the process of self-generation of additional information through cognitive mediation.

More the additional access to persuasive arguments, more will be the individual change in opinions, attitudes, values and judgements in the direction of arguments. On the basis of results, it can be concluded that the direct exchange of information in a lively interactive session will be a more efficient process to bring change and polarisation than the mere exposure to comparison stimuli.

In essence, this study offers two major conclusions. First, the access to additional persuasive information determines polarisation. Second, the active exchange of persuasive information in a lively interactive session brings more polarisation than the passive self-generation of few persuasive information following social comparison.

4

FACTORS INFLUENCING POLARISATION

Any theoretical validity can be ascertained in two ways : (a) by experimentally manipulating the independent variables of theoretical interest and observing their impact on dependent variables, and (b) by relating the traits and variables of theoretical interest to dependent variables. The first procedure was followed in earlier chapter. The second procedure is adopted in this study to test the theories in the light of third objective discussed in review of literature. An attempt is made to find out the relationships of variables at individual, message and group levels with shifts in preference.

Situational Variable at the Individual Level

The most common usage of ego involvement refers to the general interest in, concern about or commitment to a specific position on an issue (Freedman, 1964; Rhine & Polowniak, 1971; Kiesler, Collins, & Miller, 1969). The change in ego involvement is associated with the receipt of persuasive information and change in attitude (Rhine and Polowniak, 1971; Sherif & Sherif, 1969). When the initial ego involvement on an issue was high, the receipt of persuasive information did not exert any influence on attitude change. The ego-involving issue is heavily processed and much information is integrated prior to the receipt of persuasive information (Isenberg, 1986). Thus, the extent of ego-involvement and its change are dependent on the availability of persuasive arguments. If additional access to persuasive arguments brings polarisation, the ego involvement in polarised positions will increase. Second, in PAT the subjects' additional access to persuasive arguments following group discussion favours the initial valued alternatives on items. Subjects become more knowledgeable about the valued alternatives on items and shift their responses in the direction of arguments (Vinokur, Trope, & Burnstein, 1975). Therefore, the subjects will perceive the items more interesting and meaningful following polarisation. Third, cognitive strain is the expansion of mental effort by the subject to select a preference on an issue. It was reported that statistical training constituting a new learning reduced the cognitive strain of male subjects in probabilistic information processing (Schoemaker, 1979). Similar cognitive learning also takes place following the additional access to persuasive arguments and polarisation occurs. Therefore, in accordance with PAT, the expansion of mental effort to select posterior preferences on dilemma items will reduce than the mental effort expanded to select prior preferences.

Message and Interpersonal Variable

In PAT, the additional access to persuasive arguments following group discussion brings polarisation. The persuasive arguments are generally novel and valid (Vinokur & Burnstein, 1978b). Other investigators have pointed out the useful and supportive characteristics of arguments (Brock, Albert, & Becker, 1970). They are no less important for the arguments to be persuasive. The amount of additional access to persuasive arguments following group discussion does not remain same for all the subjects. Few persuasive arguments remain available to the subjects who take initially lenient valued positions on items. They gain access to many additional persuasive arguments following group discussion and accordingly yield larger shifts in preference. The reverse happens to the subjects who take extreme valued positions on items initially. The former subjects are likely to perceive more favourably the arguments received during discussion than the latter. Hence, the subjects who perceive more favourably the arguments received during discussion are likely to yield more shifts in preference. Second, in attitudinal and judgemental tasks, the content of group discussion determines the socio-emotional climate of interpersonal behaviour in group. The evaluation of group discussion and interaction are studied popularly with Bales's interaction process analysis (1950). This covers three major socio-emotional dimensions of interpersonal behaviour : (a) dominant *vs.* submissive, (b) friendly *vs.* unfriendly, and (c) controlled *vs.* expressive. This emphasises the process of communication rather than the content of communication in group. In fact, when subjects discuss the attitudinal and judgemental tasks in temporary group, the content of discussion influences primarily the socio-emotional process of interaction. Therefore, knowledge about the issue, critical thinking, pointed contribution, clarification of meaning etc. demand their inclusion in evaluation of group discussion and interaction. Those benefiting from the content of discussion are likely to perceive favourably the group discussion on both content and process and yield larger shifts than others. In other words, more the subjects evaluate favourably the group discussion and interaction, they are likely to prefer extreme valued options on dilemma items and yield more shifts in preference. Third, attitude is considered as a combination of cognitive, affective and active components towards a particular object, situation or person. All conventional scales of attitude tap at the best the affective or feeling component only. When the content and process of interpersonal relationships during interaction become satisfying to subjects, they induce favourable feelings towards the group and reinforce shifts in preference. Therefore, more the favourable attitude of subjects towards their groups, they are likely to yield more shifts in preference. Fourth, the content and process of interpersonal interaction in temporarily formed group determine directly the subjects' perception regarding the competency of their partners in group. The perceived competency of partners is also shown to influence shifts (Verma & Sinha, 1981). Subjects perceiving trust, cooperation and encouragement from others and internalising the norm of the group on each item, evaluate favourably the competency of their partners in group. They are likely to yield more shifts in preference following group interaction.

Individual Trait

Sociability is one of the important traits for effective interpersonal behaviour. The high sociable individuals seek out the company of others and love them, like informal conversation and meet people easily, remain happy and comfortable in social situations. The low sociable individuals enjoy solo activities, find difficulty in talking about others in public and withdraw themselves from social reality (Eysenck, 1970). High sociability goes with extraversion and low with introversion. High sociable individuals are likely to display more socially desirable behaviour after observing the norm of others in social situations than the low sociable individuals. According to the image-maintenance and self-enhancement strategies of SCT (Brown, 1965, 1974; Myers, 1978; Myers, Bruggink, Kersting, & Schlosser, 1980; Myers, Wojcicki, & Aardema, 1977), when the desirable norms on dilemma items will be disclosed during group discussion, the higher sociable individuals tend to internalise these norms, hold more valued preferences and yield more shifts in preference.

The ability to manage and control self-presentation through verbal and non-verbal behaviour is a prerequisite for effective interpersonal behaviour. Observing the expressive behaviour of others in social situation, some individuals become vigilant to present the appropriate patterns of expression and experience to match with others. They are the self-monitoring (SM) individuals. They regulate their self-presentations by tailoring their actions in accordance with the immediate situational cues (Snyder, 1974, 1979). This is a face-saving device, a conscious desire to gain social approval and a willingness to display impression management tactics. Although the high need for approval subjects give socially desirable responses to gain social approval, this variable does not relate to shifts in preference (Lamm, Schaude, & Trommsdorff, 1971). The high need for approval subjects are also unfriendly, non-conversational and do lack appropriate self-control abilities and skills to modify their self-presentations (Bem, 1972; Zaidel & Mehrabian, 1969). The SM trait, therefore, appears to be a more appropriate conceptualisation for image-maintenance strategy of SCT than the need for approval. Snyder (1974) initially proposed five components of SM construct. Observing the psychometric weaknesses of five components, Lennox and Wolfe (1984) reported two sound components of self-monitoring construct : (a) the SM subjects are sensitive to the self-presentation and expressive behaviour of others in social situations, (b) they use these cues for modifying and managing their own self-presentations. When the valued norms on items are disclosed during discussion, the high self-monitoring subjects are more likely to accept these norms on items and yield more shifts in preference for managing their self-presentations.

In accordance with SCT, when the group norm on each item is disclosed during group discussion, the conformity pressure operates on initial moderates to comply with the emerging group norm (Sanders & Baron, 1977, p.304). Therefore, those having the higher tendencies to conform are likely to accept readily the group norms on items and yield more shifts in preference.

In accordance with SCT, the individual perceives himself to be more risky and more cautious than his assumed peers on risky and cautious items respectively (Myers, 1982). Those who take valued preferences on dilemma items are evaluated more favourably by others on dimensions of self (Jellison & Riskind, 1979; Verma & Sinha, 1981). The subjects who perceive themselves to be highly competent on different dimensions of self, after disclosure of valued norms on items following group interaction and discussion, are more likely to accept the valued norms and yield more shifts to protect their self-images.

Since this is an extension of the earlier work, only one condition is taken and the same dilemma items of the earlier study are used.

Method

Sample

A total of 88 students (Male = 56, Av. age = 20.49; Females = 32, Av. age = 20.125) from post-graduate departments of Sambalpur University, Jyoti Vihar, Orissa participated as subjects in this study. The study was conducted in two phases. The subjects individually filled up the questionnaires and returned them in the first phase. The real experiment started in second phase.

TABLE 4.1: Sample Characteristics

Sex	Subject	Average age	Education
Male	56 (14)	20.490	Post-graduate (1st year)
Female	32 (8)	20.125	-do-
Total	88 (22)	20.360	

Number of groups is given in parentheses.

Since group size and sex had no differential impact on shifts, no attempt was made to take groups of different size and to replicate equal number of males and females. In second phase, the subjects run in individuals and in four-person groups (Table 4.1). Twelve to twenty subjects participated in each session. Each session took about one hour and thirty minutes.

Materials

In the first phase, the subjects were instructed in the questionnaire to express freely their feelings and opinions. The questionnaire measured the following constructs.

(a) *Sociability*

The 13-item questionnaire of Eaves and Eysenck (1975) was used to measure sociability. This was a shorter version test. Only one item (original item number 36 but 5 in our questionnaire) was slightly modified ('Can you usually let yourself go and enjoy yourself a lot at a get-together of your friends?') to suit Indian context. Three responses of yes (score = 1), undecided (score = 0.5) and no (score = 0) were given against each item and subjects were instructed to encircle one that applied to them. Six of the items were positively keyed and the rest were negatively keyed.

The sociability scores of the subjects on 13-items were split into odd and even categories. The odd and even item scores correlated very significantly among themselves (0.423, P < .001) and with the total score of sociability (0.903, 0.722, P < .001). The split-half reliability of the test by Spearman-Brown formula was highly significant (0.594, P < .001)

(b) *Self-monitoring (SM)*

The SM was measured by the shorter and revised version test of Lennox and Wolfe (1984). The test had two subscales : (a) ability to modify self-presentation (AMSP), and (b) sensitive to the expressive behaviour of others (SEBO). AMSP contained 7-items and SEBO 6-items. The response format against each item was given on a six-point scale ranging from certainly and always true (score = 5) to certainly and always false (score = 0). Only two items in AMSP were reversely keyed. The subjects were asked to indicate the extent to which each statement was true or false to them.

The scores of the subjects on AMSP and SEBO correlated very significantly with the total score of SM (0.797, 0.805, P < .001) as a measure of internal consistency. The scores on two sub-scales of SM also correlated significantly among themselves (0.282, P < .01). The two sub-scale scores were used singly as well as jointly as suggested by the authors.

(c) *Concern for Appropriateness (CA)*

The CA scale (Lennox & Wolfe, 1984) was used to measure the conformity tendency. The scale consisted of 20-items and two sub-scales : (a) cross-situational variability (CSV), and (b) attention to social comparison information (ASCI). CSV contained 7-items and ASCI 13-items. The response format and scoring pattern were similar to SM scale.

The scores on CSV and ASCI correlated very significantly with the total score of CA (0.707, 0.822, $P < .001$) as a measure of internal consistency. The two sub-scale scores correlated insignificantly among themselves (0.180). The two sub-scale scores were used separately as well as jointly as suggested by the authors.

(d) *Perceived Self-competency (PSC)*

Fifteen adjectives were drawn from different sources to measure PSC (Assor, Aronoff, & Messe, 1981; Jellison & Riskind, 1970; Pervin & Lilly, 1967; Sharan, 1977). The adjectives covered the dimensions of evaluation, activity and potency (Osgood, Suci, & Tannenbaum, 1957). The adjectives were clever, creative, intelligent, competent, active, knowledgeable, trustworthy, insightful, innovative, sincere, confident, decisive, convincing, likeable and sensitive. A six-point response scale was given against each adjective ranging from very much (score = 5) to not at all (score = 0). Subjects were instructed to choose one response against each adjective that described them appropriately. All items were positively keyed.

The scores on odd and even items correlated very significantly among themselves (0.701, $P < .001$) and with the total score of PSC (0.937, 0.906, $P < .001$). The split-half reliability of the test by Spearman-Brown formula was highly significant (0.824, $P < .001$).

Pre- and Post-test Variable

(a) *Attitudinal Judgement*

The two risky items and two cautious items of the earlier study were used. The response format below each item was given on an eleven-point Likert-scale as earlier. The average scores on two risky and two cautious items indexed the attitudes towards uncertain and certain alternatives respectively. The positive difference between pre- and post- test scores indicates shifts towards the uncertain alternative. The negative difference indicates the reverse.

(b) *Ego-involvement*

Below each dilemma item the subjects were asked : 'how important do you consider your advice to this issue?' The responses were given on an unidirectional six-point scale ranging from extremely important (score = 5) to not at all important (score = 0). The ego-involvement scores on two risky items and two cautious items were averaged to obtain an estimation of ego-involvement for each set of items. The negative difference of ego-involvement scores from pre- to post-test indicates the increase in ego-involvement.

(c) *Item Perception*

Two questions were asked to measure item perception : 'to what extent is this item (a) *interesting*, and (b) *meaningful* to you?' The response descriptions were given on an unidirectional six-point scale ranging from not at all (score = 0) to extremely interesting or meaningful (score=5).

The scores on each item of item perception obtained for two risky and two cautious items were averaged for each subject. The pre-test scores of the subjects on 'interesting' and 'meaningful' dimensions correlated very significantly with the total score of item perception and among themselves for risky set (0.785, 0.846, 0.335, $P < .001$) and cautious set of items (0.829, 0.766, 0.327, $P < .001$). The two item scores of item perception were added to obtain an estimation of item perception for each set of dilemma items. The negative difference between pre- and post-test scores of item perception indicates the increase in favourable item perception.

(d) *Cognitive Strain*

Two questions were asked to measure cognitive strain : '(a) how much *effort* do you put into evaluating this issue? and (b) how *difficult* do you find recommending your advice on this issue?' Other investigators measured similarly the cognitive strain (Cacioppo, Petty, & Morris, 1983; Schoemaker, 1979). The response descriptions against each item were given on an unidirectional six-point scale ranging from very much (score = 5) to not at all (score = 0).

The scores on each item of cognitive strain obtained for two risky and two cautious items were averaged for each subject. The pre-test scores of the subjects on two items of cognitive strain correlated significantly with the total score of cognitive strain and among themselves for risky set (0.748, 0.771, $P < .001$; 0.254, $P < .05$) and cautious set of items (0.826, 0.797, $P < .001$; 0.318, $P < .01$). The two item scores on cognitive strain were added to obtain an estimation of cognitive strain for each set of dilemma items. The positive difference between pre- and post-test scores indicates the decrease in cognitive strain.

Post-Test Variable

(a) *Argument Characteristics (AC)*

The subjects were asked to evaluate the arguments received during discussion on influential and convincing (IC), new (N), useful (U), supportive (S), and logical (L) dimensions. The response descriptions against each dimension were given on an unidirectional six-point scale ranging from not at all (score = 0) to extremely influential, new, useful etc. (score = 5). The responses on each dimension for two risky and two cautious items were averaged for each subject to obtain an estimation of each dimension for each set of items.

The subjects' scores on IC, N, U, S and L correlated very significantly with the total score of AC for risky and cautious sets of items as a measure of homogeneity of items (see Table 4.3). The scores on all dimensions were added for each set of items to index the rating of AC.

(b) *Evaluation of Group Discussion (EGD)*

The group evaluation form developed by Harnack, Fest, and Jones (1977, p.268) was slightly revised and used. Each discussant was asked to evaluate the discussion on dimensions of information (evidence of back-ground reading, knowledge about the issue and analysis of the situation), reasoning (evidence of critical thinking), co-operation (support, encouragement, responsibility for stimulating discussion and resolving conflict) and communication (contributions to the point, explanation of complex ideas and clarification of meaning). The responses against each dimension were given on a five-point scale ranging from poor (score = 1) to superior (score = 5) as recommended by the authors. The responses on each dimension for two risky and two cautious items were averaged to obtain an estimation of each dimension for each set of items. The average scores on four dimensions correlated very significantly with the total score of all the dimensions for risky (0.723, 0.653, 0.721, 0.873, P < .001) and cautious sets of items (0.711, 0.683, 0.745, 0.802, P < .001) as a measure of internal consistency. The total score on all the dimensions for each set of items indexed the evaluation of group discussion.

The discussants were also asked to report the overall effectiveness of discussion (OED) : 'how *effective* was the discussion of this issue to you?' The responses were given on an unidirectional six-point scale ranging from very much (score = 5) to not at all (score = 0). The subject scores on OED for two risky and two cautious items were averaged to obtain an estimation of OED for each set of items.

(c) *Attitude towards Group (ATG)*

Two questions were asked to measure ATG : '(a) to what extent are you *attracted* to the group with whom you discussed the issue? and (b) to what extent are you *willing to participate* with your group in a similar type of task in future?' Identical response descriptions were given against each item on an unidirectional six-point scale ranging from highly (score = 5) to not at all (score = 0). The scores on two items correlated significantly among themselves (0.435, P<.001) and with the total score of ATG (0.822, 0.870, P<.001). The subject scores on two items were added to index ATG.

(d) *Perceived Competency of Partners (PCP)*

Fifteen adjectives used to measure perceived self-competency were also used to measure PCP. The response format and scoring pattern were identical except the instructions. The subjects were instructed to evaluate their group members according to their feelings and opinions on each of the adjectives.

In all these measures (except ATG) the response anchors were reversed from one dilemma item to another.

(e) *Demographic Variable*

In the last part of the questionnaire, the subjects were asked to report their name, age, sex and education to record the demographic features of the sample and to match the questionnaires of the subjects in different phases of the experiment.

Procedure

First Phase

The students were given a brief introduction in the class-room to cooperate in a social science study relating to individual differences in possession of psychological characteristics. They were handed over the questionnaires entitled 'Some aspects about' containing the measures of personality traits (sociability, self-monitoring, concern for appropriateness and perceived self — competency). They were mentioned to fill up the questionnaires at their own pace and return them the next day. They were also requested to cooperate in another phase of the study after returning the questionnaires. Nothing about the actual experiment was communicated. Next day, questionnaires were collected.

Second Phase

(a) *Pre-test*

The subjects upon arrival were distributed the 'opinion questionnaire'. It was preceded by standard instructions and examplars. After the subjects went through the instructions, the experimenter explained the instructions and answered the questions raised by the subjects. The subjects gave their responses to dilemma items, ego-involvement, item perception, cognitive strain and demographic information. On completion, the questionnaires were collected.

(b) *Experimental Manipulation*

Immediately subjects were instructed to form homogeneous sex groups of four persons each. The subjects in group were distributed fresh questionnaires containing the dilemma items and the instructions. The instructions were identical to PA condition of earlier experiment. After the subjects went through the instructions, clarifications were made by the experimenter. The subjects discussed the items in group. On completion of discussion, the questionnaires were collected and subjects were requested to return to their original positions.

(c) *Post-test*

The subjects were again given the questionnaires with the instructions for their final responses. The instructions were similar to the earlier post-test instructions in PA condition. Necessary clarifications were made by the experimenter. The questionnaire contained the measurement of attitudinal judgement, ego-involvement, item perception, cognitive strain, argument characteristics, evaluation of group discussion, attitude towards the group, competency of partners and demographic information. On completion, the questionnaires were collected. Subjects were debriefed, answered and thanked by the experimenter.

Results amd Discussion

(a) *Situational Variable*

The results reveal significant polarisation on risky and cautious sets of items following group discussion. Subjects prefer more strongly the uncertain alternative on risky items and the certain alternative on cautious items. The ego-involvement in polarised positions increases significantly. The item perception changes. Items become more interesting and meaningful to the subjects following group discussion than before. Although the cognitive strain decreases in selecting posterior preferences than selecting prior preferences, the decrease is not significant on any sets of items (Table 4.2).

Unfortunately, ego-involvement is used in two different ways by different authors. The general usage refers to the interest in, concern about or commitment to a particular position on an issue. It has also referred to the interest in and concern about an issue without reference to a specific position (Freedman, 1964). When ego-involvement is tied to the specific position, it has increased in polarised preferences. The direct access to additional persuasive arguments and self-generation of arguments favouring the valued alternatives on items following group discussion have increased the ego-involvement in polarised preferences.

TABLE 4.2: Change in Ego-involvement, Item Perception and Cognitive Strain

Item set	Variable (V)	Mean			t-value $(V_1 - V_2)^a$
		Pre-test (V_1)	Post-test (V_2)	Change (V_1-V_2)	
Risky	Item score	3.938	2.949	0.989	4.631***
	Ego-involvement	3.188	3.665	–0.477	–3.743***
	Item perception	6.415	7.034	–0.619	–3.329**
	Cognitive Strain	5.222	5.051	0.171	0.953
Cautious	Item Score	8.642	9.955	–1.313	–5.169***
	Ego-involvement	3.642	4.080	–0.438	–3.432***
	Item perception	6.148	6.761	–0.631	–3.165**
	Cognitive strain	5.165	4.778	0.387	1.908

* p <.05 (two tailed).
** p <.01 (two tailed).
*** p <.001 (two tailed).
a All are two tailed t-values except the shifts in preference.

If change in ego-involvement depends directly on persuasive arguments availability, it will increase in valued pre-test preferences. Second, high ego-involvement in pre-test preferences will decrease the subsequent shifts in preference. The low ego-involvement subjects in pre-test are likely to gain access to many additional persuasive arguments following group discussion and are likely to yield larger shifts in preference. First, the initial preference scores on two sets of items are split into class intervals (see Fig. 4.1). The average ego-involvement decreases in neutral preferences (5.5 – 6.5) and gradually increases in moderate (3.0 – 5.0; 7.0 – 9.0) and extreme preferences (1.0 – 2.5; 9.5 – 11.0) on risky and cautious sets of itêms except one deviation. On cautious set of items the ego-involvement in neutral preferences increases than in moderate uncertain preferences. On cautious items, generally a few individuals prefer the non-valued uncertain preferences which may partly account for this inconsistency. Otherwise, as the initial preferences increase in valued or non-valued direction, the levels of ego-involvement also continually increase. The trend is more sharp in the valued direction of items than in the non-valued direction. Second, the subjects are arranged into high (*N*=29),moderate (*N* = 29), and low (*N* =30) ego-involvement groups on the basis of their ego-involvement in initial preferences. As inferred, ego-involvement in initial preferences relates inversely to the subsequent shifts in preference (Fig. 4.2). The low ego-involvement group yields highest average shifts in preference followed by moderate and high ego-involvement groups on both sets of items. It supports a similar finding of another investigator (Freedman, 1964). When a subject is exposed to the discrepant positions of others on an issue, there arises a tendency within him to change in the direction of others. Under condition of high ego-involvement in initial position, this relationship breaks down. Even high discrepancies with others produce little or no change. Under condition of low ego-involvement, greater change occurs with greater discrepancies. Thus, the extent of ego-involvement and its change depend upon the availability of persuasive arguments.

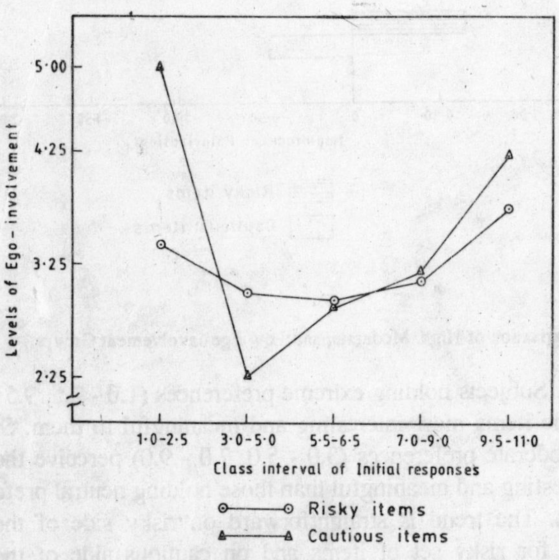

FIG. 4.1: Levels of Ego-involvement in Initial Responses.

The subjects perceive the dilemma items more interesting and meaningful following the access to additional persuasive arguments. This agrees with the commitment version (Moscovici & Zavalloni,

1969, p.128). If informational influence associates with the change in item perception, the item perception in pre-test is likely to increase directly with the initial preference. As done earlier, the preference scores of the subjects are split into class intervals on both sets of items. The average item perception scores are plotted against these class intervals (Fig. 4.3). The item perception increases favourably with the

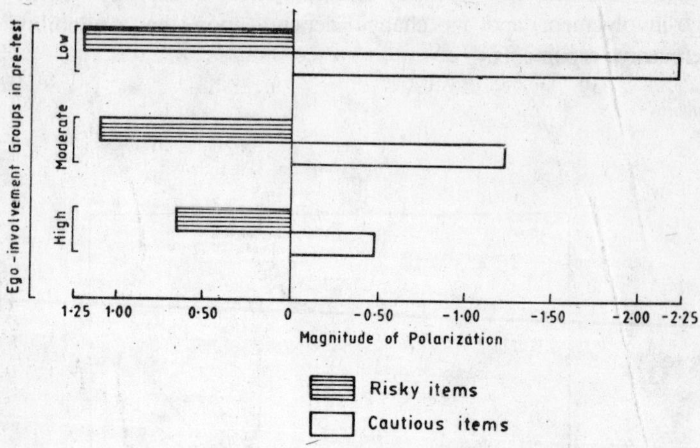

FIG. 4.2: **Polarisation of High, Moderate, and Low Ego-involvement Groups.**

preference. Subjects holding extreme preferences (1.0 - 2.5, 9.5 - 11.0) perceive the items most interesting and meaningful to them. Subjects holding moderate preferences (3.0 - 5.0, 7.0 - 9.0) perceive the items more interesting and meaningful than those holding neutral preferences (5.5 - 6.5). The trend is straightforward on risky side of the scale continuum for risky set of items and on cautious side of the scale continuum for cautious set of items. However, there is a deviation. On risky set of items, subjects holding neutral preferences perceive the items more interesting and meaningful in comparison to those holding moderate conservative preferences. On risky items, generally fewer subjects prefer the non-valued conservative preferences which may partly account for this deviating trend. By and large, as the availability of persuasive arguments increases in holding initial preferences, the item perception increases favourably. It follows directly that more favourable the initial item perception, lower will be the shift in preference. The subjects on the basis of their initial item perception scores are arranged into high (N = 29), moderate (N = 29), and low (N = 30) item perception groups. The low item perception group yields more average shift in preference followed by moderate and high item perception groups on both sets of items (Fig. 4.4). The subjects in low item perception group possessed initially fewer persuasive arguments favouring their preferences. They have gained access to many persuasive arguments favouring the valued alternatives on items following group discussion. Accordingly, they have yielded more shifts in preference than the subjects in other groups. Thus, the initial item perception increases favourably with the extreme initial preferences; changes following group discussion; and relates inversely to the yield of shifts in preference.

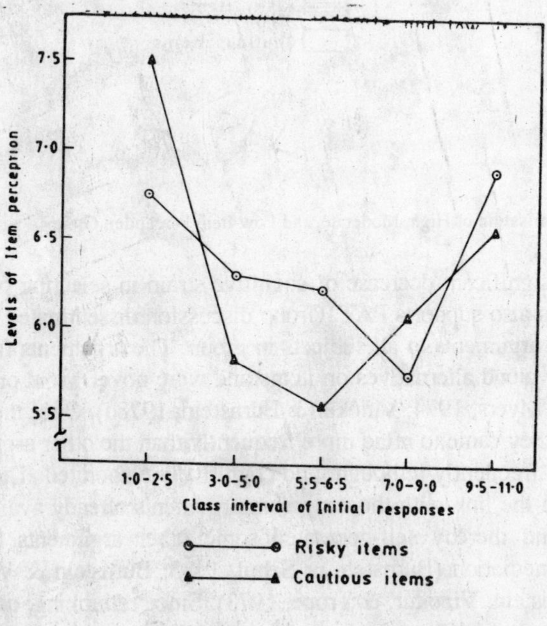

FIG. 4.3: Levels of item Perception Against the Class Interval of Initial Responses.

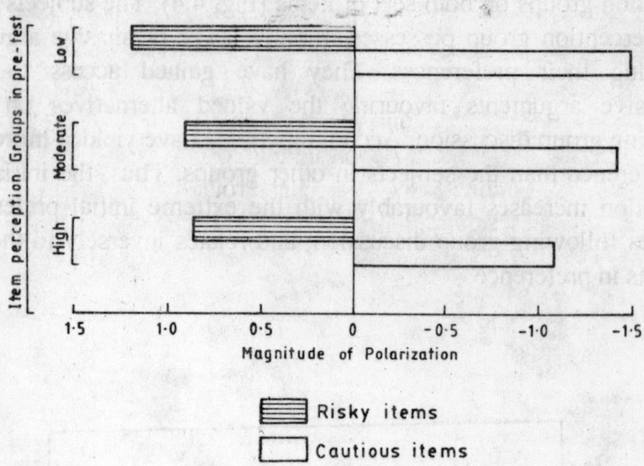

FIG. 4.4: Polarisation of High, Moderate, and Low Item Perception Groups.

The insignificant decrease of cognitive strain in selecting posterior preferences also supports PAT. Group discussion disseminated the few persuasive arguments to all subjects in group. The arguments favoured the initial valued alternatives on items and were novel, valid or cogent (Bishop & Myers, 1974; Vinokur & Burnstein, 1978b). Once they were available, they came to mind more frequently than the other arguments. They were frequently rethought and cognitively elaborated. They tried to establish the link with the congruent arguments already available in memory and thereby self-generated some other arguments through cognitive mediation (Burnstein & Schul, 1983; Burnstein & Vinkour, 1975; Burnstein, Vinokur, & Trope, 1973). Since rethinking, cognitive elaboration and self-generation of persuasive arguments continued following group discussion, cognitive strain did not decrease significantly in selecting the posterior preferences.

(b) *Message and Interpersonal Variable*

It appears essential to see how the argument dimensions evaluated during discussion are related directly among themselves and with the total score of argument characteristics (Table 4.3). The different argument dimensions are related significantly among themselves and with the total score of argument characteristics. The correlations of different argument dimensions with the total score of argument characteristics reveal more contribution of logical, useful, influential and convincing dimensions to total argument ratings than new and supportive dimensions. The former three components explain 42.12 per cent to 56.55 per cent variability of total argument ratings, while the latter two components explain 26.42 per cent to 30.80 per cent variability of total argument ratings on two sets of items. An examination of mean ratings indicates the dissemination of low novel arguments during group discussion. Despite the highly significant shifts in preference following group discussion, the perceived novelty of arguments does not appear to be an important argument characteristic as stated earlier (Vinokur & Burnstein, 1978b). The correlations indicate that the novel arguments are not supportive to the subjects during discussion. The perceived logicality or validity appears to be the most important argument characteristic. It explains the highest amount of variability in argument ratings. The logical arguments are also highly influential and convincing, new, useful and supportive to the subjects during group discussion.

TABLE 4.3 : **Correlations Among Argument Characteristics (AC) — Influential and Convincing (IC), New (N), Useful (U), Supportive (S) and Logical (L)**

Item set	Character-istic	Correlation					
		IC	N	U	S	L	AC
Risky	N	0.179*	1.000				
	U	0.341**	0.239**	1.000			
	S	0.189*	—0.178*	0.534***	1.000		
	L	0.301**	0.352**	0.309**	0.243*	1.000	
	Total(AC)	0.649***	0.526***	0.670***	0.555***	0.725***	1.000
	Mean	3.159	1.744	3.409	3.222	3.210	14.744
Cautious	N	0.266**	1.000				
	U	0.193*	0.227*	1.000			
	S	0.215*	—0.192*	0.380***	1.000		
	L	0.316**	0.181*	0.520***	0.396***	1.000	
	Total(AC)	0.667***	0.514***	0.673***	0.548***	0.752***	1.000
	Mean	2.830	1.517	3.381	3.347	3.301	14.375

* p < .05.
** p< .01.
*** p<.005.

When the subjects perceive more favourably the arguments received during discussion, their shifts in preference increase in valued directions. The correlation between the two variables is quite substantial on both sets of items. However, content and process of group discussion can be recorded either by an outside observer or by group members. Yet, none is free from lacunae. It becomes difficult for an outside observer to record each and every aspect of interaction and discussion. Similarly, when group members evaluate each other, it becomes difficult for a member to be a participant, an observer and a critic of his friends. In attitudinal and judgemental tasks, the outcomes are intangible. Therefore, the group member evaluation claims advantage over evaluation done by an outsider. The individual evaluation of group discussion (on dimensions of information, reasoning, cooperation, communication) varies directly with shifts in preference at a less reliable level of significance (see Burnstein & Vinokur, 1973, p. 132; Burnstein, Vinokur, & Trope, 1973, p. 243). Moreover, shifts are derived differences and subjects are differentially sensitive to the reception and yielding components of persuasive information (McGuire, 1969) received during discussion. So, consideration of such a liberal level of significance ($P < .07$) is not unjustified. As a further validation, effectiveness of discussion increases with shifts in preference on both sets of items (Table 4.4). On the whole, when the subjects perceive favourably the arguments received during discussion, evaluate favourably the group discussion and effectiveness of discussion, their shifts in preference increase following group discussion. The attitude towards group and the perceived competency of partners in group fail to vary significantly with the magnitude of shifts in preference. Of course, these correlations remain in expected directions on both sets of items. While the items measuring the attitude towards the group and perceived competency of partners in group incorporate predominantly the assessment of interpersonal transactions, the items evaluating group discussion assess predominantly the contents of discussion. It is, therefore, understood that the contents of discussion are more important to polarisation following group discussion than the interpersonal transactions in group.

(c) *Individual Trait*

None of the personality variables relate presumably and consistently either to polarised preferences or to shifts in preference on both sets of items (Table 4.5). The 'attention to social comparison information' varies directly with the conservative post-test preferences on risky set of items. The 'tendencies to conform (CA)' vary positively with conservative posterior preferences irrespective of item sets. Also, as the subjects perceive themselves to be more competent, their polarised preferences increase in valued direction on risky items. Only when the 'sensitivity to the expressive behaviour of others' increases, the shifts

TABLE 4.4: Correlations of Argument Characteristics (AC), Evaluation of Group Discussion (EGD), Overall Effectiveness of Discussion (OED), Attitude Towards Group (ATG) and Perceived Competency of Partners (PCP) with Shifts in Preference ($R_1 - R_2$)

Item set	Variable (V)	Mean	SD	Correlations $V(R_1 - R_2)$
Risky	AC	14.744	3.680	0.286***
Cautious		14.375	3.833	–0.216**
Risky	EGD	13.739	2.137	0.206*
Cautious		13.824	2.376	–0.207*
Risky	OED	3.443	0.804	0.217**
Cautious		3.472	0.936	–0.370****
Risky	ATG	6.989	2.332	0.130
Cautious				–0.168
Risky	PCP	51.307	8.657	0.128
Cautious				–0.041

* $p < .07$ (two tailed). *** $p < .01$ (two tailed).
** $p < .05$ (two tailed). **** $p < .001$(two tailed).

in preference on cautious set of items decrease. It is difficult to draw any safe conclusion from these empirical inconsistencies. Indeed, sensitivity to the expressive behaviour of others captures directly the initial valued preferences on both sets of items. The subjects' perceived self-competency varies directly with the initial valued preferences on risky set of items only. Although the scores on sociability and self-monitoring display a tendency to increase with the initial valued preferences on items, the correlations fail to reach significance. Perhaps, the scores on sensitivity to the expressive behaviour of others, self-monitoring, sociability and self-competency in combination with the initial preferences on dilemma items predict the shifts in preference. In multiple correlations, all the personality variables in combination with initial preferences predict the shifts in preference on both sets of items. An indepth inquiry of multiple correlations reveals some other interesting facts. Initial preferences correlate significantly with shifts in preference on risky set of items (0.593) and on cautious set of items (0.734). Initial preferences explain 35.17 per cent variability of shifts in preference on risky set of items and 53.88 per cent variability of shifts in preference on cautious set of items. This indicates that the initial availability of persuasive arguments to the subjects determines directly the initial preferences and inversely the shifts in preference. The personality variables in combination with initial preferences explain 35.28 per cent to 38.81 per cent variability of shifts in preference on risky set of items and 53.88 per cent to 55.95 per cent variability of shifts in preference on cautious set of items. If one interpolates the explained variability of shifts by initial preferences to the above values, some of the personality variables like attention to social comparison information and tendencies to conform (CA) do not explain more than 3.5 per cent variability of shifts in preference on risky set of items and 2.07 per cent variability of shifts in preference on cautious set of items. Thus the impact of personality variables on shifts in preference is very negligible. These deny the role of comparison process to induce shifts.

Conclusions

The pre-test ego-involvement in positions and item perception vary directly with the pre-test preferences on items, change following group discussion and relate inversely to shifts in preference. Since the levels of ego-involvement and of item perception influence the initial preferences and shifts in preference, they are the moderator variables of polarisation. Their variations and changes are quite consistent with the explanations of PAT. The insignificant decrease of cognitive strain in selecting the posterior preferences also supports the explanations of PAT.

Despite the low novelty of disseminated arguments during group discussion, the risky and cautious preferences polarise following group discussion. The logicality of disseminated arguments explains the largest percentage variability of argument ratings and relates significantly to other argument dimensions. The favourable perception of the arguments, evaluation of group discussion and overall effectiveness of discussion influence directly the shifts in preference.

The attitude towards group and the perceived competency of partners in group fail to relate significantly with the magnitude of shifts in preference. Further probe on these reveals that polarisation is influenced profoundly by the information content of discussion rather than by the socio-emotional climate of group during discussion. These findings add credence to PAT.

TABLE 4.5: Correlations of Sociability (S), Ability to Modify Self-presentation (AMSP), Sensitive to the Expressive Behaviour of Others (SEBO), Self-monitoring (SM), Cross-situational Variability (CSV), Attention to Social Comparison Information (ASCI), Concern for Appropriateness (CA) and Perceived Self-competency (PSC) with Initial Preferences (R_1), Polarised Preferences (R_2) and Shifts in Preference (R_1-R_2)

Item set	Variable (V)	Mean (V)	SD (V)	Correlation			
				V.R_1	V.R_2	V(R_1-R_2)	(R_1-R_2) .VR_1
Risky	S	5.778	2.340	–0.130	–0.027	0.170	0.600***
Cautious				0.132	0.078	0.078	0.734***
Risky	AMSP	23.330	4.290	0.046	–0.062	0.110	0.599***
Cautious				0.009	–0.054	0.049	0.735***
Risky	SEBO	18.795	4.369	–0.224*	–0.182	–0.074	0.596***
Cautious				0.263*	0.008	0.264*	0.738***
Risky	SM	42.125	6.933	–0.112	–0.153	0.022	0.600***
Cautious				0.171	–0.029	0.197	0.738***
Risky	CSV	18.409	6.800	0.116	0.097	0.036	0.594***
Cautious				0.030	0.159	–0.087	0.742***
Risky	ASCI	36.011	8.451	0.133	0.271*	–0.112	0.623***
Cautious				0.047	0.161	–0.071	0.742***
Risky	CA	54.420	11.761	0.163	0.251*	–0.060	0.613***
Cautious				0.051	0.208*	–0.102	0.748***
Risky	PSC	49.614	9.450	–0.245*	–0.214*	–0.067	0.598***
Cautious				0.036	–0.098	0.110	0.739***

* $p < .05$ (two tailed).
** $p < .01$ (two tailed).
*** $p < .001$ (two tailed).

Previously, comparison theory was tested by experimentally manipulating the independent variable. Here it is studied on the basis of trait relations. None of the personality variables relates consistently either to the polarised preferences or to the magnitude of shifts in preference. The personality variables like attention to social comparison information and concern for appropriateness alone hardly explain 2 per cent to 3 per cent variability of shifts. The results provide very poor support to the mediating role of comparison process for inducing shifts.

All these findings limit the scope of comparison process to explain shifts. The resultant shifts are neither due to image maintenance and self-enhancement strategies nor due to bandwagon pressure. The informational influence is the cause of polarisation for which Burnstein (1982) has argued and justified recently. The earlier chapter also supported it.

5

EPILOGUE

Out of the three studies discussed here, the first one is concerned with methodology and the last two with theories. They should, therefore, be of interest to methodologists and theorists who are divergent in their approaches.

As Davis (1971) has argued persuasively, the interest in research increases as it disconfirms prior beliefs. To assist in revision of beliefs, this chapter summarises the results of three studies and blends the findings in a conceptual framework. It also discusses the implications and suggests avenues for further research.

General Findings

The first study addresses two major questions : whether the shifts on dilemma items are contaminated by the risk-oriented instructions; and whether the dilemma items measure the attitudinal judgement. Risky, neutral and cautious items are used in three parallel forms. The items in one form contain the so-called risk-oriented instructions with the words 'lowest' and 'at least' and the response descriptions below each item in percentage of chances. It is called percentage form. The items in other two forms incorporate the neutral instructions. In one form, the responses below each item remain in probability of chances and in the other in Likert-type scale. They are called probability form and attitudinal judgement form.

The risky and cautious sets of items, irrespective of risk-oriented and neutral instructions, yield significant choice shift and polarisation following group discussion and consensus. Further scrutiny reveals that the risky and cautious sets of items in percentage form, containing the risk-oriented instructions, yield slightly more shifts than the same items in probability form. The effect of risk-oriented instructions is subtle. The negligible effect is primarily psychometric one. Its inclusion decreases the pre-test scores on conventionally used dilemma items and facilitates the yield in shifts correspondingly. The items in attitudinal judgement form yield comparable shifts as the items in percentage form, and slightly larger shifts than the items in probability form. The responses to each of the risky and cautious items in attitudinal judgement form correlate positively with the responses to same items in other two forms. The low probability (or percentage) on risky items and the high probability on cautious dilemma items tap the uncertain and certain preferences in Likert-type scale respectively. The usual risky and cautious dilemma items with or without risk-oriented instructions measure the attitudinal judgement. The items in attitudinal judgement form also guarantee many other advantages. The study recommends the use of dilemma items in attitudinal judgement form.

Many other findings are also found. When the initial mean of an item remains in risky or conservative side of the scale continuum, it yields risky shift or cautious shift accordingly. While the variance of preferences decreases following choice shift, it does not so happen following polarisation. Choice shift and polarisation occur in between-subjects design but they decrease on risky set of items in probability form. This study clarifies the shaky difference between choice shift and polarisation. It suggests a concentration on polarisation phenomenon for further research understanding the commonness in intensification of initial inclination to both choice shift and polarisation.

The second study, using the dilemma items in attitudinal judgement form, tests whether informational influence is the basis of polarisation. It evaluates the concepts of persuasive argument theory and social comparison theory. The concepts are utilities' ratio, certainty and confidence, ideal preference and satisfaction. Three conditions are taken : (a) a persuasive argument condition followed by group discussion, (b) a social comparison condition followed by position comparison in group, and (c) a control condition followed by a buffer task.

The persuasive arguments available to the subjects initially evaluate the outcome utilities relatively to make the uncertain preference attractive on risky set of items and the certain preference attractive on cautious set of items. The certainty and confidence in and satisfaction with valued preferences increase directly. Ideal preferences become more extreme in valued directions than self preferences.

Significant polarisation occurs on risky and cautious sets of items following group discussion and social comparison. The outcome utilities and utilities' ratio change as per the subjective expected utility model. The subjects feel more confident and satisfied with their polarised preferences than with their prior preferences. Posterior ideal preferences become more extreme in valued directions than prior ideal preferences only in persuasive argument condition. These changes do not occur in control condition. The changed utilities' ratio, certainty and confidence, ideal preference and satisfaction vary directly with the polarised preferences. The magnitude of shifts in utilities' ratio, certainty and confidence, ideal preference and satisfaction correlates directly with the magnitude of yield in polarisation. But the correlations between shifts in satisfaction and shifts in preference, remaining in expected directions, fail to reach significance in social comparison condition. Higher certainty and confidence in and satisfaction with initial preferences, lower the subsequent shifts in preference. The magnitude of change in one variable brings the proportionate change in others with a few exceptions in social comparison condition. Changes in conceptual parameters along with shifts in preference become larger in persuasive argument condition in comparison to social comparison condition. While subjects receive persuasive verbal information, non-verbal information actively and self-generate additional persuasive information following group discussion, they only self-generate additional persuasive information following position comparison. The subjects' access to more information following discussion changes the conceptual parameters very significantly and yields larger polarisation accordingly. The passive self-generation of a few persuasive information following comparison changes the conceptual parameters of the theories significantly with occasional failures. It also yields smaller polarisation.

Females do not yield larger shifts in preference than males consistently. Bigger groups do not yield more shifts in preference in comparison to smaller groups. The heterogeneity in initial preferences of groups does not influence shifts in preference. These deny the mediating role of conformity pressure in inducing polarisation. The inverse relationship between initial valued preferences and shifts in preference provides further support to informational influence hypothesis. Thus, informational influence proves to be the basis of polarisation in both the theories.

The third study again tests two theories by relating the variables at individual, message and group levels to shifts in preference. The initial preferences following group discussion polarise in valued directions of items. The initial ego-involvement in positions and item perception vary directly with the pre-test preferences on items. They relate inversely to shifts in preference and change following group discussion. The cognitive strain decreases, albeit insignificantly, in selecting posterior preferences than in selecting prior preferences. The argument ratings, evaluation of group discussion and overall effectiveness of discussion influence directly the shifts in preference. These variations support the persuasive argument theory.

Many personality variables supporting the self-enhancement and image maintenance strategies of social comparison theory do not vary in expected directions. They correlate insignificantly with polarised preferences and with shifts in preference. Some of the personality variables like attention to social comparison information and concern for appropriateness alone hardly explain 2 per cent to 3 per cent variability of shifts. Their effects on shifts are negligible. These findings thus do not support the social comparison theory.

While the first study recommends the use of dilemma items in Likert-scale and a concentration on polarisation phenomenon for further research, the last two studies using dilemma items provide consistent support to persuasive argument theory.

Conceptual Framework

The risky and cautious dilemma items measure the attitudinal judgement towards uncertain and certain alternatives respectively. The risky items value the uncertain alternative and the cautious items value the certain alternative. Polarisation occurs on these items irrespective of response formats and instructions.

When a person evaluates the alternatives on an issue to state his preference, he retrieves ideas, images and thoughts from memory describing the attributes of alternatives. The images, ideas and thoughts in memory comprise of information. The amount of retrievable information depends upon his past experience, knowledge about the issue and current analysis of the situation. When the information favours one alternative to the other, his preference reflects this preponderance.

On dilemma items, the available information to the individual values the uncertain alternative and its outcome on risky items and the certain alternative and its outcome on cautious items. The relative evaluation of outcome utilities (as per SEU model) predicts the preferences. The person feels confident and satisfied with the increasing value preferences on items. The ideal preferences increase with the valued preferences on items. The individual ego-involvement in valued preferences increases and he perceives the items interesting and meaningful. The valued preferences on items are associated with the availability of more information to the individual. More information availability influences the supporting variables of two theories accordingly.

The individual gains access to some additional persuasive verbal information favouring the valued alternatives on items and non verbal information following discussion with others. The argumentation, repetition and rehearsal of information in an active interactive session increase the cogency of information. The additional cogent information tries to link and activate the earlier congruent information (before discussion) available in memory. As a result of rethinking and cognitive elaboration upon the additional information, some other persuasive information self-generates through cognitive mediation favouring the valued alternatives on items. Larger polarisation and larger shifts in conceptual parameters of the theories occur following group discussion because of the individual's additional access to persuasive verbal information, non verbal information and self-generated information. The relative evaluation of outcome utilities changes. The person feels more confident and satisfied with his polarised preferences than with his prior preferences. He gives more values internally (ideal preference), the uncertain preference on risky items and the certain preference on cautious items than earlier. The magnitude of change in relative evaluation of outcome utilities, confidence, satisfaction and ideal preference varies directly with the magnitude of yield in polarisation. The magnitude of these changes relate significantly among themselves because they are activated proportionately by the access to additional information. The person feels more involved in his polarised preferences than in his prior preferences. The items become more interesting and meaningful to him than earlier. The person evaluates the information characteristics and discussion favourably depending upon his magnitude of yield in polarisation. Since the cognitive elaboration and rethinking on persuasive information continue following group discussion, the cognitive strain does not decrease sharply in selecting posterior preferences.

When the person compares his opinion with others on an issue, he finds the discrepant positions of others. He tries to think and justify why others have taken different positions than him on the same issue. He self-generates some additional persuasive information favouring the discrepant preferences of others that revises his own preference.

The comparison of preferences on dilemma items with others leads the person to self-generate additional persuasive information favouring the valued preferences of others. Only this self-generated information revises his preferences, relative evaluation of outcome utilities, confidence, ideal preference and satisfaction. All these variables behave similarly as they behave following group discussion. However, the shifts in all the variables become smaller following social comparison than the shifts in these variables following group discussion. Even the affective state of satisfaction does not increase significantly with polarised preferences on risky items following social comparison, and shifts in satisfaction fail to vary significantly with shifts in preference. The passive self-generation of few persuasive information following social comparison can account for smaller polarisation and smaller shifts in conceptual parameters of the two theories (see Fig. 5.1). It is difficult to explain comparison-induced shifts without some sort of informational influence. Many personality traits reflecting a concern for others' opinions and a tendency to be aware of differences between one's own opinion and that of others – traits that should augment the impact of social comparison – do not relate to polarisation.

The availability of persuasive information to the person directly determines the strength of his initial preferences on items. The amount of additional access to persuasive information following group discussion or comparison determines his yield of shifts in preference. Both the variables, therefore, relate inversely. Moreover, higher certainty in, ego-involvement in and satisfaction with initial preferences along with the favourable item perception before discussion, lower the subsequent magnitude of yield in polarisation. Additional access to persuasive verbal information, non verbal information and/or self-generated information proves to be the basis of attitudinal judgement polarisation.

This is a theory of awareness. When the awareness in the cognitive field increases depending upon the access to additional persuasive information, polarisation occurs accordingly. If the discussion or comparison with others does not increase the knowledge of the person

FIG. 5.1: Flow Chart to Demonstrate Polarisation Following the Access to Additional Persuasive Information.

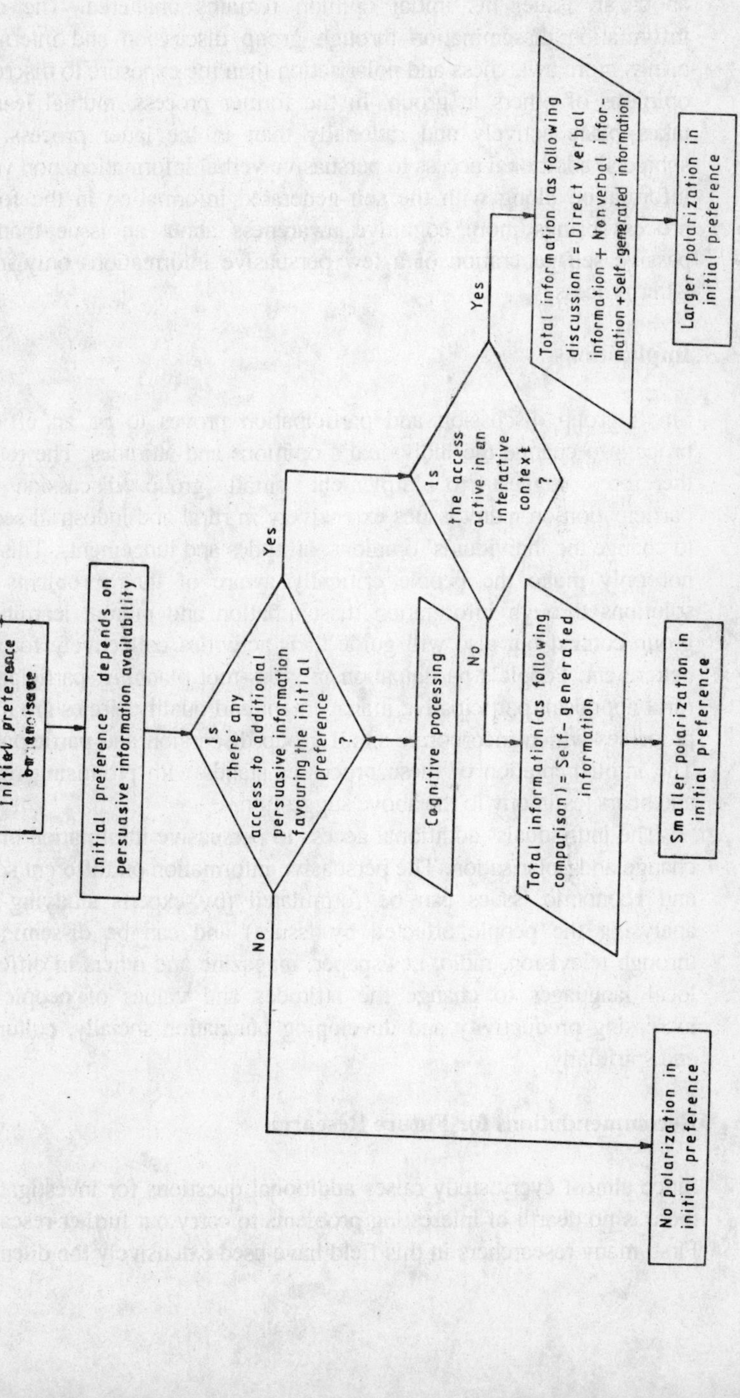

about an issue, his initial opinion remains unaltered. The direct information dissemination through group discussion and interaction brings more awareness and polarisation than the exposure to discrepant opinions of others in group. In the former process, mutual learning takes place actively and rationally than in the latter process. The subjects' additional access to persuasive verbal information, non verbal information along with the self-generated information in the former process brings more cognitive awareness about an issue than the passive self-generation of a few persuasive informations only in the latter process.

Implications

Small group discussion and participation proves to be an efficient process to change the individual's opinions and attitudes. The results, therefore, suggest to implement small group discussion and participation on many issues extensively in rural and industrial sectors to change the individuals' opinions, attitudes and judgements. This will not only make the people critically aware of their problems and solutions through information dissemination and mutual learning in group context but also will guide their activities collectively for their betterment. People's participation in grass-root planning, participatory rural appraisal, participative management and quality circles are a few processes which incorporate small group discussion and participation. The implementation of these processes stands with promising results and bears testimony to the above suggestion.

The individuals' additional access to persuasive information brings change and polarisation. The persuasive information on different social and economic issues can be formulated (by experts studying and analysing the people affected by issues) and can be disseminated through television, radio, newspaper, magazine and others in different local languages to change the attitudes and values of people for increasing productivity and developing our nation socially, culturally and spiritually.

Recommendations for Future Research

Since almost every study raises additional questions for investigation, there is no dearth of interesting problems to carry out further research. First, many researchers in this field have used extensively the dilemma items only. The conceptual framework which emerged here can be extended to perceptual tasks for understanding the basic, substantive issues in this field. Second, persuasive information is proved to be the sole determinant of change and polarisation. The characteristics of information as well as its mode of presentation (verbal, visual etc.) can be thoroughly studied to increase the impact of information. Third, the self-generation of information through cognitive mediation is not clearly known. It has remained as an inferential postulation. Once it will be known, the same model can be imputed into the computer so that it can self-generate information and take decisions in many critical situations. It will provide a technique to simulate intelligence in computer and will be a real achievement in the field of artificial intelligence. Researches are going on to answer some of these questions.

APPENDIX I

SAMPLE QUESTIONNAIRE (STUDY I)

OPINION QUESTIONNAIRE (FORM A)

Instructions

In the following pages, you will find a series of situations that are likely to occur in everyday life. The central person in each situation is faced with a choice between two alternative courses of action: an uncertain alternative with unsure outcomes, which we might call *X*, and a certain alternative with a known sure outcome, which we might call *Y*.

For each situation in the following pages, you will be asked to give your judgement to what extent you recommend alternative *X* or alternative *Y* for the central person in each situation.

An example: "Bibhu is a prisoner in a war camp. Conditions in the camp are quite bad; hard physical labour, poor diet, no medical treatment, etc. He notes a possibility of an escape. If he succeeds, he will enjoy freedom again but if he fails, he will be executed by the enemy."

Try to place yourself in the position of Bibhu. You would recommend strongly, moderately or slightly for Bibhu either to remain in the camp (i.e., certain alternative) or to attempt the escape (i.e., uncertain alternative that would either result in success or failure). For example, suppose you desired to recommend moderately for Bibhu to attempt the escape, then you would tick the following scale as indicated:

Please put a tick mark (√) against the statement that best expresses your advice.

– Strongly recommend to remain in the camp
– Moderately recommend to remain in the camp
– Slightly recommend to remain in the camp
– Undecided
– Slightly recommend to attempt the escape
√ Moderately recommend to attempt the escape
– Strongly recommend to attempt the escape

Read each situation carefully before giving your judgement. Try to place yourself in the position of the central person in each of the situations.

There is no time limit and you can take your own time. However, you should consider the problems carefully.

– Ananda, an electrical engineer, is married and has one child. He has been working for a large electronics corporation since graduating from college five years ago. He is assured of a life-time job with a modest, though adequate salary, and liberal pension benefits upon retirement. On the other hand, he has little chance of a significant salary increase before retirement. While attending a convention, Ananda is offered a job with a small, newly founded company which has a highly uncertain future. The new job would pay more to start and would offer the possibility of a share in the ownership if the company survived the competition of the larger firms.

Imagine that you are advising Ananda. Please put a tick mark (√) against the statement that best expresses your advice.

- Strongly recommend to take the new job
- Moderately recommend to take the new job
- Slightly recommend to take the new job
- Undecided
- Slightly recommend to stick to the old job
- Moderately recommend to stick to the old job
- Strongly recommend to stick to the old job

– Binod, a 45-years old accountant, has recently been informed by his physician that he has developed a severe heart ailment. The disease would be sufficiently serious to force Binod to change many of his strong life habits – reducing his work load, drastically changing his diet, giving up favourite leisure-time pursuits and others. The physician suggests that a delicate medical operation could be attempted which, if successful, would completely relieve the heart condition. But its success could not be assured, and in fact, the operation might prove fatal.

Imagine that you are advising Binod. Please put a tick mark (√) against the statement that best expresses your advice.

- Strongly recommend to carry on with the heart ailment

- Moderately recommend to carry on with the heart ailment
- Slightly recommend to carry on with the heart ailment
- Undecided
- Slightly recommend to undergo operation
- Moderately recommend to undergo operation
- Strongly recommend to undergo operation

– Hari is currently a first class post-graduate degreeholder in Chemistry who is eager to pursue study leading to Ph.D. degree. He has been accepted by both University *X* and University *Y*. University *X* has a world-wide reputation for excellence in Chemistry. While a degree from University *X* would signify outstanding training in this field, the standards are so very rigorous that only a fraction of the candidates actually receive the degree. University *Y*, on the other hand, has much less of a reputation in Chemistry, but almost everyone admitted is awarded the Ph.D. degree, though the degree has much less prestige than the corresponding degree from University *X*.

Imagine that you are advising Hari. Please put a tick mark (√) against the statement that best expresses your advice.

- Strongly recommend to enroll in University *X*
- Moderately recommend to enroll in University *X*
- Slightly recommend to enroll in University *X*
- Undecided
- Slightly recommend to enroll in University *Y*
- Moderately recommend to enroll in University *Y*
- Strongly recommend to enroll in University *Y*

– Dilip is the captain of College *X*'s football team. College *X* is playing its traditional rival, college *Y*, in the final game of the season. The game is in its final seconds. Dilip's team, college *X*, is behind in the score. College *X* has time to run one more play. Dilip, the captain, must decide whether it would be best to settle for a tie score with a play which would be almost certain to work or, on the other hand, should he try a more complicated and risky play which would bring victory if it succeeded, but defeat if not.

Imagine that you are advising Dilip. Please put a tick mark (√) against the statement that best expresses your advice.

- Strongly recommend to attempt the certain play

- Moderately recommend to attempt the certain play
- Slightly recommend to attempt the certain play
- Undecided
- Slightly recommend to attempt the risky play
- Moderately recommend to attempt the risky play
- Strongly recommend to attempt the risky play

– Mohan is contemplating marriage to Miss Tapasi, a girl whom he has known for a little more than a year. Recently, however, a number of arguments have occurred between them, suggesting some sharp differences of opinion in the way each views certain matters. Indeed, they decide to seek advice from a well-known relative as to whether it would be wise for them to marry. On the basis of the suggestions offered by their relative, they realise that a happy marriage, while possible, would not be assured.

Imagine that you are advising Mohan and Miss Tapasi. Please put a tick mark (√) against the statement that best expresses your advice.

- Strongly recommend to marry
- Moderately recommend to marry
- Slightly recommend to marry
- Undecided
- Slightly recommend not to marry
- Moderately recommend not to marry
- Strongly recommend not to marry

– Gopal, a married 30-year old research physicist, has been given a five-year appointment by a major university laboratory. As he thinks about the five years, he realises that he might work on a difficult, long-term problem which, if a solution could be found, would resolve basic scientific issues in the field and bring high scientific honours. If no solutions were found, Gopal would have little to show for his five years in the laboratory, and this would make it hard for him to get a good job afterwards. On the other hand, he could, as most of his professional associates are doing, work on a series of short-term problems where solutions would be easier to find, but where the problems are of lesser scientific importance.

Imagine that you are advising Gopal. Please put a tick mark (√) against the statement that best expresses your advice.

- Strongly recommend to work on a difficult, long-term problem
- Moderately recommend to work on a difficult, long-term problem
- Slightly recommend to work on a difficult, long-term problem
- Undecided
- Slightly recommend to work on easy, short-term problems
- Moderately recommend to work on easy, short-term problems
- Strongly recommend to work on easy, short-term problems

– Ramesh is about to board a plane at the airport at the beginning of his overseas vacation. Although he has been looking forward to this trip for sometime, he is troubled because he awoke in the morning with a severe abdominal pain. Because he has never flown before, he thinks that the pain may simply be an upset stomach brought on by anticipation of the flight. Although he is not far from a hospital where he knows he will obtain quick attention, he realises that a visit to the hospital will cause him to miss his flight which in turn will seriously disrupt his vacation plans. The pain has gotten more severe in the last few minutes.

Imagine that you are advising Ramesh. Please put a tick mark (√) against the statement that best expresses your advice.

- Strongly recommend to go to the hospital
- Moderately recommend to go to the hospital
- Slightly recommend to go to the hospital
- Undecided
- Slightly recommend to board the plane
- Moderately recommend to board the plane
- Strongly recommend to board the plane

– Dipak and his wife Sarita have been attempting to have a child for a number of years. Sarita is now pregnant, but a complication has arisen. The doctor has advised Dipak and Sarita that if the pregnancy is allowed to progress, Sarita's life could be in danger. If further complications do develop, the doctor will not be able to save the child and may not be able to save Sarita. If the pregnancy is terminated at this time, it will be impossible for Sarita to become pregnant again.

Imagine that you are advising Dipak and Sarita. Please put a tick mark (√) against the statement that best expresses your advice.

- Strongly recommend to continue the pregnancy
- Moderately recommend to continue the pregnancy
- Slightly recommend to continue the pregnancy
- Undecided
- Slightly recommend to terminate the pregnancy
- Moderately recommend to terminate the pregnancy
- Strongly recommend to terminate the pregnancy

– Bimal is a writer who is said to have considerable creative talents but who so far has been earning a comfortable living by writing short stories. Recently he has come up with an idea for a potentially significant novel. If it could be written and accepted, it might have considerable literary impact and be a big boost to his career. On the other hand, if he was not able to work out his idea or if the novel was a flop, he would have expended considerable time and energy without remuneration.

Imagine that you are advising Bimal. Please put a tick mark (√) against the statement that best expresses your advice.

- Strongly recommend to keep writing short stories
- Moderately recommend to keep writing short stories
- Slightly recommend to keep writing short stories
- Undecided
- Slightly recommend to write the novel
- Moderately recommend to write the novel
- Strongly recommend to write the novel

Personal Data

1. Name : ____________ 2. Sex : Male . . ./Female . . . (tick one)
3. Age : ____________ 4. Class : ____________

OPINION QUESTIONNAIRE (FORM B)

Instructions

In the following pages, you will find a series of situations that are likely to occur in everyday life. The central person in each situation is faced with a choice between two alternative courses of action, which we might call *X* and *Y*. Alternative *X* is more desirable and attractive than alternative *Y*, but the probability of attaining or achieving *X* is less than that of attaining or achieving *Y*.

For each situation in the following pages, you will be asked to indicate the *minimum* changes of success you would demand before recommending that the more attractive and desirable alternative, *X*, be chosen.

An example : "Ashok is a prisoner in a war camp. Conditions in the camp are quite bad; hard physical labour, poor diet, no medical treatment, etc. He notes a possibility of an escape. If he succeeds, he will enjoy freedom again but if he fails, he will be executed by the enemy."

Try to place yourself in the position of Ashok. What should the lowest chances of success be before you would recommend to give the uncertain alternative (i.e., attempting the escape) a try? For example, suppose you felt the chances had to be at least 70 per cent (i.e., 70 per cent chance that the escape would be successful and 30 per cent chance that it would not be successful) that Ashok would succeed in escaping in order for him to attempt it, then you would tick (√) the following scale as indicated :

Ashok would attempt the escape if at least :

– The chances are 10 per cent that Ashok will succeed.
– The chances are 20 per cent that Ashok will succeed.
– The chances are 30 per cent that Ashok will succeed.
– The chances are 40 per cent that Ashok will succeed.
– The chances are 50 per cent that Ashok will succeed.
– The chances are 60 per cent that Ashok will succeed.
√ The chances are 70 per cent that Ashok will succeed.
– The chances are 80 per cent that Ashok will succeed.
– The chances are 90 per cent that Ashok will succeed.
– Place a tick mark here if you think Ashok should *not* attempt the escape, no matter what the percentage of chances.

Read each situation carefully before giving your judgement. Try to place yourself in the position of the central person in each of the situations.

Before you start, it is important to remember that you are *not* being asked your opinion on what you feel the chances *really* are, but rather what you feel the *minimum* chances of success would have to be before it would be advisable for the central person to choose the uncertain alternative than to choose the certain one.

There is no time limit and you can take your own time. However, you should consider the problem carefully.

OPINION QUESTIONNAIRE (FORM C)

Instructions

In the following pages, you will find a series of situations that are likely to occur in everyday life. The central person in each situation is faced with a choice between two alternative courses of action, which we might call *X* and *Y*. Alternative *X* is more desirable and attractive than alternative *Y*, but the probability of attaining or achieving *X* is less than that of attaining or achieving *Y*.

For each situation in the following pages, you will be asked to indicate the chances of success you would demand before recommending that the more attractive and desirable alternative, *X*, be chosen.

An example : "Prasanta, a successful businessman who participated in a number of civic activities, has been approached by the leaders of his political party as a possible candidate in the next election. Prasanta's party is a minority party though it won occasional elections in the past. Prasanta would like to hold political office, but to do so would involve a serious financial sacrifice, since the party has insufficient campaign funds."

Try to place yourself in the position of Prasanta. What should the chances of success be before you would recommend to give the uncertain alternative (i.e., contesting for the political office) a try? For example, suppose you felt the chances had to be 5 in 10 (i.e., 50 per cent chance that he would win the election and 50 per cent chance that he would not win the election) that Prasanta would win the election in order for him to run for political office, then you would tick (√) the following scale as indicated :

Prasanta would run for political office if the chances are :

– 1 in 10 that Prasanta would win the election.
– 2 in 10 that Prasanta would win the election.
– 3 in 10 that Prasanta would win the election.
– 4 in 10 that Prasanta would win the election.

√ 5 in 10 that Prasanta would win the election.
– 6 in 10 that Prasanta would win the election.
– 7 in 10 that Prasanta would win the election.
– 8 in 10 that Prasanta would win the election.
– 9 in 10 that Prasanta would win the election.
– Place a tick mark here if you think Prasanta should *not* run for political office, no matter what the probabilities.

Read each situation carefully before giving your judgement. Try to place yourself in the position of the central person in each of the situations.

Before you start, it is important to remember that you are being asked your opinion on what you feel the chances of success would *really* have to be before it would be advisable for the central person to choose the uncertain alternative than to choose the certain one.

There is no time limit and you can take your own time. However, you should consider the problems carefully.

SAMPLE QUESTIONNAIRE (STUDY II)

OPINION QUESTIONNAIRE (Pre-test instructions)

Instructions

In the following pages, you will find a series of situations that are likely to occur in everyday life. The central person in each situation is faced with a choice between two alternative courses of action : an uncertain alternative with unsure outcomes, which we might call *X*, and a certain alternative with a known sure outcome, which we might call *Y*.

For each situation in the following pages, you will be asked to give your judgement as to what extent you recommend alternative *X* or alternative *Y* for the central person.

An example : "Bibhu is a prisoner in a war camp. Conditions in the camp are quite bad; hard physical labour, poor diet, no medical treatment, etc. He notes a possibility of an escape. If he succeeds, he will enjoy freedom again but if he fails, he will be executed by the enemy."

Imagine that you are advising Bibhu. You would recommend very strongly, strongly, moderately, slightly or very slightly for Bibhu either to remain in a camp (i.e., certain action) or to attempt the escape (i.e., uncertain action that would either result in success or failure). *For example,* suppose you desired to recommend moderately for Bibhu to attempt the escape, then you would tick the following scale as indicated :

Please put a tick mark (√) against the statement that best expresses your advice.

- Very strongly recommend to remain in the camp
- Strongly recommend to remain in the camp
- Moderately recommend to remain in the camp
- Slightly recommend to remain in the camp
- Very slightly recommend to remain in the camp
- Undecided
- Very slightly recommend to attempt the escape

- – Slightly recommend to attempt the escape
- √ Moderately recommend to attempt the escape
- – Strongly recommend to attempt the escape
- – Very strongly recommend to attempt the escape

After this you are asked to report (by putting a tick mark at the appropriate place) about your level of certainty with your response to each situation.

Then you are presented with a scale to evaluate the *possible outcomes* as you feel about them. *For example*, in the above situation there are three possible outcomes of uncertain and certain actions : failing in attempt to escape (failure of the uncertain action), succeeding in escape (success of the uncertain action), not attempting to escape, thereby remaining in the camp (certain action). For Bibhu, suppose, you would prefer succeeding in escape to remaining in the camp. Another possibility you would prefer remaining in the camp to failing in escape. So the three possible outcomes as you feel for Bibhu will not be equally attractive. Therefore, you are asked to report your feelings about the outcomes of the situations in the questionnaire. *Suppose* you feel that succeeding in escape is moderately desirable, moderately good, very beneficial, and very rewarding, then you will put the tick marks on the four dimensions given against this outcome, i.e., Escape attempted and it resulted in success :

	very	mode-rately	sli-ghtly	nei-ther	sli-ghtly	mode-rately	very	
desirable	....	√	....	....	....	....	....	undesirable
bad	....	....	....	....	....	√	....	good
beneficial	√	....	....	....	....	....	....	harmful
punishing	....	....	....	....	....	....	√	rewarding

However, 'neither' refers to the mid-point that specify for each dimension neither desirable nor undesirable, neither bad nor good, neither beneficial nor harmful, and neither punishing nor rewarding. Before *neither* in this scale 'slightly', 'moderately', and 'very' relate to the left-hand side of each dimension whereas after *neither* in this scale 'slightly', 'moderately', and 'very' relate to the right-hand side of each dimension. This is just *one example.* For each situation in the questionnaire you are asked to evaluate the three possible outcomes as you feel about them. After that some questions are asked, and you are *to give your responses by putting tick marks at the appropriate places or as per instructions.*

Read each situation and the related aspects carefully before giving your response.

SATISFACTION/DISSATISFACTION MEASUREMENT

Instructions Name : ———

Now go through each situation and reply to a question just below that asks about your level of satisfaction or dissatisfaction with your initial response to each situation (Give tick mark at the place that expresses your feelings best).

– Hari is currently a first class post-graduate degree holder in Chemistry who is eager to pursue study leading to the Ph.D. degree. He has been accepted by both University *X* and University *Y*. University *X* has a world-wide reputation for excellence in Chemistry. While a degree from University *X* would signify outstanding training in this field, the standards are so very rigorous that only a fraction of the candidates actually receive the degree. University *Y*, on the other hand, has much less of a reputation in Chemistry, but almost everyone admitted is awarded the Ph.D. degree, though the degree has much less prestige than the corresponding degree from University *X*.

To what extent you feel satisfied or dissatisfied with your initial response to this situation?

Highly satis-fied	Moderately satis-fied	Slightly satis-fied	Neut-ral	Slightly dissatis-fied	Moderately dissatis-fied	Highly dissatis-fied
–	–	–	–	–	–	–

– Gopal, a married 30-year-old research physicist, has been given a five-year appointment by a major university laboratory. As he thinks about the five years, he realises that he might work on a difficult, long-term problem which, if a solution could be found, would resolve basic scientific issues in the field and bring high scientific honours. If no solutions were found, Gopal would have little to show for his five years in the laboratory, and this would make it hard for him to get a good job afterwards. On the other hand, he could, as most of his professional associates are doing, work on a series of short-term problems where solutions would be easier to find, but where the problems are of lesser scientific importance.

To what extent you feel satisfied or dissatisfied with your initial response to this situation?

Highly satis-fied	Moderately satis-fied	Slightly satis-fied	Neut-ral	Slightly dissatis-fied	Moderately dissatis-fied	Highly dissatis-fied
–	–	–	–	–	–	–

– Ramesh is about to board a plane at the airport at the beginning of his overseas vacation. Although he has been looking forward to this trip for sometime, he is troubled because he awoke in the morning with a severe abdominal pain. Because he has never flown before, he thinks that the pain may simply be an upset stomach brought on by anticipation of the flight. Although he is not far from a hospital where he knows he will obtain quick attention, he realises that a visit to the hospital will cause him to miss his flight which in turn will seriously disrupt his vacation plans. The pain has gotten more severe in the last few minutes.

To what extent you feel satisfied or dissatisfied with your initial response to this situation?

Highly satis-fied	Moderately satis-fied	Slightly satis-fied	Neut-ral	Slightly dissatis-fied	Moderately dissatis-fied	Highly dissatis-fied
–	–	–	–	–	–	–

– Dipak and his wife Sarita have been attempting to have a child for a number of years. Sarita is now pregnant, but a complication has arisen. The doctor has advised Dipak and Sarita that if the pregnancy is allowed to progress, Sarita's life could be in danger. If further complications do develop, the doctor will not be able to save the child and may not be able to save Sarita. If the pregnancy is terminated at this time, it will be impossible for Sarita to become pregnant again.

To what extent you feel satisfied or dissatisfied with your initial response to this situation?

Highly satis-fied	Moderately satis-fied	Slightly satis-fied	Neut-ral	Slightly dissatis-fied	Moderately dissatis-fied	Highly dissatis-fied
–	–	–	–	–	–	–

POST-TEST QUESTIONNAIRE

(Instructions are given in Chapter 3)

– Dipak and his wife Sarita have been attempting to have a child for a number of years. Sarita is now pregnant, but a complication has arisen. The doctor has advised Dipak and Sarita that if the pregnancy is allowed to progress, Sarita's life could be in danger. If further complications do develop, the doctor will not be able to save the child and may not be able to save Sarita. If the pregnancy is terminated at this time, it will be impossible for Sarita to become pregnant again.

Imagine that you are advising Dipak and Sarita. Please put a tick mark (√) against the statement that best expresses your advice.

- Very strongly recommend to terminate the pregnancy
- Strongly recommend to terminate the pregnancy
- Moderately recommend to terminate the pregnancy
- Slightly recommend to terminate the pregnancy
- Very slightly recommend to terminate the pregnancy
- Undecided
- Very slightly recommend to continue the pregnancy
- Slightly recommend to continue the pregnancy
- Moderately recommend to continue the pregnancy
- Strongly recommend to continue the pregnancy
- Very strongly recommend to continue the pregnancy

How sure are you of your response to this situation?

Very sure	Quite sure	Moderately sure	Slightly sure	Not sure at all
–	–	–	–	–

To what extent you feel satisfied or dissatisfied with your response to this issue?

Highly satis-fied	Moderately satis-fied	Slightly satis-fied	Neut-ral	Slightly dissatis-fied	Moderately dissatis-fied	Highly dissatis-fied
–	–	–	–	–	–	–

Rate the three *possible outcomes as you feel about them* each on four dimensions given below for Dipak and Sarita.

(1) Pregnancy allowed to continue and complications *do not* arise :

	very	moderately	slightly	neither	slightly	moderately	very	
desirable	....	....	....	....	....	....	....	undesirable
bad	....	....	....	....	....	....	....	good
beneficial	....	....	....	....	....	....	....	harmful
punishing	....	....	....	....	....	....	....	rewarding

(2) Pregnancy allowed to continue and complications arise :

	very	moderately	slightly	neither	slightly	moderately	very	
undesirable	....	....	....	....	....	....	....	desirable
good	....	....	....	....	....	....	....	bad
harmful	....	....	....	....	....	....	....	beneficial
rewarding	....	....	....	....	....	....	....	punishing

(3) Their condition if pregnancy is terminated :

	very	moderately	slightly	neither	slightly	moderately	very	
desirable	....	....	....	....	....	....	....	undesirable
bad	....	....	....	....	....	....	....	good
beneficial	....	....	....	....	....	....	....	harmful
punishing	....	....	....	....	....	....	....	rewarding

– Ramesh is about to board a plane at the airport at the beginning of his overseas vacation. Although he has been looking forward to this trip for sometime, he is troubled because he awoke in the morning with a severe abdominal pain. Because he has never flown before, he thinks that the pain may simply be an upset stomach brought on by anticipation of the flight. Although he is not far from a hospital where he knows he will obtain quick attention, he realises that a visit to the hospital will cause him to miss his flight which in turn will seriously disrupt his vacation plans. The pain has gotten more severe in the last few minutes.

Imagine that you are advising Ramesh. Please put a tick mark (√) against the statement that best expresses your advice.

- Very Strongly recommend to board the plane
- Strongly recommend to board the plane
- Moderately recommend to board the plane
- Slightly recommend to board the plane
- Very slightly recommend to board the plane
- Undecided
- Very slightly recommend to go to the hospital
- Slightly recommend to go to the hospital
- Moderately recommend to go to the hospital
- Strongly recommend to go to the hospital
- Very strongly recommend to go to the hospital

How sure are you of your response to this situation?

Very sure	Quite sure	Moderately sure	Slightly sure	Not sure at all
–	–	–	–	–

To what extent you feel satisfied or dissatisfied with your response to this issue?

Highly satis-fied	Moderately satis-fied	Slightly satis-fied	Neut-ral	Slightly dissatis-fied	Moderately dissatis-fied	Highly dissatis-fied
–	–	–	–	–	–	–

Rate the three *possible outcomes as you feel about them*, each on four dimensions given below for Ramesh.

(1) Boarding plane; pain *does not* get more severe :

	very	mode-rately	sli-ghtly	nei-ther	sli-ghtly	mode-rately	very	
desirable	....	....	....	....	....	....	....	undesirable

bad	....	....	....	....	....	....	....	good
beneficial	....	....	....	....	....	....	....	harmful
punishing	....	....	....	....	....	....	....	rewarding

(2) Boarding plane; pain gets more severe :

	very	mode-rately	sli-ghtly	nei-ther	sli-ghtly	mode-rately	very	
undesirable	....	....	....	....	....	....	....	desirable
good	....	....	....	....	....	....	....	bad
harmful	....	....	....	....	....	....	....	beneficial
rewarding	....	....	....	....	....	....	....	punishing

(3) Missing flight, visiting hospital; having pain diagnosed and treated :

	very	mode-rately	sli-ghtly	nei-ther	sli-ghtly	mode-rately	very	
desirable	....	....	....	....	....	....	....	undesirable
bad	....	....	....	....	....	....	....	good
beneficial	....	....	....	....	....	....	....	harmful
punishing	....	....	....	....	....	....	....	rewarding

– Gopal, a married 30-year old research physicist, has been given a five-year appointment by a major university laboratory. As he thinks about the five years, he realises that he might work on a difficult, long-term problem which, if a solution could be found, would resolve basic scientific issues in the field and bring high scientific honours. If no solutions were found, Gopal would have little to show for his five years in the laboratory, and this would make it hard for him to get a good job afterwards. On the other hand, he could, as most of his professional associates are doing, work on a series of short-term problems where solutions would be easier to find, but where the problems are of lesser scientific importance.

Imagine that you are advising Gopal. Please put a tick mark (√) against the statement that best expresses your advice.

- Very strongly recommend to work on easy, short-term problems
- Strongly recommend to work on easy, short-term problems
- Moderately recommend to work on easy, short-term problems
- Slightly recommend to work on easy, short-term problems
- Very slightly recommend to work on easy, short-term problems
- Undecided
- Very slightly recommend to work on a difficult, long-term problem
- Slightly recommend to work on a difficult, long-term problem
- Moderately recommend to work on a difficult, long-term problem
- Strongly recommend to work on a difficult, long-term problem
- Very strongly recommend to work on a difficult, long-term problem

How sure are you of your response to this situation?

Very sure	Quite sure	Moderately sure	Slightly sure	Not sure at all
–	–	–	–	–

To what extent you feel satisfied or dissatisfied with your response to this issue?

Highly satisfied	Moderately satisfied	Slightly satisfied	Neutral	Slightly dissatisfied	Moderately dissatisfied	Highly dissatisfied
–	–	–	–	–	–	–

Rate the three *possible outcomes as you feel about them*, each on four dimensions given below for Gopal.

(1) Works on a difficult, long-term problem and finds the solution :

	very	moderately	slightly	neither	slightly	moderately	very	
desirable	....	....	....	....	....	...	....	undesirable
bad	....	....	....	....	....	....	....	good
beneficial	....	....	....	....	....	....	....	harmful
punishing	....	....	....	....	....	....	....	rewarding

(2) Works on a difficult, long-term problem and *finds no* solution :

	very	mode-rately	sli-ghtly	nei-ther	sli-ghtly	mode-rately	very	
undesirable	....	....	....	....	....	....	....	desirable
good	....	....	....	....	....	....	....	bad
harmful	....	....	....	....	....	....	....	beneficial
rewarding	....	....	....	....	....	....	....	punishing

(3) Works on easy, short-term problems and finds solutions :

	very	mode-rately	sli-ghtly	nei-ther	sli-ghtly	mode-rately	very	
desirable	....	....	....	....	....	....	....	undesirable
bad	....	....	....	....	....	....	....	good
beneficial	....	....	....	....	....	....	....	harmful
punishing	....	....	....	....	....	....	....	rewarding

– Hari is currently a first class post-graduate degree holder in Chemistry who is eager to pursue study leading to the Ph.D. degree. He has been accepted by both University *X* and University *Y*. University *X* has a world-wide reputation for excellence in Chemistry. While a degree from University *X* would signify outstanding training in this field, the standards are so very rigorous that only a fraction of the candidates actually receive the degree. University *Y*, on the other hand, has much less of a reputation in Chemistry, but almost everyone admitted is awarded the Ph.D. degree, though the degree has much less prestige than the corresponding degree from University *X*.

Imagine that you are advising Hari. Please put a tick mark (√) against the statement that best expresse your advice.

- Very strongly recommend to enroll in University *X*
- Strongly recommend to enroll in University *X*
- Moderately recommend to enroll in University *X*
- Slightly recommend to enroll in University *X*
- Very slightly recommend to enroll in University *X*
- Undecided
- Very slightly recommend to enroll in University *Y*

– Slightly recommend to enroll in University *Y*
– Moderately recommend to enroll in University *Y*
– Strongly recommend to enroll in University *Y*
– Very strongly recommend to enroll in University *Y*

How sure are you of your response to this situation?

Very sure	Quite sure	Moderately sure	Slightly sure	Not sure at all
–	–	–	–	–

To what extent you feel satisfied or dissatisfied with your response to this issue?

Highly satis-fied	Moderately satis-fied	Slightly satis-fied	Neut-ral	Slightly dissatis-fied	Moderately dissatis-fied	Highly dissatis-fied
–	–	–	–	–	–	–

Rate the three *possible outcomes as you feel about them*, each on four dimensions given below for Hari.

(1) Goes to University *X* and receives the degree :

	very	mode-rately	sli-ghtly	nei-ther	sli-ghtly	mode-rately	very	
desirable	....	....	....	....	....	....	....	undesirable
bad	....	....	....	....	....	....	....	good
beneficial	....	....	....	....	....	....	....	harmful
punishing	....	....	....	....	....	....	....	rewarding

(2) Goes to University *X* and *does not* receive the degree :

	very	mode-rately	sli-ghtly	nei-ther	sli-ghtly	mode-rately	very	
undesirable	....	....	....	....	....	....	....	desirable
good	....	....	....	....	....	....	....	bad
harmful	....	....	....	....	....	....	....	beneficial
rewarding	....	....	....	....	....	....	....	punishing

(3) Goes to University *Y* and receives the degree :

	very	moderately	slightly	neither	slightly	moderately	very	
desirable	....	....	....	....	....	....	....	undesirable
bad	....	....	....	....	....	....	....	good
beneficial	....	....	....	....	....	....	....	harmful
punishing	....	....	....	....	....	....	....	rewarding

Please go through the situations once more. For each situation, indicate the response for which you have the highest regard by putting 'R' on the left side of the response categories.

Personal Data

1. Name : ——————— 2. Sex : Male . . ./Female . . . (tick one)
3. Age : ——————— 4. Class : ———————

SAMPLE QUESTIONNAIRE (STUDY III)

SOME ASPECTS ABOUT YOU

Answer the questions listed below. Your answers will be strictly utilised for research purpose only. So feel as free as possible to express your feelings and opinions to the questions.

Section 1

1. Name : ________________ 2. Sex : Male . . ./Female . . . (tick one)

3. Age : ________________ 4. Class : ________________

Section 2

Now work through the 13 questions given below putting circle around the *Yes* or the *No*. If your find it impossible to decide one way or the other for any reason, put a circle around the e.g. '?'.

1. Do you suddenly feel shy when you want to talk to an attractive stranger? Yes ? No
2. Generally, do you prefer reading to meeting people? Yes ? No
3. Do you like going out a lot? Yes ? No
4. Do you prefer to have few but special friends? Yes ? No
5. Can you usually let yourself go and enjoy yourself a lot at a get-together of your friends? Yes ? No
6. Do other people think of you as being very lively? Yes ? No
7. Are you mostly quiet when you are with other people? Yes ? No
8. If there is something you want to know about, would you rather look it up in a book than talk to someone about it? Yes ? No

9.	Do you hate being with a crowd who play jokes on one another?	Yes ? No
10.	Do you like talking to people so much that you never miss a chance of talking to a stranger?	Yes ? No
11.	Would you be unhappy if you could not see lots of people most of the time?	Yes ? No
12.	Do you find it hard to really enjoy yourself at a lively party?	Yes ? No
13.	Can you easily get some life into a rather dull party?	Yes ? No

Section 3

A list of adjectives related to important personality characteristics is given below. Six categories of answers – very much, much, moderate, little, very little, and not at all – are given against each adjective. Read each adjective carefully and put a tick mark (√) against the category *which describes you appropriately.*

	Very much	Much	Moderate	Little	Very little	Not at all
1. Clever :	....	....	....	....	....	....
2. Creative :	....	....	....	....	....	....
3. Intelligent :	....	....	....	....	....	....
4. Competent :	....	....	....	....	....	....
5. Active :	....	....	....	....	....	....
6. Knowledgeable :	....	....	....	....	....	....
7. Trustworthy :	....	....	....	....	....	....
8. Insightful :	....	....	....	....	....	....
9. Innovative :	....	....	....	....	....	....
10. Sincere :	....	....	....	....	....	....
11. Confident :	....	....	....	....	....	....
12. Decisive :	....	....	....	....	....	....
13. Convincing :	....	....	....	....	....	....
14. Likeable :	....	....	....	....	....	....
15. Sensitive :	....	....	....	....	....	....

Section 4

Given below are 33 statements concerning your personal reactions to a number of different situations. No two statements are exactly alike, so consider each statement carefully before answering. Six categories of answers are given against each statement.

If a statement to you is :

Certainly, Always True	encircle CT
Generally True	encircle GT
Somewhat True, But with Exception	encircle ST
Somewhat False, But with Exception	encircle SF
Generally False	encircle GF
Certainly, Always False	encircle CF

1. In social situations, I have the ability to alter my behaviour if I feel that something else is called for. CT GT ST SF GF CF
2. I have the ability to control the way I come across to people depending on the impression I wish to give them. CT GT ST SF GF CF
3. When I feel that the image I am portraying is not working, I can readily change it to something that does. CT GT ST SF GF CF
4. I have trouble changing my behaviour to suit different people and different situations. CT GT ST SF GF CF
5. I have found that I can adjust my behaviour to meet the requirements of any situation I find myself in. CT GT ST SF GF CF
6. Even when it might be to my advantage, I have difficulty in putting up a good front. CT GT ST SF GF CF
7. Once I know what the situation calls for, it is easy for me to regulate my actions accordingly. CT GT ST SF GF CF
8. I am often able to read people's true emotions correctly through their eyes. CT GT ST SF GF CF
9. In conversations, I am sensitive to even the slightest change in the facial expression of the person I am conversing with. CT GT ST SF GF CF

10. My powers of intuition are quite good when it comes to understanding others' emotions and motives. CT GT ST SF GF CF
11. I can usually tell when others consider a joke to be in bad taste, even though they may laugh convincingly. CT GT ST SF GF CF
12. I can usually tell when I have said something inappropriate by reading it in the listener's eyes. CT GT ST SF GF CF
13. If someone is lying to me, I usually know it at once from that person's manner of expression. CT GT ST SF GF CF
14. I tend to show different sides of myself to different people. CT GT ST SF GF CF
15. In different situations and with different people, I often act like very different persons. CT GT ST SF GF CF
16. Although I know myself, I find that others do not know me. CT GT ST SF GF CF
17. Different situations can make me behave like very different people. CT GT ST SF GF CF
18. Different people tend to have different impressions about the type of person I am. CT GT ST SF GF CF
19. I am not always the person I appear to be. CT GT ST SF GF CF
20. I sometimes have the feeling that people do not know who I really am. CT GT ST SF GF CF
21. It is my feeling if everyone else in a group is behaving in a certain manner, this must be the proper way to behave. CT GT ST SF GF CF
22. I actively avoid wearing clothes that are not in style. CT GT ST SF GF CF
23. At parties I usually try to behave in a manner that makes me fit in. CT GT ST SF GF CF
24. When I am uncertain how to act in a social situation, I look to the behaviour of others for cues. CT GT ST SF GF CF

25. I try to pay attention to the reactions of others to my behaviour in order to avoid being out of place. CT GT ST SF GF CF
26. I find that I tend to pick up slang expressions from others and use them as part of my own vocabulary. CT GT ST SF GF CF
27. I tend to pay attention to what others are wearing. CT GT ST SF GF CF
28. The slightest look of disapproval in the eyes of a person with whom I am inter acting is enough to make me change my approach. CT GT ST SF GF CF
29. It's important to me to fit in to the group I am with. CT GT ST SF GF CF
30. My behaviour often depends on how I feel others wish me to behave. CT GT ST SF GF CF
31. If I am the least bit uncertain as to how to act in a social situation, I look to the behaviour of others for cues. CT GT ST SF GF CF
32. I usually keep up with clothing style changes by watching what others wear. CT GT ST SF GF CF
33. When in a social situation, I tend not to follow the crowd, but instead behave in a manner that suits my particular mood at the time. CT GT ST SF GF CF

Check that you have answered all the questions.

OPINION QUESTIONNAIRE (Pre-test Instructions)

Instructions

In the following pages, you will find a series of situations that are likely to occur in everyday life. The central person in each situation is faced with a choice between two alternative courses of action: an uncertain alternative with unsure outcomes, which we might call *X*, and a certain alternative with a known sure outcome, which we might call *Y*.

For each situation in the following pages, you will be asked to give your judgement as to what extent you recommend alternative *X* or alternative *Y* for the central person.

An example : "Bibhu is a prisoner in a war camp. Conditions in the camp are quite bad; hard physical labour, poor diet, no medical treatment, etc. He notes a possibility of an escape. If he succeeds, he will enjoy freedom again but if he fails, he will be executed by the enemy."

Imagine that you are advising Bibhu. You would recommend very strongly, strongly, moderately, slightly or very slightly for Bibhu either to remain in the camp (i.e., certain action) or to attempt the escape (i.e., uncertain action that would either result in success or failure). *For example*, suppose you desired to recommend moderately for Bibhu to attempt the escape, then you would tick the following scale as indicated :

Please put a tick mark (√) against the statement that best expresses your advice.

– Very strongly recommend to remain in the camp
– Strongly recommend to remain in the camp
– Moderately recommend to remain in the camp
– Slightly recommend to remain in the camp
– Very slightly recommend to remain in the camp
– Undecided
– Very slightly recommend to attempt the escape
– Slightly recommend to attempt the escape
√ Moderately recommend to attempt the escape
– Strongly recommend to attempt the escape
– Very strongly recommend to attempt the escape

After this you are asked to give your responses to some questions given under each situation or issue [by putting tick marks at the appropriate places (√) that best express your feelings]. Two examples are cited here. First, suppose you are asked : How *important* do you consider your advice to this issue?

Extremely	Quite	Moderately	Somehow	Slightly	Not at all
—	—	—	√	—	—

This tick mark at the appropriate place indicates that your advice is *somehow important*. Second, suppose you are asked :

To what extent is this issue interesting and meaningful to you?

	Not at all	Slightly	Somehow	Moderately	Quite	Extremely
(i) Interesting :	....	....	....	√	....	....
(ii) Meaningful :	....	√	....	....	....	....

The tick mark in the *first line (row)* indicates that issue is *moderately interesting* and the tick mark in the *second line* indicates that the issue is *slightly meaningful* to you. These are just examples to indicate how you will give tick marks at different places to express your feelings.

Read each situation and the related aspects carefully before giving your response.

POST-TEST QUESTIONNAIRE (Without Instructions)

– Dipak and his wife Sarita have been attempting to have a child for a number of years. Sarita is now pregnant, but a complication has arisen. The doctor has advised Dipak and Sarita that if the pregnancy is allowed to progress, Sarita's life could be in danger. If further complications do develop, the doctor will not be able to save the child and may not be able to save Sarita. If the pregnancy is terminated at this time, it will be impossible for Sarita to become pregnant again.

Imagine that you are advising Dipak and Sarita. Please put a tick mark (√) against the statement that best expresses your advice.

- Very strongly recommend to terminate the pregnancy
- Strongly recommend to terminate the pregnancy
- Moderately recommend to terminate the pregnancy
- Slightly recommend to terminate the pregnancy
- Very slightly recommend to terminate the pregnancy
- Undecided
- Very slightly recommend to continue the pregnancy
- Slightly recommend to continue the pregnancy

– Moderately recommend to continue the pregnancy
– Strongly recommend to continue the pregnancy
– Very strongly recommend to continue the pregnancy

(a) How *important* do you consider your advice to this issue?

Not at all	Slightly	Somehow	Moderately	Quite	Extremely
—	—	—	—	—	—

(b) How much *effort* did you put into evaluating this issue?

Very much	Much	Moderate	Little	Very little	Not at all
–	–	–	–	–	–

(c) How *difficult* do you find recommending your advice on this issue?

Not at all	Very little	Little	Moderate	Much	Very much
–	–	–	–	–	–

(d) To what extent is this issue interesting and meaningful to you?

	Extre-mely	Quite	Mode-rately	Some-how	Slightly	Not at all
(i) Interesting :	....	....	....	....	....	....
(ii) Meaningful :	....	....	....	....	....	....

(e) To what extent is the information received during the *discussion of this issue* influential and convincing, new, useful, supportive, and logical to you?

	Not at all	Slightly	Some-how	Mode-rately	Quite	Extre-mely
(i) Influential & convincing :	....	....	....	....	....	....
(ii) New :	....	....	....	....	....	....
(iii) Useful :	....	....	....	....	....	....
(iv) Supportive :	....	....	....	....	....	....
(v) Logical :	....	....	....	....	....	....

(f) Evaluate the group *discussion of this issue* according to your opinions and feelings.

Rating scale : 1. Poor, 2. Below average, 3. Average, 4. Excellent, 5. Superior.

Did the discussant. . .	Evaluation (tick one number per each question)
(i) . . . show evidence of background reading, knowledge about the issue, and analysis of the situation?	1 2 3 4 5
(ii) . . . show evidence of critical thinking?	1 2 3 4 5
(iii) . . . support, encourage others, and show the responsibility for stimulating discussion and resolving conflict?	1 2 3 4 5
iv) . . . make contributions, to the point, clear, explain complex ideas, and clarify meaning?	1 2 3 4 5

(g) How effective was the discussion of this issue to you?

Very much	Much	Moderate	Little	Very little	Not at all
–	–	–	–	–	–

– Ramesh is about to board a plane at the airport at the beginning of his overseas vacation. Although he has been looking forward to this trip for sometime, he is troubled because he awoke in the morning with a severe abdominal pain. Because he has never flown before, he thinks that the pain may simply be an upset stomach brought on by anticipation of the flight. Although he is not far from a hospital where he knows he will obtain quick attention, he realises that a visit to the hospital will cause him to miss his flight which in turn will seriously disrupt his vacation plans. The pain has gotten more severe in the last few minutes.

Imagine that you are advising Ramesh. Please put a tick mark (√) against the statement that best expresses your advice.

– Very Strongly recommend to board the plane
– Strongly recommend to board the plane

- Moderately recommend to board the plane
- Slightly recommend to board the plane
- Very slightly recommend to board the plane
- Undecided
- Very slightly recommend to go to the hospital
- Slightly recommend to go to the hospital
- Moderately recommend to go to the hospital
- Strongly recommend to go to the hospital
- Very strongly recommend to go to the hospital

(a) How *important* do you consider your advice to this issue?

Extremely	Quite	Moderately	Somehow	Slightly	Not at all
—	—	—	—	—	—

(b) How much *effort* did you put into evaluating this issue?

Not at all	Very little	Little	Moderate	Much	Very much
—	—	—	—	—	—

(c) How *difficult* do you find recommending your advice on this issue?

Very much	Much	Moderate	Little	Very little	Not at all
—	—	—	—	—	—

(d) To what extent is this issue interesting and meaningful to you?

	Not at all	Slightly	Somehow	Moderately	Quite	Extremely
(i) Interesting :	....	....	....	....	....	....
(ii) Meaningful :	....	....	....	....	....	....

(e) To what extent is the information received during the *discussion of this issue* influential and convincing, new, useful, supportive, and logical to you?

	Extre-mely	Quite	Mode-rately	Some-how	Slightly	Not at all
(i) Influential & convincing :	....	....	....	....	....	....
(ii) New :	....	....	....	....	....	....
(iii) Useful :	....	....	....	....	....	....
(iv) Supportive :	....	....	....	....	....	....
(v) Logical :	....	....	....	....	....	....

(f) Evaluate the group *discussion of this issue* according to your opinions and feelings.

Rating scale : 1. Poor, 2. Below average, 3. Average, 4. Excellent, 5. Superior.

Did the discussant. . .	Evaluation (tick one number per each question)
(i) . . .show evidence of background reading, knowledge about the issue, and analysis of the situation?	1 2 3 4 5
(ii) . . .show evidence of critical thinking?	1 2 3 4 5
(iii) . . .support, encourage others, and show the responsibility for stimulating discussion and resolving conflict?	1 2 3 4 5
(iv) . . .make contributions, to the point, clear, explain complex ideas, and clarify meaning?	1 2 3 4 5

(g) How effective was the discussion of this issue to you?

Not at all	Very little	Little	Moderate	Much	Very much
–	–	–	–	–	–

– Gopal, a married 30-year-old research physicist, has been given a five-year appointment by a major university laboratory. As he thinks about the five years, he realises that he might work on a difficult, long-term problem which, if a solution could be found, would resolve basic scientific issues in the field and bring high scientific honours. If no solutions were found, Gopal would have little to show for his five years in the laboratory, and this would make it hard for him to get a good job afterwards. On the other hand, he could, as most of his professional associates are doing, work on a series of short-term problems where solutions would be easier to find, but where the problems are of lesser scientific importance.

Imagine that you are advising Gopal. Please put a tick mark (√) against the statement that best expresses your advice.

- Very strongly recommend to work on easy, short-term problems
- Strongly recommend to work on easy, short-term problems
- Moderately recommend to work on easy, short-term problems
- Slightly recommend to work on easy, short-term problems
- Very slightly recommend to work on easy, short-term problems
- Undecided
- Very slightly recommend to work on a difficult, long-term problem
- Slightly recommend to work on a difficult, long-term problem
- Moderately recommend to work on a difficult, long-term problem
- Strongly recommend to work on a difficult, long-term problem
- Very strongly recommend to work on a difficult, long-term problem

(a) How *important* do you consider your advice to this issue?

Not at all	Slightly	Somehow	Moderately	Quite	Extremely
—	—	—	—	—	—

(b) How much *effort* did you put into evaluating this issue?

Very much	Much	Moderate	Little	Very little	Not at all
—	—	—	—	—	—

(c) How *difficult* do you find recommending your advice on this issue?

Not at all	Very little	Little	Moderate	Much	Very much
—	—	—	—	—	—

(d) To what extent is this issue interesting and meaningful to you?

	Extremely	Quite	Moderately	Somehow	Slightly	Not at all
(i) Interesting :	....	....	....	....	....	....
(ii) Meaningful :	....	....	....	....	....	....

(e) To what extent is the information received during the *discussion of this issue* influential and convincing, new, useful, supportive, and logical to you?

	Not at all	Slightly	Somehow	Moderately	Quite	Extremely
(i) Influential & convincing :	....	....	....	....	....	....
(ii) New :	....	....	....	....	....	....
(iii) Useful :	....	....	....	....	....	....
(iv) Supportive :	....	....	....	....	....	....
(v) Logical :	....	....	....	....	....	....

(f) Evaluate the group *discussion of this issue* according to your opinions and feelings.

Rating scale : 1. Poor, 2. Below average, 3. Average, 4. Excellent, 5. Superior.

Did the discussant. . .	Evaluation (tick one number per each question)
(i) . . . show evidence of background reading, knowledge about the issue, and analysis of the situation?	1 2 3 4 5
(ii) . . . show evidence of critical thinking?	1 2 3 4 5
(iii) . . . support, encourage others, and show the responsibility for stimulating discussion and resolving conflict?	1 2 3 4 5
(iv) . . . make contributions, to the point, clear, explain complex ideas, and clarify meaning?	1 2 3 4 5

(g) How effective was the discussion of this issue to you?

Very much	Much	Moderate	Little	Very little	Not at all
–	–	–	–	–	–

– Hari is currently a first class post-graduate degree holder in Chemistry who is eager to pursue study leading to the Ph.D. degree. He has been accepted by both University *X* and University *Y*. University *X* has a world-wide reputation for excellence in Chemistry. While a degree from University *X* would signify outstanding training in this field, the standards are so very rigorous that only a fraction of the candidates actually receive the degree. University *Y*, on the other hand, has much less of a reputation in Chemistry, but almost everyone admitted is awarded the Ph.D. degree, though the degree has much less prestige than the corresponding degree from University *X*.

Imagine that you are advising Hari. Please put a tick mark (√) against the statement that best expresses your advice.

- Very strongly recommend to enroll in University *X*
- Strongly recommend to enroll in University *X*
- Moderately recommend to enroll in University *X*
- Slightly recommend to enroll in University *X*
- Very slightly recommend to enroll in University *X*
- Undecided
- Very slightly recommend to enroll in University *Y*
- Slightly recommend to enroll in University *Y*
- Moderately recommend to enroll in University *Y*
- Strongly recommend to enroll in University *Y*
- Very strongly recommend to enroll in University *Y*

(a) How *important* do you consider your advice to this issue?

Extremely	Quite	Moderately	Somehow	Slightly	Not at all
–	–	–	–	–	–

(b) How much *effort* did you put into evaluating this issue?

Not at all	Very little	Little	Moderate	Much	Very much
–	–	–	–	–	–

(c) How *difficult* do you find recommending your advice on this issue?

Very much	Much	Moderate	Little	Very little	Not at all
—	—	—	—	—	—

(d) To what extent is this issue interesting and meaningful to you?

	Not at all	Slightly	Somehow	Moderately	Quite	Extremely
(i) Interesting :	....	....	....	....	....	....
(ii) Meaningful :	....	....	....	....	....	....

(e) To what extent is the information received during the *discussion of this issue* influential and convincing, new, useful, supportive, and logical to you?

	Extremely	Quite	Moderately	Somehow	Slightly	Not at all
(i) Influential & convincing :	....	....	....	....	....	....
(ii) New :	....	....	....	....	....	....
(iii) Useful :	....	....	....	....	....	....
(iv) Supportive :	....	....	....	....	....	....
(v) Logical :	....	....	....	....	....	....

(f) Evaluate the group *discussion of this issue* according to your opinions and feelings.

Rating scale : 1. Poor, 2. Below average, 3. Average, 4. Excellent, 5. Superior.

Did the discussant. . .	Evaluation (tick one number per each question)
(i) . . .show evidence of background reading, knowledge about the issue, and analysis of the situation?	1 2 3 4 5
(ii) . . .show evidence of critical thinking?	1 2 3 4 5

(iii) . . .support, encourage others, and show the responsibility for stimulating discussion and resolving conflict? 1 2 3 4 5

(iv) . . .make contributions, to the point, clear, explain complex ideas, and clarify meaning? 1 2 3 4 5

(g) How effective was the discussion of this issue to you?

Not at all	Very little	Little	Moderate	Much	Very much
–	–	–	–	–	–

Now on the basis of your overall impression, reply to these general questions.

(a) To what extent are you *attracted* to the group with whom you discussed the issues?

Highly	Quite	Moderately	Somehow	Slightly	Not at all
—	—	—	—	—	—

(b) To what extent are you *willing to participate* with your group in a similar type of task in future?

Not at all	Slightly	Somehow	Moderately	Definitely	Highly
–	–	–	–	–	–

(c) A list of adjectives related to important personality characteristics is given below. Six categories of answers – very much, much, moderate, little, very little, and not at all – are given against each adjective. Read each adjective carefully and according to your feelings and opinions, put a tick mark (√) against the category *which describes your group members appropriately*.

	Very much	Much	Moderate	Little	Very little	Not at all
1. Clever :	....	....	....	....	....	....
2. Creative :	....	....	....	....	....	....
3. Intelligent :	....	....	....	....	....	....
4. Competent :	....	....	....	....	....	....

5. Active :	....	....	....	....	....	....
6. Knowledgeable :	....	....	....	....	....	....
7. Trustworthy :	....	....	....	....	....	....
8. Insightful :	....	....	....	....	....	....
9. Innovative :	....	....	....	....	....	....
10. Sincere :	....	....	....	....	....	....
11. Confident :	....	....	....	....	....	....
12. Decisive :	....	....	....	....	....	....
13. Convincing :	....	....	....	....	....	....
14. Likeable :	....	....	....	....	....	....
15. Sensitive :	....	....	....	....	....	....

Personal Data

1. Name : ________________ 2. Sex : Male . . ./Female . . . (tick one)

3. Age : ________________ 4. Class : ________________

APPENDIX II

APPENDIX TABLE 2.1: Correlation among the Items in Pre-test Scores of AJF

Item No.	Risky Items (R)				Cautious Items (C)				Neutral		
	3	4	6	9	1	5	7	8	2	ΣR[b]	ΣC[c]
1(3)[a]	1.00										
2(4)	0.07	1.00									
3(6)	0.10	0.27*	1.00								
4(9)	0.08	0.08	–0.01	1.00							
5(1)	0.27*	–0.02	–0.07	0.10	1.00						
6(5)	–0.04	–0.11	–0.04	0.04	0.20*	1.00					
7(7)	–0.10	–0.02	–0.04	0.00	0.02	0.27*	1.00				
8(8)	0.00	–0.03	–0.29**	–0.26	0.02	0.07	0.06	1.00			
9(2)	0.13	0.13	–0.02	0.09	0.07	–0.03	–0.03	–0.04	1.00		
10 (ΣR)	0.45***	0.66***	0.58***	0.57***	0.10	–0.07	–0.06	–0.27*	0.14	1.00	
11 (ΣC)	0.07	–0.08	–0.19	0.04	0.57***	0.68***	0.58***	0.47***	–0.01	–0.12	1.00
Mean	1.79	3.14	2.64	3.21	4.71	4.27	5.56	5.54	2.42	10.79	20.09
SD	1.62	2.30	2.00	2.42	2.38	2.26	2.25	2.08	1.71	4.80	5.17

* $p < .05$

** $p < .01$

*** $p < .005$, df. = 64

a Numbers in parentheses are the serial number of the items in the pre-test questionnaire.

b Total of Risky Item Scores.

c Total of Cautious Item Scores.

APPENDIX TABLE 2.2: Correlation among the Items in Pre-test Scores of PRF

Item No.	Risky Items (*R*)				Cautious Items (*C*)				Neutral		
	3	4	6	9	1	5	7	8	2	ΣR^b	ΣC^c
1(3)[a]	1.00										
2(4)	–0.07	1.00									
3(6)	0.11	0.43***	1.00								
4(9)	0.31**	0.18	0.43***	1.00							
5(1)	–0.07	0.04	0.38***	0.19	1.00						
6(5)	–0.24*	0.13	0.08	0.05	0.11	1.00					
7(7)	–0.14	0.19	0.29*	0.04	0.12	0.30**	1.00				
8(8)	–0.15	0.29**	0.41***	0.26*	0.31**	0.13	0.08	1.00			
9(2)	0.39***	0.24*	0.35***	0.27*	0.16	–0.19	0.07	0.24*	1.00		
10 (ΣR)	0.55***	0.60***	0.74***	0.72***	0.20	–0.00	0.14	0.26*	0.49***	1.00	
11 (ΣC)	–0.24*	–0.25*	–0.45***	0.16	0.61***	0.63***	0.68***	0.52***	0.09	–0.22*	1.00
Mean	5.44	5.98	6.14	5.02	7.44	7.28	6.84	7.58	6.23	22.58	29.14
SD	3.10	2.98	2.62	2.60	2.91	2.82	3.40	2.11	2.59	7.27	6.99

* $p < .05$
** $p < .01$
*** $p < .005$, df.=62
a Numbers in parentheses are the serial number of the items in the pre-test questionnaire.
b Total of Risky Item Scores.
c Total of Cautious Item Scores.

APPENDIX TABLE 2.3: Correlation among the Items in Pre-test Scores of PEF

Item No.	Risky Items (R)				Cautious Items (C)				Neutral		
	1	4	6	8	2	3	5	9	7	ΣR[b]	ΣC[c]
1(1)[a]	1.00										
2(4)	0.34***	1.00									
3(6)	0.19	0.38***	1.00								
4(8)	0.29**	0.39***	0.20	1.00							
5(2)	0.02	0.01	–0.23*	–0.15	1.00						
6(3)	–0.27*	–0.06	–0.12	0.10	0.21*	1.00					
7(5)	–0.06	–0.09	–0.06	–0.15	–0.02	0.18	1.00				
8(9)	0.11	0.12	0.02	0.04	0.07	0.26*	0.15	1.00			
9(7)	–0.07	0.27*	0.11	0.30***	–0.15	–0.06	–0.12	–0.04	1.00		
10 (ΣR)	0.64***	0.77***	0.66***	0.69***	–0.13	–0.12	–0.13	0.10	0.23*	1.00	
11 (ΣC)	–0.10	–0.01	–0.17	–0.05	0.52***	0.75***	0.45***	0.62***	–0.15	–0.12	1.00
Mean	5.32	5.55	5.40	5.49	7.89	6.65	6.60	7.26	6.34	21.77	28.40
SD	2.48	2.68	2.82	2.75	3.02	3.52	2.49	2.92	2.65	7.38	7.14

* $p < .05$

** $p < .01$

*** $p < .005$, df.=63

a Numbers in parentheses are the serial number of the items in the pre-test questionnaire.

b Total of Risky Item Scores.

c Total of Cautious Item Scores.

BIBLIOGRAPHY

Allport, F.H., A structuronomic conception of behaviour : Individual and collective I. Structural theory and the master problem of social psychology. *Journal of Abnormal and Social Psychology,* 1962, **64,** 3-30.

Anderson, N.H., & Graesser, C. C., An information integration analysis of attitude change in group discussion. *Journal of Personality and Social Psychology,* 1976, **34**, 210-222.

Asch, S.E., Studies of independence and conformity : I. On minority of one against a unanimous majority. *Psychological Monographs,* 1956, **70**, (9, whole No. 417).

Assor, A., Aronoff, J., & Messe, L., Attribute relevance as a moderator of the effects of motivation on impression formation. *Journal of Personality and Social Psychology,* 1981, **41,** 789-796.

Bagozzi, R.P., An examination of the validity of two models attitude. *Multivariate Behavioral Research,* 1981, **16,** 323-359.

Bales, R.F., *Interaction process analysis.* Cambridge, Mass. : Addison-Wesley, 1950.

Barnlund, D.C., Comparative study of individual, majority and group judgement. *Journal of Abnormal and Social Psychology,* 1959, **58,** 55-60.

Baron, R.S., & Roper, G., Reaffirmation of social comparison views of choice shifts : Averaging and extremity effects in an autokinetic situation. *Journal of Personality and Social Psychology,* 1976, **33,** 521-530.

Baron, R.S., Monson, T.C., & Baron, P.H., Conformity pressure as a determinant of risk taking : Replication and extension. *Journal of Personality and Social Psychology,* 1973, **28,** 406-413.

Bateson, N., Familiarisation, group discussion, and risk-taking. *Journal of Experimental Social Psychology,* 1966, **2,** 119-129.

Baumhart, R., *An honest profit.* N.Y. : Holt, 1968.

Bell, P.R., & Jamieson, B.D., Publicity of initial decisions and risky shift phenomenon. *Journal of Experimental Social Psychology,* 1970, **6**, 329-345.

Belovicz, M.W., & Finch, F.E., A critical analysis of the "risky shift" phenomenon. *Organisational Behaviour and Human Performance,* 1971, **6**, 150-168.

Bem, D.J., Constructing cross-situational consistencies in behaviour : Some thoughts on Alker's critique of Mischel. *Journal of Personality,* 1972, **40**, 17-26.

Beyth-Marom, R., How probable is probable ? Numerical translation of verbal probability expressions. *Journal of Forecasting,* 1982, **1**, 257-269.

Bishop, G.D., & Myers, D.G., Informational influence in group discussion. *Organisational Behaviour and Human Performance,* 1974, **12**, 92-104.

Blascovich, J., & Ginsburg, G.P., Emergent norms and choice shifts involving risk. *Sociometry,* 1974, **37**, 205-218.

Blascovich, J., & Ginsburg, G.P., Conceptual analysis of risk-taking in "risky-shift" research. *Journal for the Theory of Social Behaviour,* 1978, **8**, 217-230.

Blascovich, J., Ginsburg, G.P., & Howe, R. C., Blackjack and the risky shift, II : Monetary stakes. *Journal of Experimental Social Psychology,* 1975, **11**, 224-232.

Blascovich, J., Ginsburg, G. P., & Howe, R.C., Blackjack, choice shifts in the field. *Sociometry,* 1976, **39**, 274-276.

Blascovich, J., Ginsburg, G.P., & Veach, T.L., A pluralistic explanation of choice shifts on the risk dimension. *Journal of Personality and Social Psychology,* 1975, **31**, 422-429.

Blascovich, J., Veach, T.L., & Ginsburg, G.P., Blackjack and the risky shift. *Sociometry,* 1973, **36**, 42-55.

Bornstein, R.F., Leone, D.R., & Galley, D.J., The generalisability of subliminal mere exposure effects: Influence of stimuli perceived without awareness on social behaviour. *Journal of Personality and Social Psychology,* 1987, **53**, 1070-1079.

Bower, G.H., Cognitive psychology : An interpretation. In W.K. Estes (Ed.), *Handbook of learning and cognitive processes,* Hillside, N.J. : Erlbaum Associates, 1975.

Brenner, S.N., & Molander, E.A., Is the ethics of business changing ? *Harvard Business Review,* 1977, 57-71.

Brim, O.G, Jr., Attitude content-intensity and probability expectations. *American Sociological Review,* 1955, **20,** 68-76.

Brock. T.C., Communication discrepancy and intent to persuade as determinants of counter argument production. *Journal of Experimental Social Psychology,* 1967, **3,** 296-309.

Brock, T.C., Albert, S.M., & Becker, L.A., Familiarity, utility, and supportiveness as determinants of information receptivity. *Journal of Personality and Social Psychology,* 1970, **14,** 292-301.

Brown, R., *Social psychology.* Y.N. : Free Press, 1965.

Brown, R., Further comment on the risky shift. *American Psychologist,* 1974, **29,** 468-470.

Burns, J. F., An extremity-variance analysis of group decisions involving risk. Unpublished doctoral dissertation, Massachusetts Institute of Technology, Cambridge, Mass., 1967.

Burnstein, E., An analysis of group decisions involving risk. *Human Relations,* 1969, **22,** 381-395.

Burnstein, E., Persuasion as argument processing. In H. Brandstatter, J.H. Davis, & G. Stocker-Kreichgauer (Eds.), *Group decision making.* London: Academic Press, 1982.

Burnstein, E., & Katz, S., Individual commitment to risky and conservative choices as a determinant of shifts in group decisions. *Journal of Personality,* 1971, **39,** 564-580.

Burnstein, E., & Schul, Y., Group polarisation. In H.H. Blumberg, A.P. Hare, V. Kent, & M. Davies (Eds.), *Small groups and social interaction.* N.Y.: Wiley, 1983.

Burnstein, E., & Vinokur, A., Testing two classes of theories about group induced shifts in individual choice. *Journal of Experimental Social Psychology,* 1973, **9,** 123-137.

Burnstein, E., & Vinokur, A., What a person thinks upon learning he has chosen differently from others : Nice evidence for the persuasive arguments explanation of choice shifts. *Journal of Experimental Social Psychology,* 1975, **11,** 412-426.

Burnstein, E., & Vinokur, A., Persuasive argumentation and social comparison as determinants of attitude polarisation. *Journal of Experimental Social Psychology,* 1977, **13,** 315-332.

Burnstein, E., Vinokur, A., & Pichevin. M., What do differences between own, admired and attributed choices have to do with group induced shifts in choice. *Journal of Experimental Social Psychology,* 1974, **10,** 428-443.

Burnstein, E., Vinokur, A., & Trope, Y., Interpersonal comparison versus persuasive argumentation : A more direct test of alternative explanations for group induced shifts in individual choice. *Journal of Experimental Social Psychology,* 1973, **9,** 236-245.

Burnstein, E., Miller, H., Vinokur, A., Katz., S., & Crowley, J., Risky shift is eminently rational. *Journal of Personality and Social Psychology,* 1971, **20,** 462-471.

Cacioppo, J.T., & Petty, R.E., Effects of message repetition and position on cognitive response, recall, and persuasion. *Journal of Personality and Social Psychology,* 1979, **37,** 97-109.

Cacioppo, J.T., Petty, R.E., & Morris, K.J., Effects of need for cognition on message evaluation, recall, and persuasion. *Journal of Personality and Social Psychology,* 1983, **45,** 805-818.

Carlsmith, J.M., Ellsworth, P.C., & Aronson, E., *Methods of research in social psychology.* Mass. : Addison-Wesley, 1976.

Carlson, J.A., & Davis, C.M., Cultural values and the risky shifts : A cross-cultural test in Uganda and the United States. *Journal of Personality and Social Psychology,* 1971, **20,** 392-399.

Cartwright, D., Risk taking by individuals and groups : An assessment of research employing choice dilemmas. *Journal of Personality and Social Psychology,* 1971, **20,** 361-378.

Castore, C.H., Group discussion and prediscussion assessment of preferences in the risky shift. *Journal of Experimental Social Psychology,* 1972, **8,** 161-167.

Chaiken, S., Heuristic versus systematic information processing and the use of source versus message cues in persuasion. *Journal of Personality and Social Psychology,* 1980, **39,** 752-766.

Clark, R.D. III., & Willems, E.P., Where is the risky shift? Dependence on instructions. *Journal of Personality and Social Psychology,* 1969, **13,** 215-221.

Clark, R. D. III., Crockett, W.H., & Archer, R.L., Risk as value hypothesis : The relationship between perception of self, others, and the risky shift. *Journal of Personality and Social Psychology,* 1971, **20,** 425-429.

Clausen, G.S.T., Risk taking in small groups. Unpublished doctoral dissertation, University of Michigan, 1965.

Coch, L., & French, J.R.P., Overcoming resistance to change. In D. Cartwright, & A. Zander (Eds.), *Group dynamics : Research and theory,* Evanston, III: Row, Peterson, 1960.

Coleman, J.F., Blake, R.R., & Mouton, J.S., Task difficulty and conformity pressures. *Journal of Abnormal and Social Psychology,* 1958, **57,** 120-122.

Conroy, W.J., Katkin, E.S., & Barnette, W.L., Modification of smoking behaviour by the use of a self confrontation technique. Paper presented at meetings of the Southeastern Psychological Association, New Orleans, 1973.

Cook, T.D., & Campbell, D.T., The design and conduct of quasi-experiments and true experiments in field settings. In M.D. Dunnette (Ed.), *Handbook of industrial and organisational psychology,* Chicago: Rand McNally, 1976.

Coombs, C.H., & Pruitt, D.G., Components of risk in decision making : Probability and variance preferences. *Journal of Experimental Psychology,* 1960, **60,** 265-277.

Cronbach, L.J., & Furby, L., How should we measure 'change' — or should we ?. *Psychology Bulletin,* 1970, **74,** 68-80.

Davis, J.H., Group decision and social interaction : A theory of social decision schemes. *Psychological Review,* 1973, **80,** 97-125.

Davis, M.S., That's interesting!. *Philosophy of Social Science,* 1971, **1,** 309-344.

Davis, J.H., Hoppe, R.A., & Hornseth, J.P., Risk-taking : Task, response pattern, and grouping. *Organisational Behaviour and Human Performance,* 1968, **3,** 124-142.

Davis, J.H., Kerr, N., Sussmann, M., & Rissman, A.K., Social decision schemes under risk. *Journal of Personality and Social Psychology,* 1974, **30,** 248-271.

Deutsch, M., & Gerard, H.B., A study of normative and informational social influences upon individual judgement. *Journal of Abnormal and Social Psychology,* 1955, **51,** 629-636.

Doise, W., Intergroup relations and polarisation of individual and collective judgements. *Journal of Personality and Social Psychology,* 1969, **12,** 136-143.

Eagly, A.H., Comprehensibility of persuasive arguments as a determinant of opinion change. *Journal of Personality and Social Psychology,* 1974, **29,** 758-773.

Eagly, A.H., & Warren, R., Intelligence, comprehension, and opinion change. *Journal of Personality,* 1976, **44,** 226-242.

Eaves, L., & Eysenck, H., The nature of extraversion : A genetical analysis. *Journal of Personality and Social Psychology,* 1975, **32,** 102-112.

Ebbesen, E.B., & Bowers R.J., Proportion of risky to conservative arguments in a group discussion and choice shift. *Journal of Personality and Social Psychology,* 1974, **29,** 316-327.

Edwards, W., Variance preferences in gambling. *American Journal of Psychology,* 1954, **67,** 441-452.

Eysenck, H.J., *Readings in extraversion-introversion.* London: Staple Press, 1970.

Feldman, K.A., & Newcomb, T.M., *The impact of college on students.* San Francisco : Jossey-Bass, 1969.

Ferguson, D.A., Vidmar, N., Effects of group discussion on estimates of culturally appropriate risk levels. *Journal of Personality and Social Psychology,* 1971, **20,** 436-445.

Festinger, L., A theory of social comparison processes. *Human Relations,* 1954, **7,** 117-140.

Festinger. L., *A theory of cognitive dissonance.* Stanford : Stanford University Press, 1957.

Fields, J.M., & Schuman, H., Public beliefs about the beliefs of the public. *Public Opinion Quarterly,* 1976, **40,** 427-448.

Fischhoff, B., Watson, S., & Hope, C., Defining risk. *Policy Sciences,* 1984, **17,** 123-139.

Fishbein, M., & Ajzen, I., Attitudes and opinions. *Annual Review of Psychology,* 1972, **23,** 487-544.

Fishbein, M., & Ajzen, I., *Belief, attitude, intention and behaviour.* Reading, Mass. : Addison-Wesley, 1975.

Flanders, J.P., & Thistlethwaite, D.L., Effects of familiarisation and group discussion upon risk taking. *Journal of Personality and Social Psychology,* 1967, **5,** 91-98.

Fortenberry, J.C., & Smith, L. A., A comparison of risk selections. *Human Factors,* 1981, **23,** 693-700.

Fowler, H., *Curiosity and exploratory behaviour.* New York : Macmillan, 1965.

Fraser, C., Gouge, G., & Billig, M., Risky shifts, cautious shifts, and group polarisation. *European Journal of Social Psychology,* 1971, **1,** 7-30.

Freedman. J.L., Involvement, discrepancy, and change. *Journal of Abnormal and Social Psychology,* 1964, **69,** 290-295.

Freire, P., *Pedagogy of the oppressed.* London : Penguin, 1977.

Fromkin, H.L., Effects of experimentally aroused feelings of undistinctiveness upon valuation of scarce and novel experiences. *Journal of Personality and Social Psychology,* 1970, **16,** 521-529.

Fromkin, H.L., Feelings of interpersonal undistinctiveness : An unpleasant affective state. *Journal of Experimental Research in Personality,* 1972, **6,** 178-185.

Fromm, E., *Escape from freedom.* N.Y. : Farrah and Rinehart, 1941.

Gaskell. G.D., Thomas, E.A.C., & Farr, R.M., Effects of pretesting on measures of individual risk preferences. *Journal of Personality and Social Psychology,* 1973, **25,** 192-198.

Goethals, G.R., & Darley, J., Social comparison theory : An attributional approach. In J. Suls, & R. Miller (Eds.), *Social comparison processes : Theoretical and empirical perspective,* Washington, D. C. : Hemisphere Press, 1977.

Goethals, G.R., & Zanna, M.P., The role of social comparison in choice shifts. *Journal of Personality and Social Psychology,* 1979, **37,** 1469-1476.

Greenwald, A.G., Cognitive learning, cognitive response to persuasion and attitude change. In A. G. Greenwald, T.C. Brock, & T.M. Ostrom (Eds.), *Psychological foundations of attitudes.* New York : Academic Press, 1968.

Grube, J. W., Can values be manipulated arbitrarily? A replication that controls for regression effects. *Personality and Social Psychology Bulletin,* 1982a, **8,** 528-533.

Grube, J.W., Value discrepancy, dissatisfaction, and naturally occurring value change. Paper presented at the 20th ICAP, Edinburgh, Scotland, 1982b.

Hamid, P. N., & Flay, B.R., Changes in locus of control as a function of value modification. *Journal of Social and Clinical Psychology,* 1974, **13,** 143-150.

Harnack, R.V., Fest, T.B., & Jones, B.S., *Group discussion theory and technique.* N.J. : Prentice-Hall, 1977.

Higbee, K.L., Expression of "Walter Mitty-ness" in actual behaviour. *Journal of Personality and Social Psychology,* 1971, **20,** 416-422.

Himmelfarb, S., & Eagly, A.H., *Readings in attitude change.* N.Y.: Wiley, 1973.

Hinsz, V. B., & Davis, J.H., Persuasive arguments theory, group polarisation, and choice shifts. *Personality and Social Psychology Bulletin,* 1984, **10,** 260-268.

Hong, L. K., Risky shift and cautious shift : Some direct evidence on the cultural-value theory. *Social Psychology,* 1978, **41,** 342-346.

Hopkins, S.W. Jr., Behavioural and attitude changes produced from dissonance created between intra-personal values and attitudes.

Unpublished doctoral dissertation, University of Texas, Austin, 1973.

Horney, K., *The neurotic personality of our time.* New York : Norton, 1937.

Hovaland, C.I., Effects of the mass media of communication. In G. Lindzey (Ed.), *Handbook of social psychology*, Cambridge, Mass. : Addison-Wesley, 1954.

Isenberg, D.J., Group polarisation : A critical review and meta-analysis. *Journal of Personality and Social Psychology,* 1986, **50,** 1141-1151.

Jellison, J., & Arkin, R., Social comparison of abilities : A self presentation approach to decision-making in groups. In J. Suls, & R.L. Miller (Eds.), *Social comparison processes : Theoretical and empirical perspectives,* Washington D.C. : Hemisphere Press, 1977.

Jellison, J.M., & Riskind, J., A social comparison of abilities interpretation of risk-taking behaviour. *Journal of Personality and Social Psychology,* 1970, **15,** 375-390.

Johnson, C.D., & Davis, J.H., Risk taking and decision schemes. *Organisational Behaviour and Human Performance,* 1972, **8,** 159-175.

Johnston, L. Jr., The immediate and short-term effects of group discussion and individual study on risk levels. Unpublished doctoral dissertation, Florida State University, 1968.

Kahan. J.P., A subjective probability interpretation of the risky shift. *Journal of Personality and Social Psychology,* 1975, **31,** 977-982.

Kaplan, M.F., Discussion polarisation effects in a modified jury decision paradigm : Informational influences. *Sociometry,* 1977, **40,** 262-271.

Kaplan, M.F., & Miller, C.E., Judgements and group discussion : Effect of presentation and memory factors on polarisation. *Sociometry,* 1977, **40,** 337-343.

Keating, J.P., & Brock, T.C., Acceptance of persuasion and the inhibition of counter argumentation under various distraction tasks. *Journal of Experimental Social Psychology,* 1974, **10,** 301-309.

Kiesler, C.A., Collins, B.A., & Miller, N., *Attitude change.* N.Y. : Wiley, 1969.

Kiesler, C.A., & Kiesler, S.B., *Conformity.* Reading, Mass. : Addison-Wesley, 1969.

Knapp, M.L., *Nonverbal communication in human interaction.* N.Y. : Holt, 1972.

Knox, R. E., & Safford, R.K., Group caution at the race track. *Journal of Experimental Psychology,* 1976, **12,** 317-324.

Kogan, N., & Wallach, M.A., *Risk taking : A study in cognition and personality.* N.Y. : Holt, 1964.

Kogan. N., & Wallach, M.A., Group risk taking as a function of members' anxiety and defensiveness levels. *Journal of Personality,* 1967a, **35,** 50-63.

Kogan, N., & Wallach, M.A., The risky shift phenomenon in small decision-making groups : A test of the information exchange hypothesis. *Journal of Experimental Social Psychology,* **3,** 1967b, 75-85.

Lambert, R., Extremisation du comportement de prise de risque en groupe et modele majoritaire. *Psychologie Francaise,* 1969, **14,** 113-125.

Lambert, R., Extremisation due risque en groupe. *Journal de la Societe de Statistique de Paris,* 1971, **112,** 11-22.

Lamm, H., Will an observer advise higher risk-taking after hearing a discussion of the decision problem ? *Journal of Personality and Social Psychology,* 1967, **6,** 467-471.

Lamm, H., & Myers, D.G., Machiavellianism, discussion time, and group shift. *Social Behaviour and Personality,* 1976, **4,** 41-48.

Lamm, H., Schaude, E., & Trommsdorff, G., Risky shift as a function of group members' value of risk and need for approval. *Journal of Personality and Social Psychology,* 1971, **20,** 430-435.

Lamm, H., Trommsdorff, G., & Rost-Schaude, E., Self-image, perception of peers' risk acceptance and risky shift. *European Journal of Social Psychology,* 1972, **2,** 255-272.

Laughlin, P.R., & Earley, P.C., Social combination models, persuasive arguments theory, social comparison theory, and choice shift. *Journal of Personality and Social Psychology,* 1982, **42,** 273-280.

Laughlin, P.R., Kerr, N.L., Davis, J.H., Halff, H.M., & Marciniak, K.A., Group size, member ability, and social decision schemes on an intellective task. *Journal of Personality and Social Psychology,* 1975, **31,** 522-535.

Lenihan, K.J., Perceived climates as a barrier to housing desegregation. Unpublished manuscript, Columbia University : Bureau of Applied Social Research, 1965.

Lennox, R. D., Wolfe, R.N., Revision of the self-monitoring scale. *Journal of Personality and Social Psychology* , 1984, **46,** 1349-1364.

Levinger, G., & Schneider, D.J., A test of the "risk is a value" hypothesis. *Journal of Personality and Social Psychology,* 1969, **11,** 165-169.

Lewin, K., Group decision and social change. In T.M. Newcomb, & E.L. Hartley (Eds.), *Readings in social psychology,* N.Y. : Holt , 1947.

Lindsay, P.H., & Norman. D.A., *Human information processing: An introduction to psychology.* N.Y. : Academic Press, 1974.

Madaras, G.R., & Bem, D.J., Risk and conservatism in group decision-making. *Journal of Experimental Social Psychology,* 1968, **4,** 350-365.

Madsen, D.B., Issue importance and choice shifts : A persuasive arguments approach. *Journal of Personality and Social Psychology,* 1978, **36,** 1118-1127.

Marquis, D.G., Individual responsibility and group decisions involving risk. *Industrial Management Review,* 1962, **3,** 8-23.

Maslow, A.H., *Toward a psychology of being.* N.Y. : Van Nostrand, 1962.

McCauley, C.R., Extremity shifts, risk shifts and attitude shifts after group discussion. *European Journal of Social Psychology,* 1972, **2,** 417-436.

McCauley, C., Teger, A.I., & Kogan, N., Effect of the pretest in the risky shift paradigm. *Journal of Personality and Social Psychology,* 1971, **20,** 379-381.

McCauley, C., Stitt, C.L., Woods, K., & Lipton, D., Group shift to caution at the race track. *Journal of Experimental Social Psychology,* 1973, **9,** 80-86.

McGuire, W.J., Inducing resistance to persuasion : Some contemporary approach. In L. Berkowitz (Ed.), *Advances in experimental social psychology,* N.Y.: Academic Press, 1964.

McGuire, W.J., The nature of attitudes and attitude change. In G. Lindzey, & E. Aronson (Eds.), *Handbook of social psychology,* Reading, Mass. : Addison-Wesley, 1969.

McGuire, W.J., Attitude change : The information processing paradigm. In C.G. McClintock (Ed.), *Experimental social psychology,* N.Y. : Holt, 1972..

McKeachie, W.J., Psychology at age 75 : The psychology teacher comes into his own. *American Psychologist,* 1968, **23,** 551-557.

Mehrabian, A., *Silent messages.* Belmont, California : Wadsworth Publishing Company, 1971.

Moscovici, S., & Zavalloni, M., The group as a polariser of attitudes. *Journal of Personality and Social Psychology,* 1969, **12,** 125-135.

Moscovici, S., Doise, W., & Dulong R., Studies in group decision II : Difference of positions, differences of opinion and group polarisation. *European Journal of Social Psychology,* 1972, **2,** 385-400.

Muehleman, T., Robinson, F., & Emerson, D., Shifts in preference in moral reasoning. *Journal of Social Psychology,* 1984, **125,** 287-293.

Myers, D.G., Enhancement of initial risk tendencies in social situations. Unpublished doctoral dissertation, University of Iowa, 1967.

Myers, D.G., Summary and bibliography of experiments on group-induced response shift. *JSAS Catalog of Selected Documents in Psychology,* 1973, **3,** 123.

Myers, D.G., Interpersonal comparison processes in choice dilemma responding. *Journal of Psychology,* 1974, **86,** 287-292.

Myers, D.G., Polarising effects of social comparison. *Journal of Experimental Social Psychology,* 1978, **14,** 554-563.

Myers, D.G., Polarising effects of social interaction. In H. Brandstatter, J. H. Davis, & G. Stocker-Kreichgauer (Eds.), *Group decision making,* London: Academic Press, 1982.

Myers, D.G., & Arenson, S.J., Enhancement of dominant risk tendencies in group discussion. *Psychological Reports,* 1972, **30,** 615-623.

Myers, D.G., & Bach, P. J., Discussion effects on militarism-pacifism: A test of the group polarisation hypothesis. *Journal of Personality and Social Psychology,* 1974, **30,** 741-747.

Myers, D.G., & Bishop, G.D., Discussion effects on racial attitudes. *Science,* 1970, **169,** 778-789.

Myers, D.G., & Bishop, G.D., The enhancement of dominant attitudes in group discussion. *Journal of Personality and Social Psychology,* 1971, **20,** 386-391.

Myers, D.G., & Lamm, H., The group polarisation phenomenon. *Psychological Bulletin,* 1976, **83,** 602-627.

Myers, D.G., Bach, P.J., & Schreiber, F.B., Normative and informational effects of group interaction. *Sociometry,* 1974, **37,** 275-286.

Myers, D.G., Wojcicki, S.B., & Aardema, B.S., Attitude comparison : Is there ever a bandwagon effect ? *Journal of Applied Social Psychology,* 1977, **7,** 341-347.

Myers, D.G., Wong, D.W., & Murdoch, P., Discussion arguments, information about others' responses, and risky shift. *Psychonomic Science,* 1971, **24,** 81-83.

Myers, D.G., Bruggink, J.B., Kersting, R.C., & Schlosser, B.A., Does learning others' opinions change one's opinions ? *Personality and Social Psychology Bulletin,* 1980, **6,** 253-260.

Nagel. T.W., & O'Driscoll, M.P., Group Polarisation in a real life context : Analysis of choice shift in an educational situation. *Australian Journal of Psychology,* 1978, **30,** 229-240.

Newcomb, T.M., *Personality and Social Change : Attitude formation in a student community.* New York : Dryden, 1943.

Nordhoy, F., Group interaction in decision-making under risk. Unpublished master's thesis, Massachusetts Institute of Technology, School of Industrial Management, 1962.

O'Gorman, H.J., & Garry, S.L., Pluralistic ignorance — A replication and extension. *Public Opinion Quarterly,* 1976, **40,** 449-458.

Orne, M. T., Demand characteristics and concept of quasi-controls. In R. Rosenthal, & R.L. Rasnow (Eds.), *Artifact in behavioural research,* N.Y. : Academic Press, 1969.

Osgood, C.E., Suci, G.J., & Tannenbaum, P.H., *The measurement of meaning.* Urbana, Illinois. : University of Illinois Press, 1957.

Penner, L.A., Interpersonal attraction toward a black person as a function of value importance. *Personality,* 1971 **2,** 175-187.

Pennington, D.F. Jr., Haravey, F., & Bass, M.B., Some effects of decision and discussion on coalescence, change, and effectiveness. *Journal of Applied Psychology,* 1958, **42,** 404-408.

Pervin, L.A., & Lilly, R.S., Social desirability and self-ideal, self ratings on the semantic differential. *Educational Psychology Measurement,* 1967, **27,** 845-853.

Petty, R.E., & Cacioppo, J.T., Forewarning, cognitive responding and resistance to persuasion. *Journal of Personality and Social Psychology,* 1977, **35,** 645-655.

Petty, R.E., Wells, G.L., & Brock, T.C., Distraction can enhance or reduce yielding to propaganda : Thought disruption versus effort justification. *Journal of Personality and Social Psychology,* 1976, **34,** 874-884.

Pruitt, D.G., The "Walter Mitty" effect in individual and group risk taking. *Proceedings of the 77th Annual Convention of American Psychological Association,* 1969, **4,** 425-426.

Pruitt, D.G., Choice shifts in group discussion : An introductory review. *Journal of Personality and Social Psychology,* 1971a, **20,** 339-360.

Pruitt, D.G., Conclusions : Towards an understanding of choice shifts in group discussion. *Journal of Personality and Social Psychology,* 1971b, **20,** 495-510.

Pruitt, D.G., & Teger, A.I., Is there a shift toward risk in group discussion? If so, is it a group phenomenon? If so, what causes it ? Paper presented at the American Psychological Association Convention, Washington, D.C., 1967.

Rabow, J., Fowler, F.J., Bradford, D.L., Hofeller, M.A., & Shibuya, Y., The role of social norms and leadership in risk-taking. *Sociometry,* 1966, **29,** 16-27.

Rettig, S., Group discussion and predicted ethical risk taking. *Journal of Personality and Social Psychology,* 1966, **3,** 629-633.

Rettig, S., Trust and locus of control in predictive judgements of unethical behaviour. *Proceedings of the 80th Annual Convention of the American Psychological Association,* 1972, 221-222.

Rettig, S., Risky shift and information flow in relation to predicted ethical risk taking. *Journal of Social and Economic Studies,,* 1979, **7,** 237-247.

Rhine, R. J., & Polowniak, W.A.J., Attitude change, commitment, and ego involvement. *Journal of Personality and Social Psychology,* 1971, **19,** 247-250.

Rim, Y., Personality and group decisions involving risk. *Psychological Record,* 1964a, **14,** 37-45.

Rim, Y., Social attitudes and risk-taking. *Human Relations,* 1964b, **17,** 259-265.

Rim, Y., Dominant interests and risk. *Archivio di Psicologia Neurologia e psichiatra,* 1965a, **26,** 17-25.

Rim, Y., Leadership attitudes and decisions involving risk. *Personnel Psychology,* 1965b, **18,** 423-430.

Rim, Y., Interpersonal values and risk-taking. *Psychologia,* 1966a, **9,** 120-124.

Rim, Y., Machiavellianism and decisions involving risk. *British Journal of Social and Clinical Psychology,* 1966b, **5,** 30-36.

Rim, Y., Who are the risk-takers in decision-making ? *Personnel Administration,* 1966c, **29,** 26-30.

Rokeach, M., Long-range experimental modification of values, attitudes, and behaviour. *American Psychologist,* 1971, **26,** 453-459.

Rokeach, M., *The nature of human values.* N.Y. : Free Press, 1973.

Rokeach, M., Long-term value change initiated by computer feedback. *Journal of Personality and Social Psychology,* 1975, **32,** 467-476.

Rokeach, M., Value theory and communication research. In D. Nimo (Ed.), *Communication Yearbook III.* Transaction Books, N.J. : New Bruswick, 1979a.

Rokeach, M., Change and stability in American value systems, 1968-1971. In M. Rokeach (Ed.), *Understanding human values : Individual and societal,* N.Y. : Free Press, 1979b.

Rosenthal, R., *Experimenter effect in behavioural research.* N.Y. : Appleton — Century — Crofts, 1966.

Sanders, G.S., & Baron, R.S., Is social comparison irrelevant for producing choice shifts? *Journal of Experimental Social Psychology,* 1977, **13,** 303-314.

Schoemaker, P. J.H., The role of statistical knowledge in gambling decisions : Moment vs. risk dimension approaches. *Organisational Behaviour and Human Performance,* 1979, **24,** 1-17.

Schoemaker, P.J.H., *Experiments on decisions under risk : The expected utility hypothesis.* Baston : Martinus Nijhoff, 1980.

Schroeder, H.E., The risky shift as a general choice shift. *Journal of Personality and Social Psychology,* 1973, **27,** 297-300.

Scott, W. A., Attitude measurement. In G. Lindzey, & E. Aronson (Eds.), *The handbook of social psychology* (Vol. II). Reading, Mass. : Addison-Wesley, 1968.

Sharan, M.B., *A study of role conflict and its influence on role performance.* Calcutta : Firma KLM, 1977.

Sharan, M.B., Prasad, S., & Suar, D., Factors influencing stability of the self-concept. *Creative Psychologist,* 1989, **1,** 9-17.

Shaw, M.E., A comparison of individual and small groups in the rational solution of complex problems. In T. M. Newcomb, & E.L. Hartley (Eds.), *Reading in social psychology,* New York : Holt, 1947.

Sherif, M., A study of some social factors in perception. *Archives of Psychology,* 1935,**27,** No. 187.

Sherif, M., & Sherif, C.W., *Social psychology.* New York : Harper and Row, 1969.

Silverthorne, C.P., Information input and the group shift phenomenon in risk taking. *Journal of Personality and Social Psychology,* 1971, **20,** 456-461.

Simon, H.A., A behavioural model of rational choice. *Quarterly Journal of Economics,* 1955, **69,** 99-118.

Singleton. R. Jr., Another look at the conformity explanation of group-induced shifts in choice. *Human Relations,* 1979, **32,** 37-56.

Sinha, J. B.P., & Yousuf, S.M.A., Effects of locus of control on choice shift in a cross-cultural perspective. *Journal of Social Psychology,* 1972, **88,** 177-183.

Slovic, P., & Lichtenstein, S., Relative importance of probabilities and payoffs in risk taking. *Journal of Experimental Psychology Monograph,* 1968, **78,** 1-18.

Smith, M.B., Is experimental social psychology advancing ? *Journal of Experimental Social Psychology,* 1972, **8,** 89-96.

Snyder, M., Self-monitoring of expressive behaviour. *Journal of Personality and Social Psychology,* 1974, **30,** 526-537.

Snyder, M., Self-monitoring processes. In L. Berkowitz (Ed.), *Advances in experimental social psychology,* N.Y.: Academic Press, 1979.

St. Jean, R., Reformation of the value hypothesis in group risk taking. *Proceedings of the 78th Annual Convention of the American Psychological Association,* 1970, 339-340.

Stokes, J.P., Effects of familiarisation and knowledge of others' odd choices on shifts to risk and caution. *Journal of Personality and Social Psychology,* 1971, **20,** 407-412.

Stoner, J.A.F., A comparison of individual and group decisions involving risk. Unpublished master's thesis, Massachusetts Institute of Technology, School of Industrial Management, 1961.

Stoner, J.A.F., Risky and cautious shifts in group decisions : The influence of widely held values. *Journal of Experimental Social Psychology,* 1968, **4,** 442-459.

Streufert, S., *The components of a simulation of local conflict : An analysis of the tactical and negotiations game.* (Advanced Research Projects Agency Tech. Rep., Project SD 260) Evanston, Ill : Northwestern University, 1968.

Stroebe, W., & Fraser, C., The relationship between riskiness and confidence in choice dilemma decisions. *European Journal of Social Psychology,* 1971, **1,** 519-526.

Swap, W.C., & Miller, H., Risky shift and social exchange in dyads. *Psychonomic Science,* 1969, **17,** 249-250.

Teger, A. I., & Pruitt, D.G., Components of group risk taking. *Journal of Experimental Social Psychology,* 1967, **3,** 189-205.

Teger, A. I., Pruitt, D.G., St. Jean, R., & Haaland, G.A., A re-examination of the familiarisation hypothesis in group risk taking. *Journal of Experimental Social Psychology,* 1970, **6,** 346-350.

Tesser, A., Attitude polarisation as a function of thought and reality constraints. *Journal of Research in Personality,* 1976, **10,** 183-194.

Tesser, A., Self-generated attitude change. In L. Berkowitz (Ed.), *Advances in experimental social psychology,* N.Y. : Academic Press, 1978.

Tesser, A., & Conlee, M.C., Some effects of time and thought on attitude polarisation. *Journal of Personality and Social Psychology,* 1975, **31,** 262-270.

Triandis, H.C., *Attitudes and attitude change.* New York : Wiley, 1971.

Verma, J., & Sinha, J.B.P., Cultural invariance in risky shift and its determinants. *Psychologia,* 1981, **24,** 235-238.

Vidmar, N., & Burdeny, T.C., Effects of group size and the item type in the "group shift" effect. *Canadian Journal of Behavioural Science,* 1971, **3,** 393-407.

Vinokur, A., Distribution of initial risk levels and group decisions involving risk. *Journal of Personality and Social Psychology,* 1969, **13,** 207-214.

Vinokur, A., Cognitive and affective processes influencing risk taking in groups : An expected utility approach. *Journal of Personality and Social Psychology,* 1971, **20,** 472-486.

Vinokur, A., & Burnstein, E., The effects of partially shared persuasive arguments on group-induced shifts: A group problem solving approach. *Journal of Personality and Social Psychology,* 1974, **29,** 305-315.

Vinokur, A., & Burnstein, E., Depolarisation of attitudes in groups. *Journal of Personality and Social Psychology,* 1978a, **36,** 872-885.

Vinokur, A., & Burnstein, E., Novel argumentation and attitude change : The case of polarisation following group discussion. *European Journal of Social Psychology,* 1978b, **8,** 335-348.

Vinokur, A., Trope, Y., & Burnstein, E., A decision-making analysis of persuasive argumentation and the choice-shift effect. *Journal of Experimental Social Psychology,* 1975, **11,** 127-148.

Vinokur, A., Burnstein, E., Sechrest, L., & Wortman, P. M., Group decision making by experts : Field study of panels evaluating medical technologies. *Journal of Personality and Social Psychology,* 1985, **49,** 70-84.

Wallach, M.A., & Kogan, N., Sex differences and judgement processes. *Journal of Personality,* 1959, **27,** 555-564.

Wallach, M.A., & Kogan, N., Aspects of judgement and decision-making : Interrelationships and changes with age. *Behavioural Science,* 1961, **6,** 23-36.

Wallach, M.A., & Kogan, N., The roles of information, discussion, and consensus in group risk taking. *Journal of Experimental Social Psychology,* 1965, **1,** 1-19.

Wallach, M.A., Kogan, N., & Bem, D.J., Group influence on individual risk taking. *Journal of Abnormal and Social Psychology,* 1962, **65,** 75-86.

Wallach, M.A., Kogan, N., & Burt, R.B., Group risk taking and field dependence-independence of group members. *Sociometry,* 1967, **30,** 323-338.

Weick, K.E., Organisations in the laboratory. In V.H. Vroom (Ed.), *Methods of organisational research,* Pittsburgh : University of Pittsburgh Press, 1967.

Willems, E.P., & Clark, R.D. III., Dependence of the risky shift on instructions : A replication. *Psychological Reports,* 1969, **25,** 811-814.

Zaidel, S., & Mehrabian, A., The ability to communicate and infer positive and negative attitudes facially and vocally. *Journal of Experimental Research in Personality,* 1969, **3,** 233-241.

Zajonc, R.B., Wolosin, R.J., & Wolosin, M.A., Group risk-taking under various group decision schemes. *Journal of Experimental Social Psychology,* 1972, **8,** 16-30.

INDEX